The Development of Scientific Writing
Linguistic Features and Historical Context

Discussions in Functional Approaches to Language

Series Editors: Christopher Butler, Honorary Professor, University of Wales, Swansea; Robin P. Fawcett, Emeritus Professor, Cardiff University

Editorial Board: John Bateman (University of Bremen); Joan Bybee (University of New Mexico); Huang Guowen (Sun Yat-sen University); Lachlan Mackenzie (Free University of Amsterdam); Jim Martin (University of Sydney); Jan Nuyts (University of Antwerp); Mick Short (Lancaster University); Anna Siewierska (Lancaster University); Anne-Marie Simon Vandenbergen (Ghent University); Michael Stubbs (University of Trier); Gordon Tucker (Cardiff University); Robert van Valin (University of New York at Buffalo)

The books in this series are addressed to university teachers, researchers and postgraduate students of linguistics – and bright undergraduate readers. The books are short (normally 150–200 pages) and readable but scholarly. They are all published in paperback, so ensuring a flow of lively books on central topics in functional linguistics that are within the financial reach of the intended readership.

The purpose of the series is to meet the need for a forum for discussing theoretical issues in functional approaches to language that are too large for publication in journal article form. It also welcomes descriptions of areas of language that are too large for journal publication – and works that combine both theory and description. While the series complements *Advances in Cognitive Linguistics* (also an Equinox series), it welcomes works that are both functional and oriented to the cognitive aspects of language use.

Books in this series therefore typically present and evaluate new work in theory or description or both. But they may also offer a critique of one or more previously published works of these types. In all cases, however, authors are expected to survey the relevant alternative approaches, and to say which they see as the most promising one, and why. Books in this series therefore always give reasons for preferring one position to another rather than simply describing a position – as in all good discussions.

Published:

English Tense and Aspect in Halliday's Systemic Functional Grammar: A Critical Appraisal and an Alternative, Carl Bache

Forthcoming:

Alternative Architectures for Systemic Functional Linguistics: How do we Choose?, Robin P. Fawcett

Process Types and Participant Roles in the English Clause: A New Systemic Functional Approach, Amy Neale

The Structure of Modern Irish: A Functional Account, Brian Nolan

The Development of Scientific Writing
Linguistic Features and Historical Context

David Banks

LONDON   OAKVILLE

Published by Equinox Publishing Ltd.
UK: Unit 6, The Village, 101 Amies St.,London SW11 2JW
USA: DBBC, 28 Main Street, Oakville, CT 06779
www.equinoxpub.com

First published 2008

British Library Cataloguing-in-Publication Data
A catalogue record for this book is available from the British Library.

ISBN-13   978 1 84553 316 8   (hardback)
            978 1 84553 317 5   (paperback)

Library of Congress Cataloging-in-Publication Data
Banks, David, 1943-
    The development of scientific writing : linguistic features and historical context / David Banks
      p. cm.
    Includes bibliographical references and index.
    ISBN-13: 978-1-84553-316-8 (hb)
    ISBN-13: 978-1-84553-317-5 (pb)
    1. English language—Technical English—History. I. Title.
    PE1475.B325 2007
    808'.0666—dc22
                        2007012865

Typeset by S.J.I. Service, New Delhi
Printed and bound in Great Britain by Lightning Source UK Ltd, Milton Keynes, and Lightning Source Inc., La Vergne, TN

Contents

Author's note

No one who writes a book like this does so without creating debts in many quarters. I am no exception. Hence I would like to thank all those people who have in some way contributed to the evolution and production of this book. They are too numerous to be mentioned individually, and I hope those whose names are not given here will accept my apologies, and my recognition of the value of their contributions. Nevertheless there are some whom I must thank more formally: first the *Conseil Scientifique* of the *Université de Bretagne Occidentale*, who granted me a sabbatical semester during which part of this book was originally drafted; then, those colleagues, most notably Janet Ormrod and Irina Lord, who commented on earlier drafts and enabled me to eliminate some inconsistencies, and improve the clarity of the writing; Janet Joyce, Robin Fawcett, Chris Butler and their team at Equinox for their helpful advice and encouragement; and, since some parts of this material were originally presented at various conferences and colloquia, those who attended the presentations and took part in the discussion which followed them. To all of these, my grateful thanks.

Introduction

Diachronic study of scientific text

Linguistic interest in scientific writing is frequently dated from Barber's seminal article (Barber 1962) of the early 1960s. In this, he considered such things as sentence length, number of clauses per sentence, verb forms, both finite (including passive forms) and non-finite, and lexis. Of course, there had been precursors, such as McDonald's (1929) *English and Science*, and Savory's (1953) book *The Language of Science*. McDonald's book is distinctly aimed at the practitioner, and even if Savory's book is of more linguistic intent, it was Barber's article that sparked a lasting linguistic interest in the genre. Interestingly, from our point of view, Savory's book includes a chapter on 'The growth of the language of science', and even though his remarks are restricted to questions of lexis, it still shows an awareness that scientific language is not static, but, like all forms of living language, evolves over time. It remains a fact, nevertheless, that the vast literature which has built up in the wake of Barber's article is basically concerned with contemporary scientific discourse; so it is synchronic in nature rather than diachronic, and hence, does not take the development of the language into consideration. This may be because a great deal of it has been geared to pedagogical interests, notably that of training non-anglophone scientists to write for publication in English (Cooke 1993). Recently however, there have been a few excursions into this area of the diachronic study of scientific writing, which it might be useful to look at briefly, for they are all in some way different to the sort of study I wish to present in this book.

Bazerman (1988) is a book many of whose chapters were previously published as articles. It tends then to deal with a series of separate, though related, questions. The factor that unites the book is that of the way in which scientific writing is produced. Several chapters of the book deal with historical questions, which is why it is of interest here, though this is not the case of all the chapters in his book. Chapter 3 deals with articles in the *Philosophical Transactions of the Royal Society* from 1665 to 1800. Chapter 4 deals with the controversy in which Newton was involved from the publication of his article 'A new theory of light and colours', to that of his book *Opticks*. Other chapters which deal with historical matters do so over a rather shorter time-span and are restricted to the twentieth century. The main thrust of the book is to consider the sociological situations in which these discourses were produced.

Gross (1996) (the first edition appeared in 1990), is interested in the rhetoric of science. The focus of the book is therefore on the argumentation, and the language, as encoded, is of interest only insofar as it reveals the argumentation being used. It is historical in that it looks at a number of non-contemporary texts, but these are looked at in isolation, and not in terms of historical development. Thus Watson and Crick appear in Chapter 4, Copernicus in Chapter 7, Newton in Chapter 8, and Darwin in Chapter 10. These are dealt with individually, and the fact that Copernicus did not write in English is not pertinent to Gross' objectives. Indeed, all quotations from Copernicus and other writers who wrote in languages other than English are given in English translation, underlining the fact that the way the language is encoded is immaterial to the points he wants to make.

Atkinson (1999) deals with a single, but extremely important scientific journal, the *Philosophical Transactions of the Royal Society*, already referred to in relation to Bazerman's book. This is the longest running scientific journal, for with the exception of the years 1679–1683, when it was replaced by the *Philosophical Collections*, it has been published continuously since its inception in 1665. Atkinson's approach is historical and he deals with the extensive period of 1675–1975. Since a large section of this book will also deal with the *Philosophical Transactions of the Royal Society*, over the similar period of 1700–1980, it would seem that there might be much in common between Atkinson (1999) and the present book. However, the bent of Atkinson's book is rhetorical (like Gross 1996) and sociological. Hence, he is interested, like Gross, in what is said, rather than how it is said, and how that fits into the sociological context of the time. I feel that the second of these, as will become evident, is of great importance, but the way things are said, the way discourse is encoded in language, is, for me, also of vital importance.

Valle (1999) is in some ways similar to Atkinson (1999). She also considers the *Philosophical Transactions of the Royal Society* over the period 1665–1965. Her study is more restrictive, in that it deals only with the life sciences. Once again, its objective is more sociological, in that she is concerned with the establishment of a discourse community, and the texts are useful in that context.

Gross *et al.* (2002) deal with the scientific article from the seventeenth to the twentieth century. For each of the four centuries concerned, there is one chapter that deals with the texts from a rhetorical point of view, 'Argument in the *x*th century', and one dealing more precisely with linguistic features, 'Style and presentation in the *x*th century'. While the features studied are of interest, they seem to have been selected on an *ad hoc* basis. For example, for each century a set of 'stylistic features' are considered. The list of 'stylistic features' for the seventeenth century is as follows:

Personal pronouns

Evaluative expressions

Poetic expressions

Deviant expressions

Suppressed-person passives

Objective passives

Dummy subjects

Hedges

Quantitative expressions

Citations

While some of these, like 'suppressed-person passives', can be identified on purely formal criteria, others, such as 'poetic expressions' and 'deviant expressions' must, to a certain degree, be subjective. For the eighteenth century, these features are divided into 'divergence' types and 'convergence' types. This distinction disappears in the nineteenth-century discussion, but two new features 'clausal density' and 'sentence length' are added to the list. A further two features, 'noun strings' and 'technical abbreviations' are added for the twentieth century. This lack of uniformity complicates the question of comparison between the results for the different centuries. Furthermore, this book uses examples from English, French, and German sources. This is a wonderful idea. Unfortunately, the French and German examples are given in English translation only, and hence, the reader who is interested precisely in linguistic features has no idea to what extent the translation correctly represents the features of the original.

These remarks may sound critical, but my object is not to criticize, and I would like to insist that these books are all excellent in their own ways. What I wish to point out is that they do not do the sort of thing that I wish to do in this book. So the time has perhaps come for me to spell that out in more detail. The above books all treat language as a social phenomenon, and with that I totally agree. Language is part of the social relationships which are built up within communities. It is not something which exists as some sort of independent entity, which we can, as it were, plug into communication gaps. The language is the communication, and is indistinguishable from it. It is consequently also related to the context in which it comes about, and can only be totally understood in relation to that context. Thus each natural language system is the set of meaning-making resources from which the speaker can select for communicating meanings in context. The natural language I will deal with is English, and the context which I wish to consider in this book is that of scientific research, and more precisely the written language in which that scientific research is communicated. I wish to look at the language, not just as it is today, but as it has developed since English began being used regularly as a language of scientific communication in the late seventeenth century. I hope to show, not just how the language has changed over time, but that the language changes as a function of the context of scientific research in which it is produced. Thus, the constantly changing context of scientific research and the language which is derived from that context are intimately linked.

Systemic Functional Linguistics – a suitable framework

I do not believe that it is possible to study language in some theory-neutral way. It is necessary to have some theoretical framework. The pretence of being theory-neutral is in itself a form of theory, though one which is trying to hide that fact. There are basically three possible approaches to language, and hence three broad categories of linguistic theory. The first category is that which treats language as an entity in itself and is interested primarily in the forms in which it is found. Such theories are formalist theories, and Generative Grammar is a prime example of this. The second category is that of theories which are interested in how humans create language in communication. They are thus interested in the mental processes involved in the production of language, and various forms of Cognitive Linguistics have become popular in recent years. The third category is that which is interested in how language functions; and among the various functional theories which have been developed, Systemic Functional Linguistics considers function both internally in terms of how the different parts of the language function together to construct meaning, and externally in terms of the way language functions in society as a means of communication. It is this last type of theory which provides a suitable framework for the sort of study I wish to present. This does not, of course, mean that these three categories (formal, cognitive and functional) are totally distinct, and certainly grey areas and overlaps exist, particularly between functional and cognitive approaches. Moreover, language is ultimately encoded in form, so no matter what approach is used, form has to be dealt with at some point (Banks 2004c).

This book is ostensibly a book on linguistics, or more precisely, a book on the linguistic analysis of scientific text. As such, I hope it will be of interest to practising linguists and students of linguistics. However, I hope that historians and philosophers, particularly those with an interest in the history and philosophy of science, or the history of ideas, will find what is said here relevant to their concerns. I hope that I have successfully negotiated the balancing act of providing sufficient explanation of more technical points for those less familiar with linguistic terminology, without boring those who use it on a daily basis.

Linguistics is unique as a discipline, in that it is the only discipline where the means of communicating its results constitute the object of study. Linguistics studies language but has to use language to express what it wants to say about it. It is perhaps for that reason that it finds itself at the crossroads of several other disciplines. Some linguistic theories have a common frontier, and indeed fade off into, logic; others have a similar relationship with psychology; others are on the frontier of sociology. It is this last which does the type of job necessary for the study presented here. The theory which best combines these features of functionalism and an openness to sociological matters is Systemic Functional Linguistics (Halliday 2004a; Bloor and Bloor 1995; Lock 1996; Thompson 2004; Banks 2005c), and this is the theoretical framework which lies behind the work presented in this book. I hope that the way in which the book is written, and the comparative transparency of the terminology used, will make it accessible to those less familiar with this approach. I will nevertheless give a brief outline of the relevant parts of the theory, and explain some of the concepts which will be important in the following pages.

The part of the Systemic Functional Linguistics model which is of greatest interest to us here is the part which deals with meaning. The model proposes three types of meaning, or semantic metafunctions. These are ideational, interpersonal, and textual. Ideational meaning is that part which concerns the representation of the world, whether it be the external world in which the speaker finds him/herself, or the internal world of the speaker's own mind. Interpersonal meaning concerns the relationships set up by the speaker; these may be relationships with the speaker's addressees, or with the content of the message. Textual meaning is concerned with the way in which the message is organised.

At the level of the clause, ideational meaning, since it is concerned with the representation of the world, involves consideration of processes, that is, of happenings and states, the participants that are involved in those processes, and the attendant circumstances. The relationship between the process, the participants and the circumstances is referred to as the transitivity of the clause. The following example is taken from Newton's *Opticks*.

> In a very dark Chamber, at a round Hole, about one third Part of an Inch broad, made in the Shut of a Window, I placed a Glass Prism ... (Newton 1730 [1979]: 26)

Here, we have a process, encoded in the word *placed*; it has two participants, *I*, and *a Glass Prism*. This particular process is an example of Material process (the names of functions have traditionally been capitalised in Systemic Functional Linguistics), that is, a process that takes place in a physical environment; so a Material process is one where someone does something, or something happens in the physical world. In this example, the first participant is the person who does the action of placing; he is the conscious instigator of the process. This type of participant is called the Actor. The second participant in this example is the entity that is in some way altered or modified by what takes place. In this case the prism is moved from one place to another. This is called the Affected. The rest of the clause gives the circumstances; in this case they tell us where the process takes place. It is possible to distinguish five different process types: in additional to Material process we have Mental, Relational, Verbal and Existential processes.

Mental processes are those which, as the name implies, are internal to the Subject's mind; they are processes of thought, perception, and affection. In the following example, again taken from Newton's *Opticks*, the word *suspected* encodes a Mental process.

> ... I suspected that Tincture might either wholly, or in great Measure arise from some Rays of the Spectrum scattered irregularly by some Inequalities in the Substance and Polish of the Glass ... (Newton 1730 [1979]: 30)

Here again there are two participants. The first, *I*, is the conscious entity whose mind is the cerebral site of the process; this type of participant is called the Senser. The second participant here is the contents of the *that*-clause which follows the verb. This gives us the content of the mental event, and is called the Phenomenon.

Relational processes relate to the existence or creation of a state. In the case of the creation of a state, some dynamism might be thought to be involved. Before, the state does not exist, afterwards, it does. However; the majority of Relational processes are of the existence of a state type, and in these nothing takes place. Unlike Material and Mental processes which are principally dynamic, Relational processes are basically static. A Relational process states the relationship between two entities, or between an entity and one of its properties:

> ... the Sun's Light is an heterogeneous Mixture of Rays ... (Newton 1730 [1979]: 63)

In this example (again from Newton) the Relational process, encoded by *is*, links an entity, called the Carrier, here *the Sun's Light*, to a property, called the Attribute, which is here *an heterogeneous Mixture of Rays*.

Verbal processes are processes of communication, either spoken or written:

> I have hitherto explain'd the power of Bodies to reflect and refract ... (Newton 1730 [1979]: 276)

Again in this example there are two participants; the first, *I*, is the person communicating, and the second, *the power of Bodies to reflect and refract*, is the content of the communication. The person communicating is called the Sayer, and the content of the communication is the Verbiage.

Existential processes state the existence of some entity, hence there is only one participant involved.

> There are certain Phænomena of this scatter'd Light, which when I first observed them, seem'd very strange and surprizing to me. (Newton 1730 [1979]: 289)

In this clause the *Phænomena* are said to exist, so this is termed the Existent. It is the only participant; *there* is not a participant since it does not refer to anything; it only has the grammatical role of signalling that the clause is existential in nature.

The above is not intended to be an exhaustive treatment of transitivity, and I have not gone through all the possible semantic roles which a participant can have. But I hope that the above is sufficient for those readers unfamiliar with this approach to get some idea of what this sort of analysis is like, and to follow the argumentation, where necessary, in the rest of this book.

The interpersonal component, as we have said, concerns the relationships set up by the speaker. The difference between a statement and a question involves this type of meaning, since choosing one or the other attributes roles to both the speaker and his addressee. In choosing a statement, the speaker gives himself the role of informer, while his addressee is the person informed, while if he chooses a question, he gives himself the role of questioner, and imposes the role of potential answerer on his addressee. Consider the following example from Newton's *Opticks*.

> ... is not this done by an Attraction between the Particles of the Salt of Tartar, and the Particles of the Water which float in the Air in the form of Vapours? (Newton 1730 [1979]: 376)

Compare this with the following constructed statement form.

> ... this is [not] done by an Attraction between the Particles of the Salt of Tartar, and the Particles of the Water which float in the Air in the form of Vapours.

The difference between the two is in the ordering of the words *this is done/is this done*. So this is the part which tells us whether the clause is a statement or a question; and if we are the addressees of this clause, it tells us whether the speaker is treating us as people who are being informed, or as potential answerers. This part is known as the Mood, and the rest of the clause as the Residue.

The textual metafunction, or the part of meaning that deals with the organization of the message, concerns a number of things, but the most important from our point of view is the thematic structure. This distinguishes between the Theme, which is what the speaker starts from, and consequently, in English, places at the beginning of his clause, and what is then said about it, which is the Rheme. In many ways, Rheme can be conceived negatively, simply as what is not the Theme (Fawcett 2000). In the following clause *I* is the speaker's starting point and constitutes the Theme, while the rest of the clause is the Rheme.

> I placed also two Paper Circles very near one another, the one in the red Light of one Prism, and the other in the violet light of the other. (Newton 1730 [1979]: 52)

On the other hand, in the following clause Newton takes the circumstantial phrase *In the middle of two thin Boards* as his starting point, so this is Theme, while the rest of the clause, including the Subject, *I*, is Rheme.

> In the middle of two thin Boards I made round holes a third part of an Inch in diameter ... (Newton 1730 [1979]: 45)

In any stretch of natural language, all three metafunctions are present. They are not in any hierarchical relationship, but are woven together like the strands of a tress. For purposes of study, it is necessary to talk about them individually, simply because one cannot say more than one thing at a time, but it must never be forgotten that when one particular metafunction is being discussed, the others are operating simultaneously in the same stretch of language.

Language is not just a question of meaning in some abstract sense, it is meaning in context. Language is created in, and is a part of, a social situation and it cannot be divorced from that situation. Just as language is born out of a social situation, so it feeds back into it to become a causal element in the development of that social situation. As Halliday says:

> ... the relation of the language to the social system is not simply one of expression but a more complex natural dialectic in which language actively symbolizes the social system, thus creating as well as being created by it. (Halliday 1978: 183)

Just as the semantic level of language can be seen as comprised of three metafunctions, ideational, interpersonal, and textual, so the situation can be seen as three variables, each linked to one of the semantic metafunctions. Related to the ideational metafunction, is field. Field is the activity which is going on, of which the act of communication is a part, and it includes the content of that communication. The interpersonal metafunction is related to tenor. This is the set of relationships between the persons taking part in the act of communication. The textual metafunction is related to mode. Mode is the form which the communication takes, stemming from the basic distinction between written and spoken communication. To take a simple example, the rules for the game of football have as their field the game itself, players, pitches, referees, and so on. The tenor is concerned with the relationships between the governing body of the sport, and the players, referees and club officials involved in it. The mode is written communication, intended to be read silently, but non-linearly, that is, as a reference document. To take an example more pertinent to this book, the scientific research article has as its field scientific research and the communication of the results of that research. The tenor is that of research scientists communicating with their peers in a specialised scientific domain. The mode is that of written communication, intended to be read silently, and, at least ostensibly, linearly, though there is evidence that for many scientists this is not strictly the case (Swales 1990).

These three variables of the situation have a determining role in producing the content of the metafunctions related to them. Many think of ideology as being an outer layer in this model, so that ultimately everything depends on ideology (Martin 1992; Eggins 1994). However I believe that ideology is itself part of the situation, and is best thought of as being part of tenor (Banks forthcoming).

There are two aspects of Systemic Functional Linguistics which I think are particularly important for the study of scientific text, and I shall therefore go into them in a little more detail. The first of these is a subject which has already been raised, that of thematic structure, and the second is that of grammatical metaphor, of which, more later.

Thematic structure

The concept of thematic structure is not peculiar to Systemic Functional Linguistics, and many theories use some form of this idea. However, there are some approaches which combine thematic structure and information structure as a single phenomenon, and others which distinguish between them. Systemic Functional Linguistics is of the second type. As we have seen, thematic structure is a question of the distinction between a Theme and a Rheme, where Theme is defined as the speaker's starting point. The basic unit of thematic structure is the clause. Information structure, on the other hand, distinguishes between a Given and a Focalized (Banks 2004b, 2005c), frequently called the New. The Focalized is identified by the position of the tonic accent. Consequently, its basic unit is not the clause but the tone group. In spoken language, the Focalized is audible, but in written language it depends on the aural reconstruction which the reader makes of the text, and may therefore vary, within limits, from reader to reader (Davies 1986). The focalized unit is the centre on which the speaker wants his addressee to concentrate. That is why it is frequently, though not always, information which is new to the addressee. Theories which combine thematic structure and information structure as a single phenomenon, then have the difficulty of distinguishing between two entirely different types of emphasis, which in such an approach will probably both be referred to by the same term, most commonly 'theme' or 'topic'; one of these is the emphasis given as the place where the speaker is starting from, the other is the emphasis given to the element towards which the speaker wishes to direct the addressee. It seems clearer, more coherent, and more logical to treat these two types of structure as distinct from the outset.

Even within those approaches which distinguish thematic structure as a separate phenomenon, and indeed even within Systemic Functional Linguistics, there is some disagreement as to how much of the clause should actually be included in the Theme (Berry 1996). However, the view with which I would agree is that which says that the Theme is that part of the clause up to and including the first main constituent of the clause, main constituents being those encoded as Subject, Complement, Predicator or circumstantial Adjunct. Thus, taking the following clause (again from Newton), it will be seen that the circumstantial Adjunct *At two holes made near one another in my Window-shut* is the Theme.

> At two holes made near one another in my Window-shut I placed two prisms ... (Newton 1730 [1979]: 48)

We might now make variants of this clause. The following has the Subject as Theme.

> I placed two prisms at two holes made near one another in my Window-shut.

It is also possible to have the Complement as Theme.

> Two prisms I placed at two holes made near one another in my Window-shut.

This is less common in contemporary English than it was in Newton's day, but it still occurs, particularly when there is a contrast.

> The prisms I placed at the holes, but the lenses I placed on the table.

This type of Theme, which corresponds to one of the main constituents of the clause, is called the topical Theme. Every clause has a topical Theme. It may have, but does not necessarily have, other types of Theme; these always precede the topical Theme. There are two other types of Theme which may occur; these are interpersonal Theme, and textual Theme. Interpersonal Themes are those which relate to the relationships set up by the speaker. This can be in terms of the addressee.

> Do not all fix'd Bodies, when heated beyond a certain degree, emit Light and shine ... (Newton 1730 [1979]: 340)

Here, the mood is interrogative, hence the speaker is categorised as potential answerer, and this is done by the thematisation of the Finite *do; not* is here an invitation to the speaker to agree, and can thus be included in the interpersonal Theme. The topical Theme is *all fix'd Bodies*. The speaker can also make a personal judgement about the content of his message, so that if Newton had been less sure of himself, and had said:

> Probably all fix'd Bodies, when heated beyond a certain degree, emit Light and shine.

Probably would function as an interpersonal Theme. Textual themes are those which link the clause to the rest of the discourse.

> Yet instead of the Circular Hole F, 'tis better to substitute an oblong Hole shaped like a long Parallelogram with its Length parallel to the Prism ABC. (Newton 1730 [1979]: 70)

Yet links this clause to what has been said before, indicating that the content of the clause may be contrary to the reader's expectations. *Yet* thus constitutes a textual theme. Where more than one clause combine to form a clause complex, the thematic structure can become a little more complicated. If, for example, a subordinate clause precedes its main clause, it functions in the same way that a circumstantial Adjunct does. In fact, they are doing the same job, except that instead of the group structure of the Adjunct, we now have a clause. In this case the subordinate clause functions as the (topical) Theme for the whole clause complex.

> If these Rings thus depend on the thickness of the Plate of Glass, their Diameters at equal distances from several Speculums made of such concavo-convex Plates of Glass as are ground on the same Sphere, ought to be reciprocally in a subduplicate Proportion of the thicknesses of the Plates of Glass. (Newton 1730 [1979]: 305)

In this clause complex the *if*-clause, *If these Rings thus depend on the thickness of the Plate of Glass*, functions as Theme to the rest. It is true that thematic structure is basically a structure of the clause, so that in this case we could go further and look at the thematic structure of the clauses individually; thus within the *if*-clause, *if* functions as a textual Theme, and *these Rings* as topical Theme. This however is only the internal thematic structure of a subordinate clause, which itself functions as the topical Theme of the clause complex. When we are dealing with extended text, we are interested in the text as a whole, and in this case the thematic structure at the higher (ranking clause) level will usually be more relevant. Where however the clauses are coordinate, neither can be considered to be circumstantial to the other and they can be dealt with separately.

> I placed a Prism behind the Shut in that beam to refract it towards the opposite Wall, and close behind the Prism I fixed one of the Boards ... (Newton 1730 [1979]: 45)

Here, the first clause has a topical Theme, *I*, the rest of the clause (up to *Wall*) being the Rheme. The second clause has a textual Theme, *and*, and a topical Theme *close behind the Prism*, the rest of the clause being the Rheme. So here there are two (finite) clauses at the primary or ranking level. A special case occurs when the element which functions as Theme in a clause is elided in the second.

> The Breadth of the Image answered to the Sun's Diameter, and was about two Inches and the eighth Part of an Inch, including the Penumbra. (Newton 1730 [1979]: 29)

Here there are two clauses but the Subject, *the Breadth of the Image*, is the same for each clause, and is ellipsed in the second. Some think that in terms of the thematic structure, it is necessary to reinstate this ellipsed Subject, so that each of the clauses then has its own topical Theme (Matthiessen 1995; Martin *et al.* 1997; Martin and Rose 2003). However, I dislike this tactic of rewriting the language as it appears, to make it correspond to our analytical conventions. It also means that, from the point of view of thematic structure, whether the Subject in the second clause is ellipsed or not makes no difference. So, I prefer to say that in this example there is a single Theme, *the Breadth of the Image*, but that the Rheme runs over a two-clause segment, *answered to the Sun's Diameter, and was about two Inches and the eighth Part of an Inch, including the Penumbra.*

Grammatical metaphor

The second phenomenon that I would like to deal with in a little more detail is that of grammatical metaphor (Halliday and Matthiessen 1999; Halliday 2004a; Banks 2005c). The most common way of expressing a process is by using a verb; to express an entity we usually use a noun; if we want to express a quality of an entity, we use an adjective, and so on (Ravelli 1988; Taverniers 2003). If however we cut across this system and, for example, encode a process as a noun, then what is produced is a grammatical metaphor. Consider the following passage from Newton's *Opticks*:

> And turning the Prism slowly about its Axis, until all the Light which went through one of its Angles, and was refracted by it began to be reflected by its Base, at which till then it went out of the Glass, I observed that those Rays which had suffered the greatest Refraction were sooner reflected than the rest. I conceived therefore, that those Rays of the reflected Light, which were most refrangible, did first of all by a total Reflexion became more copious in that Light than the rest, and that afterwards the rest also, by a total Reflexion, became as copious as these. (Newton 1730 [1979]: 54)

In this passage, Newton uses the verbs *refract* and *reflect*. These both refer to processes; indeed they are events which take place in the physical world, and so are examples of Material process. This is the usual or congruent way of encoding processes. Newton, however, also uses the words *refraction* and *reflexion*. These are nouns, but they still refer to the same phenomena, that is, to processes. In this case, where a noun, rather than a verb, encodes a process, the encoding is non-congruent, and we have an example of grammatical metaphor. In this passage we also see that the past participle, *reflected*, is used to describe an entity, *light*; that is, a verb is being used to encode a quality of the entity. This again is a type of grammatical metaphor.

Using grammatical metaphor produces two kinds of effect; the first of these is grammatical, the second semantic. This can be illustrated taking the nominalisation of a process as an example. Supposing we have a clause like *The government announced that taxes would rise.* The process of announcing can be nominalised, and instead of the clause, we would have the nominal group *the government's announcement that taxes would rise.* Since this contains a second process, this also could be nominalised, giving, *the government's announcement of tax increases.* This is now nominal in nature, so it can take on any of the functions which are appropriate for a nominal group, Subject, Complement, or prepositional Completive; thus as Subject we could imagine *The government's announcement of tax increases surprised everyone.* Moreover, since nouns can be modified and qualified, the nominal groups could have additional Modifiers and Qualifiers, for example, *The government's long-awaited and highly controversial announcement of inevitable tax increases made at the end of the party conference surprised everyone.* The extent to which this type of grammatical metaphor is useful can be seen if one now attempts to express the content of this clause without using grammatical metaphor. This is known as 'unpacking' (Ventola 1996). It will be immediately seen that this is difficult to do with anything like the concision of the original, and with any sort of elegance.

The change from verb form to noun form is not only grammatical in effect. Since the verb form congruently encodes a process, and the noun an entity, encoding a process in nominal form brings about semantic changes too. The fact that the process now has nominal form means that it takes on some of the quality of an entity. Entities are typically more stable and fixed than processes; processes are typically fleeting affairs, which have a beginning and an end, and are then gone forever. The process of announcing is a verbal event, and once it has taken place it is part of the past, and no longer exists. Expressing this as a noun, *announcement,* gives it more permanence and stability, as though the announcement were somehow still there. It has become a feature of, or a virtual entity in, the political environment.

Grammatical metaphor, particularly the nominalisation of processes, has become a significant feature of scientific writing; indeed, I would claim that it is particularly appropriate to scientific writing (Banks 1999, 2001a, 2003b).

The nominalisation of processes should not be confused with deverbal nouns. It is possible for a noun to encode a process, where the cognate verb just happens to be missing from the vocabulary of English. In the following example from a 1996 scientific article (Lindsay *et al.*, see Appendix 1), the words *cycle* and *flux* might be considered candidates for this class of nouns encoding processes, but where the appropriate verb does not exist.

As a result of this neutralization-reionization cycle the initial proton flux becomes a mixture of protons and fast neutral atoms. (Lindsay *et al.* 1996: 212)

In fact, the *OED* does have an entry for the verb *flux*, but it relates to the melting of metals, so does not have the relevant sense; and in any case is now obsolete. The word *cycle* is a less obvious candidate, with an OED entry 'to move or revolve in cycles', although the latest citation for this meaning is from Darwin in 1859. Whatever the status of these precise examples, they do establish the principal that a noun may encode a process in the absence of the appropriate cognate verb, and where this occurs the noun in question is an example of grammatical metaphor (Banks 2001b). At the same time, some deverbal nouns do not encode processes, for example *cook*, meaning a person who cooks, *builder*, a person who builds, and so on. These are obviously not examples of grammatical metaphor.

Michael Halliday

As has been said, the theoretical background, and the terminology used in this book are those of Systemic Functional Linguistics. This model is closely associated with the name of Michael Halliday who is usually considered to be its founding father, and its leading light. It would therefore seem appropriate to consider what Michael Halliday has himself said about scientific writing and its historical development. He has indeed given some attention to this matter and the articles he has devoted to the subject have been collected in Halliday and Martin (1993) and Halliday (2004b) (Vol. 5 of his *Collected Works*), with some items appearing in both. It should be pointed out that this present book is in no sense an attempt to test or verify the hypotheses put forward by Halliday. However, since Halliday's work in general constitutes a sort of backdrop to this book, that there is some relationship to his work is evident. The two are nevertheless different and distinct, and I think that the content of this book can in many ways be seen as complementary to Halliday's work.

In terms of approach and methodology the two are different. Halliday's work is in many ways qualititative. He does not give us the details of his textual analyses, but rather the resulting conclusions and hypotheses that can be based on them, and the arguments that can be built on them. One has the feeling that considerable analysis has preceded the production of this work, and at one point he lists Chaucer, Newton, Priestley, Dalton, Darwin and Maxwell among the scientific authors whose work he has analysed

(Halliday and Martin 1993). But the detail of this analysis remains in the background, as a presupposed basis to his main objective. Where he does give analytical detail, it is of relatively short passages given in illustration of the points he is making. The work I am going to present is largely quantitative. Since they are quantified, the phenomena I have studied can be compared in terms of their relative frequencies. Thus where Halliday's work gives us the broad sweep of the big picture, I will be frequently filling in much of the small detail which shows that the big picture is full of numerous complications, a fact which Halliday readily admits.

When he considers the development of scientific writing, Halliday starts with Chaucer's *Treatise on the Astrolabe*. He points out that in this text, the earliest known text of a technological nature to be written in English, Chaucer takes two steps towards the nominalised discourse, which Halliday takes to be symptomatic of scientific writing. Chaucer produces technical nouns and complex nominal groups with multiple Qualifiers. He describes Chaucer's text as 'a kind of technical, perhaps proto-scientific discourse' (Halliday 1988[1]: 165). He contrasts this with Newton's *Opticks*, in which he sees Newton as creating a new discourse of experimentation. Here he finds three different types of writing: first, descriptions of experiments (in contrast to Chaucer's instructions for use), with intricate clause complexes, and very little grammatical metaphor, and abstract nouns as technical terms; second, the arguments and conclusions from these, where the clause complexes are less intricate, there is some degree of grammatical metaphor, and abstract nouns appear as non-technical terms; and third, mathematical sections, where the sentences tend to be single clauses with long lexically dense nominal groups, and abstract nouns as technical mathematical terms. When he compares Chaucer with Newton, he claims that

> ... one can sense the change of direction that is being inaugurated in Newton's writing, where the grammar undergoes a kind a lateral shift that leads into "grammatical metaphor" on a massive scale. (Halliday and Martin 1993: 13)

Though this is true, it should also be borne in mind that these two texts, while both belonging to the general category of 'scientific and technical English', nevertheless have considerable generic differences. I shall go into this question in more detail later. When it comes to Priestley, whose *The History and Present State of Electricity, with Original Experiments*, published in the 1760s, he has analysed, he finds that the development has gone further. Nominal features are used to form technical taxonomies, and to summarize and package representations of processes, that is, as grammatical metaphors. These can be used for backgrounding, as Theme, or for foregrounding as

Focalised within the Rheme. Verbal features are used to relate the nominalised processes to each other or to our interpretation of them. By the time we move into the nineteenth century, where he cites Dalton's *A New System of Chemical Philosophy* (1827) and Maxwell's *An Elementary Treatise on Electricity* (1881), this has become the 'most valued model' (Halliday 1988[1]: 173). Halliday suggests two patterns of development, one of which is internal the other external. The external pattern concerns the relating of increasingly nominalised processes.

a happens; so *x* happens

→ because *a* happens, *x* happens

→ that *a* happens causes *x* to happen

→ happening *a* causes happening *x*

→ happening *a* is the cause of happening *x*

The internal pattern relates to our interpretation of this.

a happens; so we know *x* happens

→ because *a* happens, we know *x* happens

→ that *a* happens proves *x* to happen

→ happening *a* proves happening *x*

→ happening *a* is the proof of happening *x* (Halliday 1988[1]: 174))

Halliday points out that this is highly schematic. It shows the direction of change, and does not imply that the final stage is now the most common. Indeed, although it is a feature I have not attempted to quantify, I have the impression that the final stage, although it does appear in contemporary scientific articles, is still relatively rare compared with stages three and four.

Thus, grammatical metaphor is at the centre of Halliday's thought about scientific writing, and forms the cornerstone of the construction of scientific discourse. This is the point he hammers home throughout his writing on scientific discourse. In terms of the construction of discourse, he sees two reasons for this development.

One is technicality: the grammar has to create technical meanings, purely virtual phenomena that exist only on the semiotic plane, as terms of a theory; and not as isolates but organized into elaborate taxonomies. The other is rationality: the grammar has to create a form of discourse for reasoning from observation and experiment, drawing general conclusions and progressing from one step to another in sequences of logical argument. (Halliday 2004b: 123 [originally 1999])

So, a nominalised process becomes a virtual entity, taking on some of the quality of an entity, becoming more 'thing-like'. In this form it can be developed as the head of a complex nominal group with extra information in the associated Modifiers and Qualifiers. It can be, and frequently is, also used to summarise previous (non-metaphorical) material, and function as Theme, thus moving the logical argument of the text forward. The present book will I think show that while this broad sweep is largely true, it is not a smooth uncluttered process, but has many fits and starts, ups and downs, on the way. Moreover, buildings require more than one cornerstone, and it may be the case that grammatical metaphor is not the only foundation in this type of discourse. For example, Halliday's main point brings out the intricate relationship between grammatical metaphor and thematic structure, and perhaps it is possible to look at this from the Theme end of the relationship.

It is perhaps also worth pointing out that Halliday frequently illustrates his remarks with examples taken from *Scientific American*. These texts obviously fall into the general area of scientific writing, though it is not necessarily the same subgenre as appears in a research journal. *Scientific American* could, I think, be described as high quality popularisation, where 'popularisation' is in no sense derogatory. In terms of the situation variables, the two probably coincide in terms of field and mode, but differ in terms of tenor, since the presumed readerships of the two types of text are different. Halliday is presumably claiming that the relevant points that he is making are common to these two subgenres, but they could be expected to differ on some parameters too.

Halliday, then, paints the broad picture, and those who are familiar with his work point out that even when being intuitive he has a flair for pointing out features which are subsequently proved to be correct. This book in no way contradicts that picture, but complements it, and fills in some of the detail. It shows how the ongoing development is not a simple linear progression, but one that feels its way forward, groping towards the most efficient expression of the texts which emerge from the ever-changing situation.

I shall now give a brief outline of what is to be found in the rest of this book.

This study

This book will begin by considering the text, mentioned above, which is thought of as the first document of a technical nature to have been written in English, Chaucer's *Treatise on the Astrolabe*. Those linguistic features commonly associated with scientific writing, the passive, its corollary first person pronouns, and nominalisation, will be considered, and compared with an analogue present day text. Although this document is a precursor, it is necessary to move on to the seventeenth century to find English being used to any significant extent in scientific writing. Against a troubled historical background, we will consider the position of Francis Bacon, who, although not really a scientist himself, nor a person who wrote primarily in English, was to have such a great influence on the scientists of a later generation and the way they wrote in English. One of the earliest of these was Robert Boyle whose scientific writing in English is considered. After this the writing of Henry Power and Robert Hooke are compared, the first representing the biological sciences, and the second the physical. This brings us up to the founding of the Royal Society and the beginning of the *Philosophical Transactions* as its mouthpiece. This is also the period when Isaac Newton began his rise to fame. His relationship with the Royal Society, at least until he himself became President, was not an easy one, and was probably a contributory factor in his search for new ways of expressing scientific experimentation and its results. The possible influence of Latin, until then the intellectual *lingua franca*, on Newton's English is considered. Newton's English is then compared with the French of Huygens, where it would seem that the difference between an empirical and a Cartesian viewpoint leads to differences in the grammar (or lexicogrammar in systemic functional terms, since this approach considers lexis to be part of grammar). For the following three centuries, 1700–1980, a corpus of articles from the *Philosophical Transactions of the Royal Society* is used. The use of the passive is studied, and the differences over time in both the physical and biological sectors are noted. This is related to the use of first person pronouns, and again differences in the two sectors over time are noted. Similarly, grammatical metaphor, notably in the form of nominalisation of processes is studied over the period. Thematic structure is then considered, taking into account topical Theme, and the grammatical function which it conflates with, textual Theme, and interpersonal Theme. Thematic progression is also considered. A semantic typology of topical Themes is proposed, and applied to the corpus. This underlines the fact that thematic structure may well be the driving force behind other features such as passive use. Finally, a coda discusses the ways in which scientists refer to each other over this period. From this emerges a picture of the history of science over three centuries, where there are two main turning points. From the beginning of the period, the physical sciences are experimental, but the biological sector is observational. The first major change occurs in the middle of the nineteenth century when the biological sciences become, to some extent, experimental in their turn. The second major change occurs towards the end of the nineteenth or beginning of the twentieth century when the physical sciences begin to focus on mathematical modelling, a phenomenon which has not affected the biological sector by the end of the period studied. This is a striking illustration of the interrelationship of language and the context in which it is produced.

It is perhaps useful to point out that all of the analyses presented in this book were done by hand, not by computer. To some, that may sound odd, and indeed old-fashioned, in this computer-dominated day. It is true that the computer has revolutionised the way we do linguistics, and the way we think about linguistics. Nevertheless, it remains a truism that the computer is only as good as its programmer. And programmers cannot do everything. Some of the features which I have considered are not easily susceptible to computerised treatment; some of them are such that they cannot be reduced to the set of formal characteristics required for machine recognition. This provides a first justification for manual analysis. The second is rather more personal, in that I have found in experience that as the analysis progresses, certain aspects come to light, and it is fairly easy to adapt manual analysis to take this into account, whereas with a computer, modification of the parameters can involve comparatively complex program changes. Hence, for the sort of analysis which I am doing, manual analysis is more flexible.

Finally, it will be evident that this book contains a lot of numbers. The results which I have found are quantified. However, I make no claims to being a statistician, and I would avoid calling these figures statistics. No statistical tests have been applied to them, and they are presented simply as the raw facts which I found. To the extent that they give a coherent picture, they appear to be, in the ordinary language sense, significant.

In giving examples and quotations, particularly from older documents, I have attempted to keep as close to the original as possible. The so-called 'long-S' has been eliminated in favour of the standard comtemporary 's'; spaces preceding a punctuation mark have been eliminated in favour of contemporary practice in the English quotes, but not in French, where it remains the contemporary convention; but such things as capitals, italics and spelling have been retained.

Part 1
FROM CHAUCER TO NEWTON

1 Beginning with Chaucer

Where it all began

If one were to select a moment as being the time when scientific English first came into being, then the late seventeenth century would be the primary candidate. Up to that point, virtually all scientific writing had been in Latin, the academic *lingua franca* of the age, but from that moment on, more and more scientific writing was published in the vernaculars of the period. For English, Isaac Newton is frequently singled out as the person who first gave scientific English its *lettres de noblesse*. Newton had already written and published in Latin, but turned to English for his *Opticks*. This is the point that Halliday takes as being the birth of scientific English.

> For registering the birth of scientific English we shall take Newton's *Treatise on Opticks* (published 1704, written 1675–87). Newton creates a discourse of experimentation... (Halliday 1988[1]: 166)

Of course this does not mean, nor does Halliday intend us to understand, that this is the first scientific document to have been written in English. He himself, as we have already seen, precedes his discussion of Newton's book with an analysis of a much earlier text: Chaucer's *Treatise on the Astrolabe* (Chaucer 1391 [1957]). And that is probably where we should begin. Halliday sees nominalisation as being the keystone to scientific discourse (Halliday 1987,[2] 1988,[1] 1994[3]), and claims that Chaucer took the first two steps towards this nominalised form of discourse. This is evident in his use of technical nouns, both for parts of the astrolabe and for geometrical, mathematical abstractions. It is also seen in the construction of noun groups with rankshifted Qualifiers, frequently with further rankshifted Qualifiers within them. He also notes that the favoured process types are Relational in the more descriptive passages, and Mental or Material for giving instructions. Temporal and causal/conditional clause complexes use *when, if,* or *because* for hypotactic links, and *for,* or *therefore* for paratactic links. He describes the text as 'technical ... proto-scientific discourse', and says that it 'contains technical nouns, both concrete-technological and abstract-scientific; extended nominal groups, especially mathematical; clause complexes which carry forward the argument' (Halliday 1988[1]: 165).

However, if we are to use Chaucer's text as a launching pad, from which we can project forward in time to scientific discourse, and it is reasonable to do so since the *Treatise on the Astrolabe* is the earliest known text of a scientific, or at least technical, nature to have been written in English, then we must be quite clear about the type of text it is. It is certainly not a scientific text in the same sense that a scientific research article is. Chaucer's text is ostensibly addressed to his son, as it opens with the words:

> Lyte Lewys my sone, I aperceyve wel by certeyne evidences thyn abilities to lerne sciences touching nombres and proporciouns, and as wel consider I thy besy praier in special to lerne the tretys of the Astrolabie. (Chaucer 1391 [1957]: 545)

There is some doubt as to whether Chaucer actually had a son of his own. In his edition of Chaucer's works (Chaucer 1391 [1957]), Robinson points out that some have suggested that the boy who is addressed is Lewis Clifford, the son of his friend Sir Lewis Clifford. If this were so, the fact that this young boy died in 1391 could account for the fact that the *Treatise* was never completed, although this is not the only work that Chaucer left in an unfinished state. At all events, whether the addressee was his own son or not, it is evident that it was intended for a young person, for the age of his addressee is given as ten years. In pointing out that other treatises have sections that would be too difficult for him, he says:

> ... and somme of hem ben to harde to thy tendir age of ten yeer to conceive.
>
> This tretis, divided in 5 parties, wol I shewe the under full light reules and naked wordes in Englissh, for Latyn ne canst thou yit but small, my litel sone. (Chaucer 1391 [1957]: 545)

One cannot but be struck by Chaucer's pedagogical awareness. He seems to be particularly conscious of the fact that he is writing for someone who is young, and apologises to more sophisticated readers for this pedagogical approach:

> Now wol I preie meekly every discret persone that redith or herith this litel tretys to have my rude endityng for excused, and my superfluite of wordes, for two causes, the first cause is for that curious endityng and hard sentence is ful hevy at onys for such a child to lerne. And the secunde cause is this, that sothly me semith better to written unto a child twyes a god sentence, than he forgete it onys. (Chaucer 1391 [1957]: 546)

The notion that it is better to write something twice for a child, than that the child should forget it, having read it only once, is particularly charming.

Until recently Chaucer's *Treatise on the Astrolabe* had been little noticed. Curry's *Chaucer and the Medieval Sciences*, first published in 1926, with a second edition in 1960, makes no mention of it at all (Curry 1960). It is noted by Savory, but apart from pointing out that Chaucer introduced some technical terms, some directly from Latin or Greek, he goes no further (Savory 1953). Chaucer originally intended writing a book in five parts, but in the event only the Prologue and the first two parts were completed. Despite its incomplete nature, it still seems to have become a significant text at an early stage. Skeat counts no less than 22 manuscripts (Skeat 1900). Part 1 is a description of the instrument, and Part 2 contains the instructions for its use. Given this, and the fact that it was written for someone who was comparatively young, the closest contemporary equivalent would seem to be the 'how it works' type of book, aimed generally at a teenage public (Banks 1996, 1997a, 1997b). In order to investigate the possible scientific nature of this text, I shall consider three features frequently associated with scientific writing: use of the passive, use (or non-use) of personal pronouns, and nominalisation of processes. The use of these features in Chaucer's text will be compared with their use in a contemporary 'how it works' teenager's book.

The passive

Use of the passive voice is probably one of the most frequently cited characteristics of scientific writing (Banks 1994a). Technically, it is said that Middle English had no passive voice (Quirk and Wrenn 1955, Mossé 1959, Crépin 1972), but by this is meant the fact that it no longer had an inflectional passive; but it was possible to express a passive sense with a periphrastic form, using the verb *be* and the past participle, just as we still do in present-day English. As the inflectional forms of Old English fell into disuse, the periphrastic passive came into being and was in use, although rare, by the ninth century; it took until the sixteenth century for it to be fully accepted (Strang 1970), so it is reasonable to assume that it was fairly well established by the time Chaucer was writing in the late fourteenth century.

The Prologue of the *Treatise on the Astrolabe* is comparatively short, running to 94 lines in Robinson's edition (Chaucer 1391 [1957]). By comparison Part 1 is three times as long, and Part 2 just over ten times as long. In the Prologue, there are seven examples of passives, in Part 1 there are 67, and in Part 2 there are 37. Hence it is in the descriptive section, Part 1, that the passives are most frequent, and least frequent in the instructions for use, Part 2. The passives in the Prologue are almost all Mental processes, with a single example of a Verbal process. In Part 1, the commonest process type is ostensibly Verbal, with 36 examples. However, this is deceptive since 33 of these involve the same verb, *clepe*, as in:

> Of this forseide skale fro the cross lyne unto the verrey angle **is clepid** Umbra Versa, and the nethir partie is clepid Umbra recta ...[4]

> The widest of these 3 principale cercles **is clepid** the cercle of Capricorne ...

The function of these clauses is to give a definition, that is, to identify, so that although they are ostensibly cases of Verbal process, they are functioning as Relational identifying processes. There is also one case of the verb *calle*, from which the present-day English verb derives, which functions in the same way. The other process types which occur are Material or Mental. There are 21 passive Material processes, the commonest verb being *divide*, which provides nine examples:

> This zodiak **is dividid** in 12 principale divisiouns ...

> The wombe syde of thyn Astrelabie **is** also **divided** with a longe cross ...

And there are ten Mental processes, half of these being the verb *ymagyne*:

> whereas alle the remenaunt of cercles in the hevene **ben ymagyned** verrey lynes without eny latitude.

In Part 2 one finds the same phenomenon, that is, the most common process type is ostensibly Verbal, but of the 16 examples found, 15 are once again the verb *clepe*, and the single other example is *calle*, and these function, as before, as Relational identifying processes:

> Thys lyne meridional is but a maner descriptioun, or lyne ymagined, that passith upon the poles of this world and by the cenyth of oure heved. and it **is clepid** the lyne meridional ...

> To knowe the sprynge, of the dawenyng and the ends of the evenyng, the which **ben called** the two crepuscules.

Material process is the next most common type, with 12 examples:

> And thus lerned I to knowe onys for ever in which menere I shuld come to the houre of the nyght, and to myn ascendent, as verrely as **may be taken** by so smal an instrument.

> ... and tak an ascendent anon right by some manere sterre fix which that thou knowist; and forget not the altitude of the firste sterre ne thyn ascendent. And whan tha this **is don**, aspye diligently ...

Turner (1972) claims that all passives in Chaucer's *Treatise* are stative (or 'perfective') as opposed to dynamic. Despite the fact that the distinction between stative and dynamic passives is far from simple (Banks 1987), it would be true to say that Turner's claim is overstated: the two examples given above seem to be dynamic rather than stative, but at the same time a number of stative examples do occur:

> Understond wel that thy zodiak **is departed** in two halve circles ...

> ... and tak half thilke porcioun that **is excedid** and adde it to his secunde altitude ...

Part 2 also contains seven examples of Mental process:

> yit sey somme folk, so that the planetie arise in that same signe with eny degre of the forseide face in which his longitude **is rekned**, that yit is the planete *in horoscopo* ...

> To knowe the verrey degre of eny maner sterre, straunge or unstraunge, after this longitude; though he be indetermynat in thin Astralabye, sothly to the trouthe thus he **shal be knowe**.

and two examples of Relational process, both involving the verb *contene*:

> *Nota* also that the arch of the equinoxial that **is contened** or bownded bitwixe the 2 meridians is clepid the longitude of the toun.

It will be noted that this passive has a second passive participle coordinate with it. Examples of this type have been counted as constituting one occurrence rather than two. They are, in any case, very few in number.

Surprisingly, although passive forms are much less frequent in Part 2 than in Part 1, the different process types occur in roughly the same proportions in both parts (Table 1.1).

I have suggested (Banks 1997a, 1997b) that a teenager's 'how it works' book is the nearest modern equivalent to Chaucer's *Treatise*, so for

Table 1.1. Passive forms in Parts 1 and 2 of Chaucer's *Treatise*.[5]

	Part 1		Part 2	
	No.	*per cent*	*No.*	*per cent*
Material	21	31 per cent	12	32 per cent
Mental	10	15 per cent	7	19 per cent
Verbal	36	54 per cent	16	43 per cent
Relational	—	—	2	5 per cent
Total	67		37	

comparative purposes I have used one such book, *Machines and How They Work* by David Burnie (Burnie 1990). In this book the machines described are rarely those that a child might use himself; one or two are included, such as a bicycle and a camera, but the majority are more sophisticated machines such as a hovercraft or a mechanical digger. Hence the content is closer to that of Part 1, that is descriptive, rather than instructions for use. In eight pages selected at random, there were 45 examples of passives. In terms of frequency, this is closer to the frequency of Part 2 than Part 1, but more importantly, with a single exception, the examples of passives in this teenager's book are of Material process:

> ... the sewing speed and the shape of the stitches **can be controlled** very precisely.

> Four-wheel drive cars, which **are designed** to travel over rough ground, **are driven** by all their wheels.

> When the first railway and road tunnels **were built** during the last century, many of the men who dug them **were killed** trough rock-falls.

The single exception is an example of Mental process:

> The first 'horseless carriages', as they **were known**, were slow, uncomfortable and difficult to control.

So, while Chaucer's text and a comparable contemporary text may be thought of as having a similar overall frequency of passive forms, they are of different natures. Where roughly half of Chaucer's are examples of Verbal process, though frequently functioning as surrogate Relational processes, and almost a third are examples of Material process, in the contemporary text, the examples are virtually all of Material process.

Personal pronouns

In studies of the contemporary scientific research article, use of the passive is frequently seen as a way of avoiding the use of first and second person pronouns as Subject (Banks 1994a). Use of such pronouns is then in some sense the obverse of the passive, so I will now consider this question in relation to Chaucer's *Treatise*. In the Prologue there are 14 examples of first person pronoun Subjects, and 13 of these are in the first 64 lines which constitute a general introduction. There is only one example in the remainder of the Prologue which is a summary of the projected book, including the parts that were never completed. Of these 14 examples, six are Mental processes:

> ... **I aperceyve** wel by certeyne evydences thyn abilite to lerne sciences touching nombres and proporciounes ...

> ... sothly in any tretis of the Astrelabie that **I have seyn**, there be somme conclusions that wol not in alle thinges parformen her bihestes ...

and five are Verbal processes:

> **I seie** a certein of conclusions, for thre causes.

> Now **wol I preie** mekely every discret persone that redith or herith this litel tretys to have my rude endityng for excusid ...

The three remaining examples are two Material processes, one of which is a metaphor, and a Relational process:

> ... therefore **have I yeven** the a suffisant Astrolabie ...

> And with this swerd **shal I sleen** envie.

> **I n'am** but a lewd compilator of the labour of olde astrologiens ...

In Part 1 the first person pronoun Subjects are much less frequent: only eight examples for a text that is three times as long. These are, however, exclusively examples of Verbal process:

> ... for from henes forthward **I wol clepen** the heighte of any thing that is taken by the rewle 'the altitude' without moo wordes.

> Now **have I told** the twys.

In Part 2 there are 60 examples of first person pronoun Subjects. Given the relative lengths of the three sections, this means that in general they are more frequent than in Part 1, but less frequent than in the Prologue. However, probably more important than simple frequency is the fact that these examples are concentrated almost exclusively in those sections where Chaucer is providing worked examples. This he does in the first person, but otherwise first person Subjects do not occur in Part 2. Mental and Material processes are both comparatively frequent with 23 and 22 examples respectively:

> Ensample as thus: – The yeer of oure lord 1391, the 12 day of March, **I wolde knowe** the tyde of the day.

> Tho **rekned I** alle the capitale lettres fro the lyne of mydnight unto this forseide lettre X ...

> ... tho **I leide** my rewle upon this forseide 13 day ...

> Tho **turned I** myn Astrelabie ...

In addition, there are 11 cases of Verbal process:

> But natheles this rule in generall **wol I warne** the for evere ...

and four of Relational process, all in fact the verb *have*:

> And than **I had** of this conclusioun the ful experience.

In the extracts from the present-day text, first person pronouns are extremely rare. The few that do occur are plural, not singular, and have a general or inclusive sense:

> **We know** exactly who invented modern machines such as the car, the vacuum cleaner and the hovercraft.

> Although **we cannot feel** it, the atmosphere above us is very heavy.

When second person pronoun Subjects are considered in Chaucer's text, they are found to be rare in the Prologue, which has only four examples. Three of these are with Mental process verbs, and the fourth, a Relational process, is in a clause which is a grammatical metaphor for a Mental process. Second person pronoun Subjects are not particularly common in Part 1 either, where there is a total of eight, three Material processes, three Mental processes and two Relational processes. They are rather more common in Part 2, which has a total of 53. This is slightly less than the total number of first person pronouns in Part 2, but they are distributed throughout the text, and not confined to a specific sub-genre within it, as the first person pronouns are. Of these 53 examples, the majority, 30, are of Mental process:

> Thus **maist thou rekne** bothe arches, or every porcioun ...

> And by this manere of worching **maist thou se** how longe that eny sterre fix dwelleth above the erthe ...

> ... and with the poynt of it rekne in the bordure fro the sonne ariste unto that same place there **thou desirist** ...

In addition there are 14 cases of Material process:

> And whan **thou hast set** the degre of thy sonne upon as many almykanteras of height as was the altitude of the sonne taken by thy rule ...

> The same manere **maist thou worche** to knowe the quantite of the vulgar nyght.

and nine examples of Relational process:

> Now **hast thou** the height of thy pool, and the latitude of the regioun.

> ... **thou must have** a plomet hangyng on a lyne, heygher than thin heved ...

It should also be noted that Chaucer had available a singular/plural choice, which also had an interpersonal meaning, giving an intimate function to the singular choice, similar to the *tu/vous* distinction in contemporary French. Chaucer's second person pronouns are exclusively singular; there are no examples of the second person plural pronoun.

These figures, however, do not give a true idea of the presence of the second person, that is the addressee, in this text. Even in the Prologue and Part 1, the second person occurs a number of times as Complement, and frequently in the form of a possessive:

> **Thy zodiak** of **thin Astrolabie** is shapen as a compas which that contenith a large brede as after the quantitie of **thyn Astrolabie** ...

Indeed, in the Prologue and Part 1 there are 32 second person possessives, of which 11 are *thyn/thin Astrolabie*. This part of the text also has numerous injunctions to *understond wel*. Part 2 is even more imbued with the second person. The text is cast as instructions, so that imperative forms are particularly numerous, as are, once again, possessive pronouns.

In comparison, the present-day teenager's text has very few second person pronouns. The whole book has 26 chapters, and 17 have no second person pronouns at all. In those that do have a second person pronoun, this tends to occur in the introductory paragraph, frequently in a clause complex that contains a temporal or a conditional clause.

> If **you have** ever **tried** sewing, **you will know** it is a slow job.

The few possessives that occur usually do so with parts of the body:

> When you suck through a straw, the pressure in **your mouth** becomes less than that of the air outside.

So, personal pronouns are fairly numerous in Chaucer's text. First person pronouns tend to occur with Mental or Verbal processes in the Prologue, with Verbal processes in Part 1, and with Material or Mental processes in Part 2. There are also a number of second person pronouns, particularly with Mental processes in Part 2. These pronouns are always singular. In contrast, the present–day text has few personal pronouns, and the rare first person pronouns that do occur are plural.

Nominalisation

The final feature that I would like to look at in Chaucer's *Treatise on the Astrolabe* is that of the nominalisation of processes. This falls within the scope of grammatical metaphor, which is probably the commonest form of grammatical metaphor to occur in scientific writing. Halliday (1988[1]) sees the rhetorical use of grammatical metaphor as one of the innovations made by Newton, and as one of the points which marks him off from previous scientific writers.

In the Prologue there are 29 examples of nominalised processes, 24 in Part 1 and 105 in Part 2. This may be an underestimate, as there are a number of marginal cases not included. For example *manere* and *equacioun* occur sometimes but not always as nominalisations. Part 1 is descriptive, which may account for there being comparatively fewer in that section. Although there are 47 types, only seven have more than three tokens, allowing for spelling variants. The most common is *conclusioun*, which has a total of 33, 12 in the Prologue, 5 in Part 1, and 16 in Part 2:

> This **conclusioun** wol I declare in the last chapitre of the 4 partie of this tretys ...

> Another **conclusioun** to prove the latitude of the regioun.

This word, as can be seen in the last example, is the general term Chaucer uses for the various sections of Part 2. The next most common nominalisation is *declinacioun*, with a total of 18 occurrences, one in the Prologue, three in Part 1, and 14 in Part 2:

> Yif it be of the soone or of eny fix sterre, rekne hys latitude or his **declinacioun** for the equinoxiall cercel ...

> And yf it so be that thilke degre be northward fro the equinoxiall, than is his **declinacioun** north ...

The only other examples which have more than ten tokens, in fact 12 each, are *ascensioun*, which occurs only in Part 2, and *moevyng*, with two tokens in the Prologue, seven in Part 1, and three in Part 2:

> Set the heved of the signe which as the list to knowe his ***ascensioun*** upon the est orizonte ...

> ... for than shalt thou perceyve wel the **moeving** of a planete ...

In these examples, we can see the establishment of a technical vocabulary. Indeed some of these terms were probably already established as such. The following example shows Chaucer moving from the finite verb to the nominalised form, and this may well indicate a stage in the creation of technical terms:

And all that **moeveth** withinne the hevedes of these Aries and Libra, his **moevyng** is clepid northward; and all that **moevith** without these hevedes, his **moevyng** is clepid southward, as fro the equinoxiall.

There are two words which have eight tokens, *arisyng* and *declaracioun*, and two that have five, *conjunccyoun*, and *wise*:

And thys merveylous **arisyng** with a straunge degre in another signe is by cause that the latitude of the sterre fix is either north or south fro the equinoxiall.

This chapitre is so generall evere in oon that there nedith no more **declaracioun**; but forget it not.

Loke hou many houres thilke **conjunccioun** is fro the midday of the day precedent ...

And in the same **wise** maist thou seen by night, of eny sterre, whether the sterre sitte est or west, or north or south ...

In addition there are three occurrences of the words *descripcioun, experience, manere,* and *mendacioun,* two of *discencioun, eleccioun, elevacioun, endityng, feith, governaunce, nativyte, operacioun, praier* and *worchynge,* and one of *ascendyng, conditioun, depressioun, doctrine, dwellyng, eclipse, effecte, engyn, envie, enhaunsyng, equacioun, excepcioun, knowing, kouching, labour, lernyng, mesure, question, rekenyng, revolucioun, risyne, settyng, shyning, tariyng,* and *werping.*

By comparison, the contemporary teenager's text has very little in the way of nominalised processes. In eight pages taken at random there were only 12 examples. Half of these (six) were the word *movement*, the word *position* occurred twice, and there was one example each of *design, pollution, rock-falls,* and *work.*

Hence, this brief look at passive forms, personal pronouns and nominalised processes in Chaucer's *Treatise on the Astrolable* shows that passives are used to a similar extent in both this text and in a comparable modern text. Both are, however, far from the 30 per cent or so to be found in present-day scientific research articles (Banks 1994a). Whereas in the modern teenager's text they are mainly cases of Material process, in Chaucer's, half are Verbal process, the others being Material and Mental. Chaucer uses a considerable number of first person pronoun Subjects, certainly a greater rate than that of one per 35 clauses which I found in a modern corpus of scientific articles (Banks 1994a). He also uses a (smaller) number of second person pronoun Subjects. In the contemporary teenager's book, the only first person pronoun Subjects that occur are plural, and there are very few second person pronouns. Chaucer uses a significant number of nominalised processes, but considerably fewer than a modern scientific article; but the teenager's book also has very few of these. Chaucer's text consequently seems to resemble the 'how it works' text from certain points of view, but not from others. Where there are global similarities, Chaucer may be using the features in different ways to the modern text.

Before leaving Chaucer's text, it is worth looking at the way Part 2 is constructed. This is made up of 40 sections, excluding six sections of doubtful authenticity. Each section gives the instructions for the tasks to be carried out with the astrolabe. Of these 29 have the same overall lexicogrammatical structure: a non-finite infinitive clause sets out the task to be accomplished, and the instructions for doing it begin with an imperative:

> **To knowe** the altitude of the sonne or of othre celestial bodies.

> **Put** the ryng of thyn Astrelabie upon thy right thombe, and **turne** thi lift syde ageyn the light of the sonne; and **remewe** thy rewle up and doun til that the stremes of the sonne shine thorugh bothe holes of thi rewle.

> **To knowe** the altitude of the sonne in myddes of the day that is clepid the altitude meridian.

> **Set** the degre of the sonne upon the lyne meridional, and **rekne** how many degrees of almykanteras ben bitwyxe thin est orizonte and the degre of thy sonne ...

> **To fynde** the lyne meridional to dwelle fix in eny certeyn place.

> **Tak** a round plate of metal; for werpyng, the brodder the better; and **make** there upon a just compas a lite within the bordure.

This is striking since the structure is familiar due to the currency of its use in contemporary instructions. Examples like the following are fairly ubiquitous:

> **To enter** the next Prize draw, **complete** and **return** this questionnaire in the next ten days. (BT promotional competition)

> **To prime**, push bladder with a paper clip until ink fully coats silver plates. (Instructions. Hewlett Packard print cartridge)

> **To open** the door, **turn** the handle anticlockwise. (Hand-written note pinned to church door, Edlingham, Northumberland)

Here we have a structure that appears to have remained virtually the same for six centuries. If there is a difference, it would be the fact that Chaucer's infinitives are all Mental process verbs; in fact 25 of the 29 examples are the verb *knowe*, the verb *fynde* occurs twice, and the verbs *prove* and *turn* (which here means to make a mathematical conversion) once each. The contemporary examples, like those given above, tend to be of Material process.

Chaucer's *Treatise on the Astrolabe* can genuinely be seen as being where it all started, in the sense that it is the first text of a technical, if not scientific, nature to have been written in English, 'your very first ESP text', as I once called it (Banks 1997b). Moreover, one can see Chaucer using the resources of English to create the discourse he needs for this specific sub-genre. This can be seen in his use of passives, personal pronouns, and nominalised processes. In this last feature in particular it is possible to see the use and creation of a technical vocabulary, which was one of the features which led Halliday to call this document an example of 'technical ... proto-scientific discourse' (Halliday 1988[1]: 165).

2 Between Chaucer and Newton

A troubled period

It would be false to think that there was nothing of a scientific nature written in English from the late fourteenth to the late seventeenth century, but what was published in English tended to be of a more popular nature, of pedagogical or practical application, and very often on the fringes of, if not beyond, what we would now accept as genuinely scientific. The distinction between alchemy and chemistry was still very vague and fluid so that, independently of the language question, the very notion of what constituted scientific activity took a long time to emerge (Hall 1962 [1994]; Jones 1961 [1982]). The word *science* itself did not take on its modern meaning until a comparatively late date. According to the *Oxford English Dictionary*, in the fourteenth century it meant 'The state or fact of knowing'; it was 'knowledge acquired by study', and could apply to any 'recognized department of learning'. It is only in the eighteenth century that the word begins to be used in a more restricted sense, and not until the end of the nineteenth century that it takes on its contemporary meaning. Until well into the eighteenth century the word *philosophy* continued to be used to cover these branches of study. The word *scientist* is of even more recent coinage, for the first citation in the *OED* dates from 1834, and is itself instructive:

> We are informed that this difficulty [that they had no collective name] was felt very oppressively by the members of the British Association for the Advancement of Science ... *Philosophers* was felt to be too wide and too lofty a term ... *Savans* was rather assuming ... some ingenious gentleman proposed that by analogy with *artist* they might form *scientist* but this was not generally palatable.

Despite the aesthetic reticence of the members of British Association for the Advancement of Science, this was, as we all now know, the word which stuck (Banks 2004a).

Work that was cutting-edge, at least in the terms of the period, was aimed at an international readership, for whom Latin was the appropriate language. William Gilbert, in the area of physics published *De magnete* in 1600, and in physiology, William Harvey published *De motu cordis* in 1628. These were both revolutionary works, as they introduced the new experimental method into England. To understand to what extent this was revolutionary it is necessary to have some idea of the mind-set of seventeenth-century man. In the twenty-first century, we are so used to the idea of progress, of human endeavour moving inexorably onwards, even if there are temporary local ups and downs, towards some distant Teilhardian omega point (Teilhard de Chardin 1955), that it is difficult to conceive of a mind-set that turns this vision of things on its head. Living in a civilisation which is, at least partly, the result of rapid scientific and technological change over a period of more than a century, it is almost impossible to imagine a situation other than that of progress continuing indefinitely. Yet in the seventeenth century it was precisely a vision of a world in decline which prevailed. The metaphorical image of the universe was that of the human body, which grows to a peak of vitality, but then decays, and ultimately dies. For the educated man of the seventeenth century, that peak of vitality had occurred in classical Greece. By his own lifetime, the universe, and the human race, was in its old age, and consequently could not hope to rival the youth and vitality of the classical period. According to Jones, in the sixteenth century,

> Men seemed to be blind to any possible virtues in their own times. Convinced as they were that nature had about run its course, and was tottering on senile legs to a final dissolution, their eyes were all the keener to discern evidences of decay, and to read in such signs confirmation of their belief. (Jones 1961 [1982]: 24)

This image of decay was endemic, and seemed inevitable:

> ... as we see decline and decay in individual parts of nature, as for instance in man, so the universe itself must partake of the nature of its parts and pass through the cycle of youth, old age, and death. (Jones 1961 [1982]: 26)

This was a point of view that continued to hold sway throughout the seventeenth century:

> The idea of the decay of nature, frequently symbolized by the figure of giant and dwarf, traverses the whole of the seventeenth century, and crops out whenever ancients and moderns clash. (Jones 1961 [1982]: 38)

Since, according to this ideology, the highpoint of human achievement was reached in ancient Greece, experimental science was pointless. Since it was impossible to do any better than the likes of Aristotle, Galen, or Ptolemy, the only thing that could be done was to interpret, and reinterpret, what they had said for a new age. But the notion of saying something different, and hence saying that they had been wrong, was simply impossible within this framework. Moreover, since this was the prevailing view, it was also the view that was entrenched in the universities, which meant that, as the new experimental science developed from the late seventeenth century onwards, it was difficult for these new scientists, the 'moderns', to find a place in the academic system. It was only very slowly that this began to happen, for even today in such cases, it takes at least a generation for new ideas to take root and become securely implanted. In the seventeenth century, change was even more leisurely.

It would also lead us astray if we were to treat the language of this period in abstraction of the social and political events that were the backdrop to the lives of the men who created the language of the seventeenth century. Fennell describes it as a period of 'internal instability and colonial expansion' (Fennell 2001: 137), and indeed English colonial possessions in both America and India were expanding, while at home the century was one of the most turbulent in British history. The 1640s had been a period of civil war ending with the beheading of Charles I in 1649. Then came the period of the Commonwealth under Cromwell's increasingly despotic rule, followed by the restoration of the monarchy, and the return of Charles II in 1660. By comparison, the French Revolution was still more than a century in the future. In discussing the beginnings of the Royal Society in 1660, Atkinson says:

> In the England of the preceding 25 years a civil war had been fought, a king had been beheaded, and extreme political and religious repression had been endured. For part of this period English society had been on the verge of anarchy. The revival of the monarchy in 1660 was therefore looked upon not so much as an attempt to reimpose the old social order, but as a last chance to restore *any* social order. (Atkinson 1999: 15)

Francis Bacon

Francis Bacon, who was to have such a significant influence on the new scientists, and the way they wrote, lived in the years immediately preceding this upheaval, 1561–1626. Few would deny that he was to have a deep and lasting influence on the way science was organised and carried out, an influence which can still be discerned today (Butterfield 1957; Hall 1962 [1994]; Henry

2002; Jones 1961 [1982]; Vickers 1987). In some ways this is curious, for by profession he was a lawyer, who rose to the position of Lord Chancellor, before falling from grace after being condemned for corruption. In Hall's words he was 'not a scientist, not even a recognised patron of science, who yet became the most vocal prophet of science possible' (Hall 1962 [1994]: 247). If he is remembered today, it is,

> ... not so much as a scientist – he made no major discovery, formulated no scientific law, performed few original experiments – but as a propagandist for science who urged that 'natural philosophy' be given a new importance in human affairs and be organized on a new plan. (Vickers 1987, 1)

It must then be an irony of fate that he died through an experiment that went tragically wrong. Driving across snow-covered ground in 1626, when he was already in his mid-60s, he decided to experiment on the preservation of food through cold. He bought a hen, and stuffed it with snow, but in doing so caught a chill, and died from the subsequent pneumonia (Farrington 1949 [1951]; Hall 1962 [1994]). This misguided experiment was, says Hall 'a good idea in advance of its time, investigated spontaneously, unsystematically, inconclusively, but ardently' (Hall 1962 [1994]: 248). Bacon's innovative contribution was his insistence on empirical method. Experiment is the key to knowledge and learning; it is on the basis of the observed results of experiments that inductive reasoning can build up the knowledge required; this can lead to further experiment and further inductive reasoning, but the whole process is experiment-driven. This marks him off from Descartes, despite the fact that they are similar in both starting from a certain *tabula rasa*. But whereas in Descartes' case this led to deductive reasoning, where experiment was only necessary at a later stage when it was a question of the more detailed operations of nature (Butterfield 1957), for Bacon this led to a purely inductive form of reasoning based on observed data from the very start:

> The French philosopher started with the simple principle, *Cogito, ergo sum*, upon which, by means of reasoning and clear ideas, he sought to construct a sound edifice. The English philosopher, on the other hand, though insisting just as emphatically upon the necessity of purging the mind of all notions, proposed a sensuous and material basis for man to build his ideas of nature upon. (Jones 1961 [1982]: 49).

Bacon's insistence on experiment and the need to accumulate data has led some to think of his project in purely pragmatic and utilitarian terms. Thus Farrington subtitles his book on Bacon *Philosopher of Industrial Science*, and talks of 'the marriage between natural philosophy and industrial production' (Farrington 1949 [1951]: 16). He claims that for Bacon:

> ... knowledge ought to bear fruit in works, that science ought to be applicable to industry, that men ought to organize themselves as a sacred duty to improve and transform the conditions of life. (Farrington 1949 [1951]: 3)

This misconception may be due to the fact that Bacon never fully completed the writing of his *magnum opus*. His unexpected death interrupted the production of his writing and so the parts that we have available may give unwarranted weight to those parts that are complete:

> Since Bacon only completed fragments of the whole scheme, mostly the earlier parts concerned with the collection of data, he has been wrongly accused of advocating a random amassing of facts: but his plan involved theory and hypothesis as an organic part of the enterprise. (Vickers 1987: 3)

But first of all, Bacon was not concerned solely with the collection of data for its own sake; it had to be organised into the basis for the understanding of nature:

> ... Bacon did not conceive of his natural history as a haphazard collection of unorganized observations and experiments. In fact he says that little is to be expected from the intellect unless particulars are apt, well arranged, drawn up, and marshalled in some order. (Jones 1961 [1982]: 56)

This does not mean that Bacon himself always followed his own precepts with unswerving exactitude:

> Bacon by no means understood his experimental way to be pure empiricism. He had no use for random experimentation, undertaken without aim or guiding principle, however much he might at various times fall into the error of collecting diverse experiments. (Hall 1962 [1994]: 254)

So philosophical advance, and hence the advancement of scientific theory, was the ultimate goal of Bacon's project, even though this philosophy included a utilitarian vision in the form of the improvement of the human condition. On the other hand, it was not pragmatic in any purely material or pecuniary sense:

> ... in his eyes, the noblest end of natural history is not pleasure or profit, but to be, as it were, the nursing mother of philosophy, to furnish the stuff and matter of true lawful induction and thus become a solid and eternal basis of true and active philosophy. The history was to be a most comprehensive collection of experiments and observations, gathered over the whole field of nature, to furnish data from which the mind could construct a universal philosophy by means of Bacon's inductive method. (Jones 1961 [1982]: 53)

This book is about scientific writing, and it is true that Bacon did not produce what we would call scientific writing. His writing falls into the area of philosophy (in the modern sense), at best, the philosophy of science. It is nevertheless important to consider him at this point because not only was he to have an immense influence on the way science was carried out, but also the way in which scientists subsequently wrote about and described their experiments. This results partly from the way science is conceived of by Bacon, but also from what he himself wrote about scientific writing. Bacon did not espouse the use of the vernacular for scientific writing. It is true that his first major work, commonly known as *The Advancement of Learning*, was written in English. But his great project, the *Great Instauration* (*Magna Instauratio*), was, or was to be, written in Latin. The first part to be completed and published was in fact Part 2 of his project, and was called *Novum Organum*, but since this was the first part to be published, the title is frequently applied to the whole project. The second part to be published, but which constitutes Part 1 of the project, *De Augmentis Scientiarum*, was in fact a much expanded Latin translation of *The Advancement of Learning*. So Latin was the language that Bacon adopted for his major work; in other words, he fell in with the current convention of using Latin as the *lingua franca* of European intellectuals. Some of his remarks can be interpreted as pointing in the direction of a perfect language, where the sign indicates the object without passing through the filter of a natural verbal language. According to Eco (1994), Bacon's problem was to constitute an alphabet of fundamental notions, and although he never did this, his system of indexation in the *Abedcedarium novum Naturae* (1622) may have been an inspiration for future attempts in this direction. He would probably have supported the later efforts of John Wilkins who produced *An Essay Towards a Real Character and a Philosophical Language* in 1668 (Vickers 1987).

When Bacon does talk about writing style, the characteristics he espouses are those of clarity and concision, even if this results in a style which is inaesthetic. In the *Parasceve*, a short document which was published with the *Novum Organum*, he says:

> ... it is no less necessary that what is admitted should be written succinctly than that what is superfluous should be rejected; though no doubt this kind of chastity and brevity will give less pleasure both to the reader and the writer. (Robertson 1905: 404)[6]

Anything that is superfluous is to be discarded:

> ... away with antiquities, and citations or testimonies of authors; also with disputes and controversies and differing opinions, everything in short

which is philological. Never cite an author except in a matter of doubtful credit: never introduce a controversy unless in a matter of great moment. And for all that concerns ornaments of speech, similitudes, treasury of eloquence, and such like emptinesses, let it be utterly dismissed. Also let all those things which are admitted be themselves set down briefly and concisely, so that they may be nothing less than words. (Robertson, 1905: 403)

This, of course is to be understood in the context where the 'inkhorn terms' controversy was still recent and a florid style was the order of the day (Baugh 1959; Knowles 1997). It can also be seen in a context where the writings of the alchemists and Paracelsians were deliberately obscure. Some 40 years later, Boyle was to criticise their writing in the following terms:

... this equivocal way of writing is not to be endured. For in such speculative enquiries, where the naked knowledge of the truth is the thing principally aimed at, what does he teach me worth thanks that does not, if he can, make his notion intelligible to me, but by mythical terms, and ambiguous phrases darkens what he should clear up; and makes me add the trouble of guessing at the sence of what he equivocally expresses, to that of examining the truth of what he seems to deliver. (Boyle 1661 [2003]: 115)

And Bacon's blast against citations should probably seen as being against the unthinking citation of ancient, that is, classical authors, as indisputable authorities, for he later argues in favour of what he considers a correct use of citation, and, incidentally, of hedging:

With regard to the credit of the things which are to be admitted into the history; they must needs be either certainly true, doubtful whether true or not, or certainly not true. Things of the first kind should be set down simply; things of the second kind with a qualifying note, such as 'it is reported', 'they relate' ... if the instance be of importance, either from its own use or because many other things may depend on it, then certainly the name of the author should be given; and not the name merely, but it should be mentioned withal whether he took it from a report, oral or written ... or rather affirmed it of his own knowledge. (Robertson 1905: 406)

Moreover, Bacon can be said to have had a lasting influence on the generic structure of the scientific article. According to Gross 'the arrangement of the experimental report is a realization of the principles of Baconian induction' (Gross 1996: 85). These principles lead to an organization in terms of Introduction, which relates the experiment to previous experimentation and hence fits it into a research programme; Methods and Materials, so that others may judge to what extent it is valid, and if necessary reproduce it;

Results, for these form the basis of scientific knowledge; and Discussion, which since the method is an inductive one follows on the results obtained. This, of course, precisely mirrors the IMRAD (Introduction, Method, Results and Discussion) model of the contemporary research article (Swales 1990), so the current generic structure of the research article has its historic origins in Bacon's scientific programme.

Robert Boyle

One of the first to put Bacon's project into practice, and at the same time to write in English, was Robert Boyle. In searching for a genre in which to express his philosophical ideas, Bacon had opted for that of aphorisms, notably in the *Novum Organum*. Boyle, faced with the same problem for his largely philosophical work *The Sceptical Chymist* (Boyle 1661 [2003]), chose the Platonic dialogue, which enabled him to express his own ideas through the words of a fictional character, thus avoiding direct criticism. But describing experiments was a different problem. Boyle realised that scientists needed a new form to express their ideas, and to convince a sceptical readership of the validity of the new methods. As pointed out above, he attacked the alchemists for their obscure language and took over the Baconian insistence on clarity. Gotti points out that in an essay that was published anonymously:

> ... he condemns the habit that certain scientists have of using cryptic language so as not to make their discoveries comprehensible to their readers. He maintains, on the contrary, that all works should be written in clear language so that everybody can decode the contents and so improve his knowledge of the subject. This universal sharing of single discoveries is considered essential for the formation of a specialist community and for the progress of scientific thought. (Gotti 1996: 33)

He was also aware that the way a text was written had significant implications for its reception by its readers. He realised that members of the scientific community needed a new generic form in which to express themselves and to communicate effectively. In this, the stylistic flourishes of fashionable writing could only get in the way, and, like Bacon, he recommended a simpler, less florid style:

> Boyle is fully aware that a scientist's style plays an important role in the reinforcement of the perlocutionary strength of his writings and in the acceptance of his theories, and sees a strong interrelation between method of expression and success in communication. This interrelation is guaranteed in particular by the writer's adoption of a plain and unadorned style,

considered particularly appropriate to the language of science. Metaphors and literary embellishments are seen as obstacles to a clear understanding of the scientific principles outlined in the paper. (Gotti 1996: 38–39)

The genre chosen by Boyle was the experimental essay. But this was a new genre of which the features had yet to be established. This can be seen in his important book entitled *New Experiments Physico-Mechanical, Touching the Spring of the Air, and its Effects; Made, for the most Part, in a New Pneumatical Engine.* This was first published in 1660, and was cast in the epistolary form of a letter to his nephew the Lord of Dungarvan, and so bears the superficial features of this genre: 'And I am not faintly induced to make choice of this subject rather than any of the expected chymical ones to entertain your Lordship upon ... To give your Lordship then, in the first place, some account of the engine itself: it consists of ...' (Vickers 1987: 48). But the main part of the work is the description of a series of experiments, and although there are very occasional interpolations of a vocative, recalling the epistolary framework, the style has become recognizably that of scientific prose:

> By these two differing ways, My Lord, may the springs of the air be explicated. But though the former of them be that which by reason of its seeming somewhat more easy I shall for the most part make use of in the following discourse, yet I am not willing to declare peremptorily for either of them against the other. (Vickers 1987: 53)

The work uses a narrative technique, with a very short introduction, and little in the way of reflection. The general style is informative, rather than argumentative (Gotti 1996).

In previous studies of an extract from this work containing 2,708 words (Banks 1999, 2001a, 2003b), I have shown (I am here making some minor corrections) that the extract contains 64 nominalisations of processes, that is, a rate of 24 per 1,000 words, or one per 42 words of running text. Of these, almost three-quarters (73 per cent) are Material processes, with 17 per cent Verbal processes and 6 per cent Mental processes. Table 2.1 gives the details of this. Where there is more than one token of a type, the number is given in parentheses.

Although the rate here is far from that to be found in contemporary research articles where it can be as high as one per 12 words of running text, it is still possible to see the phenomenon of nominalisation being used in the creation of scientific discourse. This fits into a general pattern whereby Boyle is actively creative in the production of a new nominally-based vocabulary, which he thought necessary for the precision and clarity of this new genre.

Table 2.1. Nominalized processes in Boyle.

Material	Mental	Verbal
agitation	judgement	account (3)
bending	observation (2)	answer (2)
compression (3)	sight	comparison
condensation	thought	hypothesis
dilatation (3)	understanding	mention
drawing down		objection
endeavour		reply
expansion (2)		seconding
experience		
experiment (11)		
exsuction (2)		
motion (5)		
pressure (5)		
protrusion		
recovery		
refraction		
restitution (2)		
returning		
self-dilatation		
self-dilation		
turning (2)		
tokens: 47 (73 per cent)	tokens: 6 (9 per cent)	tokens: 11 (17 per cent)
types: 21 (62 per cent)	types: 5 (15 per cent)	types: 8 (24 per cent)

The beginnings of a technical use of the passive voice can also be discerned. According to Gotti:

> The shift from active to passive voice in these cases underlines the passing from the active role of narration of events to the description of procedures that are becoming standardized in the experimenter's repertoire or in that of scientists in general. (Gotti, 1996: 65)

In this extract there are 39 examples of the passive (cases where more than one past participle follows a single auxiliary have been counted separately); this is a rate of 14 per 1,000 words, or one per 69 words of running text. Of these, the majority, 24 (62 per cent), are Material:

> For this (to omit other likeness betwixt them) consists of many slender and flexible hairs, each of which **may** indeed, like a little spring, **be** easily **bent** or **rolled up** but will also, like a spring, be still endeavouring to stretch itself out again.

> ... though the hairs **may** by a man's hand **be bent** and **crouded** closer together ...

> ... their glass vessel, of the capacity of 32 measures, was lighter when the air **had been drawn** out of it than before ...

There are a small number, nine (23 per cent), of Verbal processes:

> And if it **be** further **objected** that the air in the bladder was violently compressed by the packthread and the sides of the bladder ...

and an even smaller number, six (15 per cent), of Mental processes:

> ... it **may** well **be doubted** whether the observation, by reason of the great difficulty, hath been exactly made ...

In a study of contemporary articles (Banks 1994a), I found that there were as many simple copulas as there were examples of the passive, roughly 30 per cent of finite verbs in each case. This is not the case in the Boyle extract, for there are less than half as many examples of the copula than there are of passives. In fact there are 18 examples of the simple copula *be*, that is, just fewer than six per 1,000 words.

The other feature which might be considered an inverse of passive use is the use of personal pronouns, particularly first person pronoun Subjects. There are 41 examples in this extract, a rate of 15 per 1,000 words, or one per 66 words of running text. An interesting feature of this is that over a third of these are plural (26 singular, 15 plural). The singular examples tend to be of Verbal or Mental process. There are 12 (46 per cent) examples of Verbal process:

> I know not whether **I need annex** that though either of the above-mentioned hypotheses, and perhaps some others, may afford us an account plausible enough of the air's spring, yet I doubt whether any of them gives us a sufficient account of its nature.

Of these, there are three which appear to be simple discourse interventions, which may function as interpersonal grammatical metaphors:

> For it may be alleged that though the air were granted to consist of springy particles (if **I may** so **speak**) yet thereby we could only give an account of the dilatation of the air in wind-guns . . .

There are almost as many, 11, examples of Mental processes:

> **I hold** it not unfit to begin with what doth constantly and regularly offer itself to our observation, as depending upon the fabric of the engine itself and not upon the nature of this or that particular experiment ...

The remaining examples are two of Relational process:

> And of this doubt I might here mention some reasons but that, peradventure, **I may** (God permitting) **have** a fitter occasion to say something of it elsewhere.

and one, perhaps marginal, example of Material process:

> Wherefore **I shall decline** meddling with a subject which is much more hard to be explicated ...

The first person plural Subjects include a certain number which have singular reference, some which are inclusive, in the sense that they include at least the reader, and perhaps the scientific community in general, and those that are totally inclusive. There is a certain ambiguity about some examples since these categories are to some extent fuzzy. Nevertheless, as many as six (out of 15) might be classed as having singular reference, and of these, three are with Verbal process verbs:

> And to this **we may add** on this occasion, that constantly upon the turning of the key to let out the air from the receiver into the emptied cylinder there is immediately produced a considerably brisk noise ...

There is one example each of Material, Mental, and Relational process. There are six examples of the inclusive type, and of these, four are of Mental process:

> So that **we need not wonder** that upon the taking off the incumbent air from any parcel of the atmosphere here below, the corpuscles whereof that undermost air consists should display themselves ...

The other examples are one each of Verbal and Relational process. The three examples of inclusive *we* are all of Material process, and all concern the air or atmosphere we live in:

> ... it will not be uneasy to conceive that that part of the atmosphere wherein **we live**, being the lower part of it, the corpuscles that compose it are very much compressed ...

Hence it is interesting to note that when Boyle uses first person pronoun Subjects, whether they be singular, or plural, with singular reference or inclusive, it is for communicating and thinking, but not for the physical actions of actually carrying out his experiments, which would have required Material process verbs. In the narrative of the experiment, passives are much more frequent than first person pronouns with active verbs.

Boyle also uses a number of second person pronoun Subjects. There are 15 in the extract, a rate of almost six per 1,000 words, or one per 180 words of running text. These are not evenly distributed throughout the extract, but are concentrated in short sections. Unlike the first person pronouns, these do occur with Material processes, which account for eight of the 15 examples:

> ... if **you open** the valve and force up the sucker again you will find that after this first exsuction **you will drive** out almost a whole cylinder full of air; but at the following exsuctions **you will draw** less and less of air out of the receiver into the cylinder ...

It will be noted that this example also contains a second person Subject with a Mental process verb (**you will find**), of which there are a total of five examples in the extract, as well as two examples of Verbal process; the following example contains one example of Mental and one of Verbal process:

> But lest **you should expect** my seconding this reason by experience and lest **you should object** that most of the experiments that have been proposed to prove the gravity of the air have been either barely proposed or perhaps not accurately tried ...

Of these 15 examples, 12 lend themselves to a general reference interpretation, like those in the first of the two above examples, whereas only three seem to have specific reference, like those in the last example.

Henry Power and Robert Hooke

Henry Power and Robert Hooke were both contemporaries of Robert Boyle. Power was four years older than Boyle and Hooke eight years younger. They were both major scientists of their time, and indeed Chapman (2005) claims that Hooke was a much greater scientist than his later reputation would have us believe. They all subscribed to the Baconian empirical programme, and were all active at the same period. Power published his *Experimental Philosophy, In Three Books: Containing New Experiments, Microscopical, Mercurial, Magnetical* in 1664, and Hooke published his *Micrographia: or Some Physiological Descriptions of Minute Bodies made by Magnifying Glasses* in 1665. Extracts from both are available in Vickers 1987. As a comparison with Boyle, I have used two short extracts from both; the Power extract is of 1004 words, and that of Hooke 1184 words. In both of these extracts they are doing the same thing: describing insects as seen through a microscope.

Both Power and Hooke use the nominalisation of processes to the same extent. There are eight examples in the Power extract, and ten in Hooke, which means that they both use this phenomenon at the rate of roughly eight per 1,000 words, one per 126 words in the case of Power, and one per 118 words in the case of Hooke. The examples used by these two writers are given in Table 2.2.

All of the examples are of Material process, with the exception of *setting on* in Power, and *sight* in Hooke. The rate is only a third of that found in Boyle, and is perhaps no more than the incidental number that would be found in any form of mature discourse. According to Halliday (2004), children do not meet ideational grammatical metaphor, of which nominalised processes are an example, before the upper levels of primary school, and so it would not be found in their normal discourse, but it is endemic to some degree in any form of adult discourse. It will also be noticed that none of the examples appears more than once in the extracts, which means that there is no indication here of these terms being used as a way of building up a technical vocabulary, as was the case in Boyle's writing.

Neither of these two writers uses the passive to any significant extent either. There are nine examples in the Power extract, which means that they occur at the rate of one per 111 words, and there are only four in the Hooke extract, which means that they occur at the rate of one per 296 words. Compared with Boyle, Power uses a little more than half as many, while Hooke uses hardly any at all. Moreover, in the Power extract, with a single exception, the passives are very much to the adjectival or stative end of the stative–dynamic cline:

> The other four legs **are cloven** and arm'd with little clea's or tallons ...

> ... two toes, both which **are lined** with two white sponges or fuzballs ...

Table 2.2. Nominalised processes in Power and Hooke.

Power	*Hooke*
Flea-biting	Access
Flexure	Habitation
Leaps	Need
Motion	Posture
Rise	Sight
Setting on	Steps
Supportance	Touch
Works	Use
	Way
	Yielding

The exception is:

> After her head **is cut off**, you shall most fairly see (just at the setting on of her neck) a pulsing particle ...

Power rarely uses first person Subject pronouns; there are only three in the extract, one of which is plural. Hooke, on the other hand, uses rather more, with 11 examples in his extract, five of which are plural. They are used with Verbal or Mental processes:

> ... what it is, **we shall** in brief **explain** by shewing that its Mechanism consists principally in two parts ...

> This Structure **I** somewhat the more diligently **survey'd** because **I could not** well **comprehend** how, if there were such a glutinous matter in those supposed Sponges ...

This means that Hooke is using these pronouns at the rate of one per 108 words, almost half the rate of Boyle's one per 66 words. In addition, Power and Hooke hardly ever use second person pronoun Subjects: there are only three in the Power extract and none at all in Hooke.

Experimental and descriptive sciences

There seem to be significant differences between the features of Boyle's writing and those of Power and Hooke, and it is reasonable to ask what this difference stems from. In his book, Boyle is describing experiments, in other words telling us what he did and what happened, whereas Power and Hooke in their books are describing what they see through their microscopes. They do not do anything apart from look. Hence the type of discourse is different. This difference could be one which for a long time separated what I have elsewhere called (Banks 1998) the ultra-hard and the not-so-hard sciences. The ultra-hard sciences are those basically in the area of physics and chemistry, while the not-so-hard sciences are those in the biological field. At this period, physics and chemistry were just beginning to emerge as an experimental discipline, whereas the biological sciences were to remain purely descriptive well into the nineteenth century. Throughout the eighteenth century, biological endeavour was concentrated on the effort of describing and classifying the huge number of new plants and animals that emerged from the newly discovered lands, and it was not until the second half of the nineteenth century, that these sciences began to take on an experimental aspect, which led to the creation of new subdisciplines such as biochemistry. Hence it is my hypothesis that it was the experimental nature of empirical physics and chemistry that instigated the search for new rhetorical ways of presenting this material. This would explain why the not-so-hard biological sciences, which were to remain non-experimental for a considerable period, had not yet begun to change, and only did so much later and at a slower rate.

A further point worth mentioning is the way in which the writing of Power, and to a lesser extent Hooke, bear the hallmarks of the style of the *virtuosi*, or gentlemen scientists, who 'had the time and leisure to advance knowledge either by collecting rarities or by promoting experiments' (Gascoigne 1994: 58). Notably this style betrays the wonder they felt at the perceived beauty of nature. Thus Power says of the common fly, 'It is a very pleasant Insect to behold' (Vickers 1987: 90), and of the horsefly, 'her eye is an incomparable pleasant spectacle' (Vickers 1987: 91). Similarly, Hooke says of the flea, 'The strength and beauty of this small creature, had it no other relation at all to man, would deserve a description' (Vickers 1987: 132). Although Boyle corresponds to the image of the *virtuoso*, being a man of means, and performing his experiments before invited guests who would bear witness to the results obtained, his style does not in general betray these features.

3 The Royal Society and Newton

The place of the Royal Society and its *Philosophical Transactions*

Into this world of Restoration England, where Boyle, and others like him, in the face of academic hostility from the universities, were attempting to put a Baconian agenda into practice, a new ingredient was forming which was to have a decisive effect on the future progress of science. From the mid-1640s, a group of men interested in the new experimental philosophy had been meeting at Gresham College in London. They were the seedbed from which the Royal Society was to spring, and in 1660 the first meeting of the group took place. The following year they requested, and obtained, a royal charter (Katzen 1980; Atkinson 1999; Valle 1999). The fact that they met in London and not in one of the university towns is significant, in that it shows the break which these men were making with the traditional forms of thought, based on the authority of classical thinkers. Their insistence on an inductive form of reasoning also marked them off from those who supported deductive reasoning, such as Descartes and his followers, who were particularly numerous in continental Europe.

> It was experimentation, as a specific form of empiricism and inductive inquiry, which the Royal Society itself saw as differentiating it from other forms of natural philosophy. This experimental philosophy was represented most distinctively by Robert Boyle, who in his own writing placed it in opposition on the one hand to *deductive rationalist* inquiry (represented in England by Hobbes, more generally by Cartesian thought), on the other to the text- and authority-oriented *Aristotelian science* practiced in the universities. (Valle 1999: 96)

The rejection of Descartes and Cartesian forms of reasoning is quite explicit in Sprat's *History of the Royal-Society*, published in 1667:

> I confess the excellent *Monsieur des Cartes* recommends to us another way in his *Philosophical Method*; where he gives this Relation of his own

progress; that after he had run through the usual Studies of youth, and spent his first years in an active life; when he retir'd to search into *Truth*, he at once rejected all the *Impressions*, which he had before receiv'd, from what he had heard, and read; and wholly gave himself over to a reflexion on the naked *Ideas* of his own mind. This he profess'd to do, that he might lay aside all his *old imaginations*, and begin anew to write on a white and unblotted *Soul*. This perhaps is more allowable in matters of *Contemplation*, and in a *Gentleman*, whose chief aim was his own delight; and so it was in his own choice, whether or no, he would go farther to seek it, than his own mind: But it can by no means stand with a practical and universal *Inquiry*. (Sprat 1667 [2003], 95-6)

Henry Oldenburg was one of the Royal Society's first secretaries, of which there were two. He was already the fulcrum in a complex web of correspondence. He received and disseminated a vast amount of scientific information, and was an inveterate letter-writer himself. This penchant for correspondence placed him in an ideal position to initiate the *Philosophical Transactions*, which, although it remained Oldenburg's private initiative, always had the blessing of the Royal Society, and was generally perceived as being its official publication. The diffusion of science through correspondence was not unusual; along with book publication, it was a common method at the time (Bazerman 1988). But it was Oldenburg who started the movement which was to make the scientific journal the cornerstone of scientific communication. He did this initially by taking something which was popular and making it an institution (Atkinson 1999). Although the Royal Society failed to instigate shared projects, and frequently functioned more like a gentlemen's club than a college, the *Philosophical Transactions* became its collective voice (Dear 1985). The ten items in the first 16-page issue in 1665 were all penned by Oldenburg himself, in the sense that he summarised items of news that he had received in his correspondence. By the time Oldenburg died in 1677, issues were more frequently of 24 pages, and sometimes as many as 40, and the degree of Oldenburg's intervention in the texts published had diminished so that full letters were printed *verbatim* and authored articles had begun to appear. However, the letter form was to have a long life, and the epistolary style continued to be used well into the nineteenth century (Katzen 1980). During the period 1679-83, it was replaced by the *Philosophical Collections*, under the editorship of Hooke, but the *Philosophical Transactions* was reinstated in 1683. The publication ceased altogether in the years 1687-90, but was then revived, and has never ceased publication since. In 1772, a committee was set up to select the contents, a move which was to lead to the contemporary system of refereeing, particularly after a decision to have more direct recourse to outside referees in 1831. The following year, 1832, the Royal Society began the *Proceedings of the Royal Society*, which was published in parallel with the *Philosophical Transactions*. Although not originally intended for papers, by 1850 papers were being published in the *Proceedings*, albeit usually shorter than those appearing in the *Philosophical Transactions*. In 1887 the *Philosophical Transactions* was split into *Series A*, for the physical sciences, and *Series B*, for the biological sciences. The *Proceedings* followed suit in 1905, when it was decided that the *Philosophical Transactions* would carry longer, more elaborate papers, while the *Proceedings* would publish shorter articles of up to 24 pages. In 1997, an even clearer division of type of material was decided on: the *Philosophical Transactions* are now devoted to review articles and monographs, while the *Proceedings* will publish research articles, though usually restricted to seven pages (Atkinson 1999; Valle 1999). Thus it would seem that from this date the onus of research publication has passed from the *Philosophical Transactions* to the *Proceedings*, a movement which had started much earlier in the twentieth century, but which is finalised in this decision.

The influence of the early editions of the *Philosophical Transactions* was immense, and even went far beyond the actual journal itself and its readers. It was imitated in other countries and its contents were frequently reprinted and translated, or otherwise reformulated in other publications:

> The *Philosophical Transactions* ranks high among the most influential of the 17th and 18th century scientific periodicals both in the degree with which it inspired imitations in other parts of Europe, and in the degree with which it supplied provender for the other scientific journals of the period. It was reprinted, abridged, abstracted, reformulated and translated in numerous editions. (Kronick 1976: 137)

From the start, those who formed the Royal Society, and indeed those in general involved in the new experimental philosophy, realised that the intellectual choices they had made implied new ways of writing. Their stance was radically different from that of those who based their thought on the authority of the ancients, and argued deductively from these premises. It followed that new rhetorical forms were necessary to express the new forms of thought. This was already evident in the writings of Bacon, and is confirmed by Sprat in his *History of the Royal-Society* (Sprat 1667 [2003]). This is scarcely a history in our contemporary sense, since the Royal Society had only been in existence for half a dozen years. It was in fact a piece of propaganda, a manifesto for the Society, which describes it as it wished to be seen by others. In a frequently quoted passage, Sprat describes the sort of language which is necessary for the recording of experimental philosophy:

> They [the Royal Society] have therefore been most rigorous in putting in execution, the only Remedy, that can be found for this *extravagance*: and that has been a constant Resolution to reject all the amplifications, digressions, and swellings of style, to return back to the primitive purity, and shortness, when men deliver'd so many *things*, almost in an equal number of *words*. They have exacted from all their members, a close, naked natural way of speaking; positive expressions; clear senses; a native easiness; bringing all things as near the Mathematical plainness, as they can; and preferring the language of Artizans, Countrymen, and Merchants, before that of Wits, or Scholars. (Sprat 1667 [2003]: 113)

This passage comes at the end of a section where he sets out to explain the Royal Society's attitude towards writing:

> ... there is one thing more, about which the *Society* has been most sollicitous; and that is, the manner of their *Discourse*: which, unless they had been very watchful to keep in due temper, the whole spirit and vigour of their *Design*, had been soon eaten out, by the luxury and redundance of *speech*. (Sprat 1667 [2003]: 111).

What follows is a diatribe against the prevailing florid style in writing which obscures clarity of thought. The following gives some idea of the flavour of Sprat's remarks:

> Who can behold, without indignation, how many mists and uncertainties, these specious *Tropes* and *Figures* have brought on our Knowledg? How many rewards, which are due to more profitable, and difficult *Arts*, have been still snatch'd away by the easie vanity of *fine speaking*? For now I am warm'd with this just Anger, I cannot with-hold my self, from betraying the shallowness of all these seeming Mysteries; upon which, *we Writers*, and *Speakers*, look so bigg. And, in few words, I dare say; that of all the Studies of men, nothing may be sooner obtained, than this vicious abundance of *Phrase*, this trick of *Metaphors*, this volubility of *Tongue*, which makes so great a noise in the World. But I spend words in vain; for the evil is now so inveterate, that it is hard to know whom to *blame*, or where to begin to *reform*. (Sprat 1667 [2003]: 112)

So this was the atmosphere within which those who espoused the new experimental philosophy were working.

Newton

And so to Isaac Newton. The man who was to become one of the greatest scientists of all time, and for some simply the greatest, was born on

Christmas Day, 1642. His father had died six months after his marriage to Hannah, Isaac's mother, so it was a fatherless child who entered the world on that Christmas morning. In 1646, when Isaac was three years old, his mother remarried. Her new husband was a local rector, Barnabas Smith, and as was natural, she went to live with him. What seems less natural is that Isaac did not accompany her, but remained on the family farm to be raised by his grandparents. This separation at such an early age, particularly as he had been raised, thus far, solely by his mother in a one-parent family, must have been traumatic, and some see it as a major factor in the development of his personality, which was to become highly introverted, and to lead him to live most of his life largely as a recluse. In 1654, having shown some aptitude for learning, he was sent to the Grammar School at Grantham, and subsequently, in 1661, he went on to Cambridge. There, he was a subsizar, which meant that, in order to pay his way, he acted as servant to more wealthy students. In 1669, at the amazingly young age of 26, Newton became Lucasian Professor of Mathematics at Cambridge. He held this chair until 1701, though he had already left Cambridge for London in 1696. The real man was, of course, more complex than his popular image. That image, the myth of the unsurpassed genius, was built up after his death, expunging any details that did not lend themselves to corroborating the desired picture (Fara 2002).

There are two factors which complicate the picture. The first of these is Newton's religious beliefs. Newton was not just a Puritan, as Auffray (2000) claims, but an Arian, or Unitarian; that is, he did not believe in the Trinity. Although this is clear from his personal papers, he kept it a closely guarded secret, for at that period such beliefs constituted a criminal offence. Had they become known, although he might not have suffered the technically possible death penalty, he would almost certainly have been hounded out of his academic position, as a heretic. However, it was also a requirement of the time that university dons take holy orders in the Anglican Church; Newton's strongly held religious beliefs were such that he would have found it impossible to take the necessary vows, and he went to great lengths to obtain a royal dispensation from the requirement to take holy orders (White 1997; Fara 2002; Gleik 2003).

The second factor is that papers which came to light in the mid-twentieth century show that Newton dabbled in alchemy right until the end of his life. Some believe it was this fact that contributed to his belief in gravity. For those, like Descartes, who were convinced of the mechanical philosophy, such an effect at a distance was impossible (White 1997; Auffray 2000; Panza 2003).

Newton's relationship with the Royal Society was in many ways a tumultuous one. He was elected a Fellow in 1672, and later that year his article 'A new theory about light and colours' appeared in the *Philosophical Transactions*. Newton, convinced of his own genius, had expected the truth of his conclusions to be evident to all. He expected his peers to be able to fill in for themselves those gaps in his writing which the argument required. This was not to be. The publication was followed by four years of often bitter controversy, initiated mainly by Hooke. Newton did not appear in person before the Royal Society; indeed he threatened to resign. His first visit did not take place until 1675, three years after his election, and he never attended regularly before he was elected President in 1703, after the death of Hooke. At this time, he had been living in London, as Master of the Mint, since 1696. Thereafter, he controlled the Royal Society in an authoritarian manner, but at the same time restored its scientific credentials, which it had been in danger of losing towards the end of the seventeenth century. Many believe that the controversy over his *Philosophical Transactions* article was responsible for the fact that although his book, *Opticks*, was virtually complete by 1687, it was not published until 1704, again following the death of Hooke. It subsequently, however, ran to four editions by 1730. It is also thought that it was this controversy that forced Newton to create new rhetorical strategies for presenting experimental accounts, thus providing the change of direction which was to lead to the genre of the scientific experimental article (Bazerman 1988; Fara 2002; Valle 1999).

However, even if Newton was searching for new means of expression, it would be false to think of him as working in some sort of vacuum. Despite his reclusive personality, he would inevitably be influenced by the culture in which he had been brought up, and within which he worked. There are at least two comparisons which are relevant from this point of view. The first is that, until this time, most scientific writing had been in Latin. Newton himself had written his *Philosophiae Naturalis Principia Mathematica*, commonly known simply as the *Principia*, in Latin, and this had been published in 1687. Latin was of course the scientific *lingua franca* of the time, and the possibility that Newton's English writing, and the innovations it contains, was influenced by the Latin that he and other scientists wrote cannot be excluded. This possible Latin influence has rarely been considered, and never in detail. Vickers (1972) simply points out the phenomenon, and Gleik (2003) discusses its sociological significance. Turner (1987) is one of the rare people to see a specifically linguistic link between Latin and scientific English. He claims that use of the passive in scientific writing is, in part, derived from Latin:

The scientific paper, a new literary form which was to be the typical vehicle of scientific information, inherited the passive from general English and from science Latin, but yet had to develop characteristic uses of it. (Turner 1972: 183)

Gross *et al.* (2002) even downplay the possible influence of Latin. In commenting on the exclusion of Latin from their corpus, they say:

This omission is not meant to slight the significance of the journals in Latin ... It is simply that the decline of Latin in the periodical literature is too precipitous for us to make evolutionary comparisons between the 17th century and later centuries. By the late 17th century, Latin was already on the way out in favour of the vernacular ... (Gross *et al.* 2002: 33)

The second type of comparison that suggests itself is that between Newton as an empirical scientist, as opposed to scientists who did not subscribe to the empiricist hypothesis. I shall first consider this question of possible Latin influence, and then the question of the influence of his empirical stance.

Newton and the influence of Latin

In a previous study (Banks 2005b), I attempted to take a first step towards testing the possible influence of Latin on Newton's writing in English. I took a short extract from Newton's *Principia*, in fact, *Lemma II*, and I compared this with the contemporary English translation by Andrew Motte, first published in 1729.[7] Since it is often claimed that Newton's use of nominalised processes is the most significant of the writing strategies that he introduced, I compared this feature in the two texts. *Lemma II* can itself be divided into three sections, which might be considered subgenres. The first is a theoretical introduction; this is followed by the mathematical demonstration; and the extract ends with a sort of coda, called the *Scholium*. The following has the relevant extracts from the introductory section of Newton's Latin text, with the nominalised processes shown in bold:

Genitam voco quantitatem omnem, quæ ex lateribus vel terminis quibuscunque in arithmetica per **multiplicationem, divisionem** & **extractionem** radicum; in geometria per **inventionem** vel contentorum & laterum, vel extremarum & mediarum proportionalium, sine **additione** & **subductione** generatur. ... Has quantitates, ut indeterminatas & instabiles, & quasi **motu fluxu**ve perpetuo crescentes vel decrescentes, hic considero; & earum **incrementa** vel **decrementa** momentanea sub nomine momentorum intelligo: ita ut **incrementa** pro momentis addititiis seu affirmativis, ac **decrementa** pro subductitiis seu negativis habeantur.

> ... Eodem recidit si loco momentorum usurpentur vel **velocitates incrementorum** ac **decrementorum** (quas etiam **motus, mutationes** & **fluxiones** quantitatum nominare licet) vel finitæ quævis quantitates **velocitatibus** hisce proportionales.

The whole section contains 168 words and there are 19 examples of nominalised process. The relevant extract from Motte's translation has 240 words, that is, more than the Latin text, as one would expect, but the extract also has 19 nominalised processes, and these all parallel those of the Latin original:

> I call any quantity a *Genitum*, which is not made by **addition** or **subduction** of divers parts, but is generated or produced in arithmetic by the **multiplication, division,** or **extraction** of the root of any terms whatsoever, in geometry by the **invention** of contents and sides ... These quantities I here consider as variable and indetermined, and increasing or decreasing as it were by a perpetual **motion** of **flux**; and I understand their momentaneous **increments** or **decrements** by the name of Moments; so that the **increments** may be esteem'd as added, or affirmative moments, and the **decrements** as subducted, or negative ones. ... It will be the same thing, if, instead of moments, we use either the **Velocities** of the **increments** and **decrements** (which may also be called the **motions, mutations,** and **fluxions** of quantities) or any finite quantities proportional to those **velocities.** ...

The 19 tokens in each text represent 13 types, and the English translations are systematically calques of the Latin. These are shown in Table 3.1.

Table 3.1. English and Latin nominalisations in *Lemma II* introduction.

addition	additio, -ionis
decrement	decrementum, -i
division	divisio, -ionis
extraction	extractio, -ionis
flux	fluxus, -us
fluxion	fluxio, -ionis
increment	incrementum, -i
invention	inventio, -ionis
motion	motus, -us
multiplication	multiplicatio, -ionis
mutation	mutatio, -ionis
subduction	subductio, -ionis
velocity	velocitas, -atis

In the second part of the text, the mathematical demonstration, nominalised processes are much less frequent. Newton's 489-word Latin text has only eight examples:

> Igitur sensus lemmatis est, ut si quantitatum quarumcunque perpetuo **motu** crescentium vel decrescentium *A, B, C,* &c. momenta, vel his proportionales **mutationum velocitates** dicantur *a, b, c,* &c. momentum vel **mutatio** geniti rectanguli *AB* fuerit *aB* +*bA,* ... Rectangulum quodvis **motu** perpetuo auctum *AB* ... Igitur laterum **incrementis** totis *a* & *b* generatur rectanguli **incrementum** *aB* + *bA.* ... Et par est **ratio** contenti sub pluribus dignitatibus.

Once again, the English text, of 618 words, has eight examples paralleling those of the Latin text:

> Wherefore the sense of the Lemma is, that if the moments of any quantities *A, B, C,* &c. increasing or decreasing by a perpetual **flux**, or the **velocities** of the **mutations** which are proportional to them, be called *a, b, c,* &c. the moment or **mutation** of the generated rectangle *AB* will be *aB* + *bA*; ... Any rectangle as *AB* augmented by a perpetual **flux**, ... Therefore with the whole **increments** *a* and *b* of the sides, the **increment** *aB* = *bA* of the rectangle is generated. ... And the **reasoning** is the same for contents under more powers ...

These eight examples represent five types. Of the Latin types, four of the five also appeared in the first section. These nominalisations are shown in Table 3.2.

It will be noted that whereas *flux* was used to translate *fluxus* in the first section, here it is used to translate *motus*. The term which is new is *ratio*, translated by *reasoning*.

In the *Scholium*, the 136-word Latin text has nine examples:

> In epistola quadam ad D. *J. Collinium* nostratem 10 Decem. 1672 data, cum descripsissem **methodum** tangentium quam suspicabar eandem esse cum **methodo** *Slusii* tum nondum communicata; subjunxi: *Hoc est unum particulare vel corollarium potius **methodi** generalis, quae extendit se citra molestum ullum **calculum**, non modo ad **ducendum** tangentes ad*

Table 3.2. English and Latin nominalisations in *Lemma II* discussion section.

flux	motus, -us
increment	incrementum, -i
mutation	mutatio, -ionis
reasoning	ratio, -ionis
velocity	velocitas, -atis

*quasvis curvas sive geometricas sive mechanicas vel quomodocunque rectas lineas aliasve curvas respicientes, verum etiam ad **resolvendum** alia abstrusiora problematum genera de curvitatibus areis, longitudinibus, centris gravitatis curvarum &c. neque (quemadmodum* Huddenii ***methodus** de maximis & minimis) ad solas restringitur æquationes illas quæ quantitatibus surdis sunt immunes. Hanc **methodum** intertexui alteri isti qua æquationum exegesin instituo reducendo eas ad series infinitas.* Hactenus epistola. Et hæc ultima verba spectant ad tractatum quem anno 1671 de his rebus scripseram. **Methodi** vero hujus generalis fundamentum continetur in lemmate præcedente.

As might now be expected, the English translation, of 175 words, has nine parallel examples:

In a letter of mine to Mr. *J. Collins*, dated *December 10. 1672* having described a **method** of Tangents, which I suspected to be the same with Slusius's **method**, which at that time was not made publick; I subjoined these words; *This is one particular, or rather a corollary, of a general **method**, which extends itself, without any troublesome **calculation**, not only to the **drawing** of Tangents to any Curve lines, whether Geometrical or Mechanical, or any how respecting right lines or other Curves, but also to the **resolving** other abstruser kinds of Problems about the crookedness, areas, lengths, centres of gravity of Curves, &c. nor is it (as* Hudden's **method** de Maximus & Minimis) limited to equations which are free from surd quantities. This **method** I have interwoven with that other of working in equations, by reducing them to infinite series. So far that letter. And these last words relate to a Treatise I composed on that subject in the year 1671. The foundation of the general **method** is contained in the preceding Lemma.

However, these represent only four types, of which two are Latin gerunds, translated by nominal *–ing* forms in English. These are shown in Table 3.3.

If the frequencies of nominalized processes are now considered, where frequency is calculated as the average number of examples per 100 words of text, they are found as shown in Figure 3.4.

It will be noted that the frequencies for the introduction are relatively high. By comparison, those for the discussion/demonstration section are low,

Table 3.3. English and Latin nominalisations in the *Lemma II Scholium*.

calculation	calculus, -i
drawing	ducendum
method	methodus, -i
resolving	resolvendum

Table 3.4. Frequencies of nominalised processes in *Lemma II*.

	Latin	*English*
Introduction	11.3	7.9
Discussion	1.6	1.3
Coda	6.6	5.1

and those for the coda fall about half-way between the two. It might be objected that the figures for the demonstration section are skewed by the fact that the section contains a large number of mathematical expressions, which by definition cannot be nominalised processes. Nevertheless, it is difficult to exclude these in a word count since they constitute an integral part of the text, and have grammatical functions. However, even if for the sake of argument these were excluded, the frequencies would only rise to 2.3 for the Latin text, and 1.5 for the English, a difference which does not significantly alter the general picture.

What this pilot study shows is that the nominalised processes of the English translation are directly derived from the original Latin text, and secondarily, that the frequency of nominalisation is subgenre sensitive. It shows that nominalisation of processes was used in scientific Latin, and this leaves open the possibility that subsequently scientific English was influenced by the Latin that all scientists of the period were familiar with, and that most of them wrote themselves. It might be argued that Newton's Latin could have been influenced by his English mother tongue. On the other hand, his Latin is certainly not a calque of English, and the fact that Latin was used as a *lingua franca* by intellectuals with a wide range of mother tongues would mitigate against its being significantly influenced by those mother tongues, since the more it was influenced, the more its use as a *lingua franca* would be reduced. My own feeling is that there is probably a complicated and two-way influence between Latin and English in the scientific writing of this period, for these scientists who were all familiar with Latin. At all events, the possible influence of Latin on Newton's writing cannot be discounted.

Newton and Huygens

We have already seen that the writing of Newton's *Opticks* (Newton 1730 [1979]) is frequently seen as a turning-point in the development of scientific writing. It is fortuitous that we also have a book on the same subject by another famous scientist of the period who wrote in a different language.

This is *Traité de la lumière* by Christiaan Huygens (1690 [1992]), which was published in 1690. Since we know that, although it was not published until 1704, Newton's *Opticks* had been virtually complete since 1687, it is reasonable to suppose that these two books were being written at the same time. Although French was not Huygens' mother tongue, he is said to have spoken it fluently. He began learning it at the age of nine, when he had already mastered Latin. For families of the rank and standing of the Huygens, it would seem that French constituted a language of domestic communication; when Huygens' father visited England as a young man, he corresponded with his parents in French. In 1666 Huygens was invited by Louis XIV to come to Paris, which he had previously visited on three occasions, to direct the founding of the *Académie Royale des Sciences*. He lived in Paris from 1666 to 1669 and from 1671 to 1681, when he returned to The Hague for reasons of health. It seems obvious that he was well integrated into French society, both civil and scientific. Hence, although he was not a native speaker, it seems reasonable to suppose that Huygens' French conforms to the standard for scientific writing of this period, and that no distortions will result from his non-native status.

In previous studies (Banks 2004a, 2005a) I have compared extracts from Newton's *Opticks* and Huygens' *Traité de la lumière*. There are virtually no other studies of this type; Gross *et al.* 2002 is a rare example, which compares a 1672 article in French by Huygens with a 1665 article in English by Henshaw. However, Gross *et al.* only use English translations of the non-English articles which they discuss, with no reference to the original languages. Their usefulness is therefore limited to ideational content and nothing can be said about the encoding choices of the authors concerned.

I studied three extracts from each book. The first extract in each is the beginning of the book, excluding the 'Advertisement' in the case of Newton, and the *Préface* in the case of Huygens. The second extract corresponds to an experimental section, though as will be seen this means something different in each case. The third extract is a discussion section, which deals with the same subject in each case. Newton's deals with 'Observations concerning the Reflexions, Refractions and Colours of thin transparent Bodies', while Huygens' deals with 'Des figures des corps diaphanes Qui servent à la Réfraction, et à la Réflexion'. The Newton extracts are referred to as N1, N2, N3, and the Huygens extracts as H1, H2, H3. The details are given in Table 3.5.

Huygens was a Cartesian, and the Cartesian method was one of deduction, where reason is paramount. Reasoning provides hypotheses, which can then be tested by experimentation, but the reasoning and hypotheses come before the experiment. Newton, as has been seen, was an empiricist, in the spirit of Bacon. The empirical programme is inductive; experimentation and

Table 3.5. Number of words in Newton and Huygens extracts.

Newton	*Huygens*
N1: 1,459	H1: 1,806
N2: 1,789	H2: 1,977
N3: 1,493	H3: 2,048
Total: 4,741	Total: 5,831
Overall total: 10572	

observation come first. Reason can then be used to build a theory on the basis of experimental results, but the experiment must come first. It is significant that Newton was incensed when critics of his 1672 paper accused him of producing 'hypotheses'. This linked him with the Cartesians, who were at the opposite pole from what he was about. According to Gross, in that 1672 paper, 'Newton clearly and uncompromisingly reverses the traditional and Cartesian roles of reason and experiment' (Gross 1996: 120). By the time of the *Opticks*, 'by piling experiment on experiment, and in each experiment, detail on detail, he created in this work an overwhelming presence for his experimental method' (Gross 1996: 122).

The two authors make their respective stances absolutely clear at the very beginning of their books. Newton starts his with the following words:

> My design in this Book is not to explain the Properties of Light by Hypotheses, but to propose and prove them by Reason and Experiments: In order to which I shall premise the following Definitions and Axioms.

Here we see Newton rejecting hypothesis, that Cartesian buzzword, as a basis for his study. In saying that he is not going to explain things through hypotheses, Newton is placing himself in diametric opposition to the Cartesians. In making this statement in such a clear and unadorned way it can clearly be read, and was probably intended to be read, as a Cartesian put-down. Huygens, on the other hand, places himself unambiguously in the Cartesian camp. The third paragraph of his book says:

> J'essaierai donc dans ce livre, par des principes reçus dans la Philosophie d'aujourd'hui, de donner des raisons plus claires et plus vraisemblables, premièrement de ces propriétés de la lumière directement étendu ; secondement de celle qui se réfléchit par la rencontre d'autres corps. Puis j'expliquerai les symptômes des rayons qui sont dits souffrir réfraction en passant par les corps diaphanes de différente espèce.

[I shall thus attempt in this book to give, according to the principles of contemporary philosophy, the clearest and most probable reasons, first for the properties of directly emitted light, and secondly of that which is reflected by contact with other bodies. Then I will explain the characteristics of rays which are said to undergo refraction by passing through translucent bodies of different types.[8]]

It is evident that *Philosophie d'aujourd'hui* here means Cartesian philosophy. Descartes is actually mentioned in the following paragraph, and is referred to frequently throughout the work.

The first extract from Newton's book (N1) begins with the above quotation and is followed, as the quotation says, by definitions and axioms. The first Huygens extract (H1) includes the above quotation and is much more discursive and more explicative than the Newton extract.

The second Newton extract (N2) is a description of experiments and of what he did while carrying out these experiments. The following gives some idea of the style of this passage:

In a very dark Chamber, at a round hole, about one third Part of an Inch broad, made in the Shut of a Window, I placed a Glass Prism, whereby the Beam of the Sun's Light, which came in at that Hole, might be refracted upwards toward the opposite Wall of the Chamber, and there form a colour'd Image of the Sun.

The second Huygens extract (H2) could also in some sense be called experimental, but not in the same sense as the Newton extract. Huygens does not describe the experimental process. The experiment is in some way there in the background, referred to as a basis for reasoning, but not recounted. The following gives some idea of this:

L'on peut donc de cette manière concevoir la transparence sans qu'il soit besoin que la matière éthérée, qui sert à la lumière, y passe, ni qu'elle trouve des pores pour s'y insinuer. Mais la vérité est que cette matière non seulement y passe, mais même avec grande facilité; de quoi l'expérience de Torricelli, dessus alléguée, est déjà une preuve.

[In this way one can conceive of transparency without any need for etherised matter, which is necessary for light, to pass through it, or for it to find pores to infiltrate. But the truth is that this matter not only passes through, but does so with the greatest ease. Torricelli's experiment, presented above, is already a proof of this.]

In the third Newton extract (N3), discussion leads Newton into more experimentation, so that he is still in the business of doing things, and hence describing the experiments he is carrying out:

Compressing two Prisms hard together that their sides (which by chance were a very little convex) might somewhere touch one another: I found the place in which they touched to become absolutely transparent, as if they had there been one continued piece of Glass.

In the third Huygens extract (H3), on the other hand, discussion leads him into the more abstract world of mathematics:

Pour démontrer ensuite que les surfaces, que ces courbes feront par leur circonvolution, dirigeront tous les rayons qui viennent sur elles du point A, en sorte qu'ils tendent vers B; soit supposé le point K dans la courbe, plus loin que n'est C; mais en sorte que la droite ZAK tombe sur la courbe, qui sert à la réfraction, en dehors; et du centre B soit décrit l'arc KS, coupant BD en S, et la droite CB en R; et du centre A l'arc DN, rencontrant AK en N.

[Then to show that the surfaces, created by the curvature of the curves, direct all the rays that fall on them from a point A in such a way that they converge on B; suppose a point K on the curve, more distant than C, but such that the straight line ZAK falls on the outside of the curve where refraction takes place; and from the centre B, let there be an arc KS, intersecting with BD at S, and the straight line CB at R; and from the centre A, an arc DN, meeting AK at N.]

In his *Principia*, Newton had established himself as one of the foremost mathematicians of his time (Panza 2003). Despite the fact that probably no more than 300 copies were printed, this work made his reputation. It would seem that Newton deliberately made this book abstruse so that only a small coterie of elite mathematicians would be able to understand it. The fact that he avoided mathematics in the *Opticks* is consequently significant, and indicates his desire to reach a wider public with this work (White 1997; Fara 2002; Gleik 2003).

I shall now attempt to compare the same features of the writing of Newton and Huygens, notably use of the passive, personal pronouns and nominalisations.

If sentence complexity, measured either as number of words per sentence, or number of finite verbs (hence finite clauses) per sentence, is considered, it is found that Huygens' sentences have more words and more finite verbs than Newton's. The relevant figures are given in Table 3.6.

Obviously, every language has its own structural specificities, but to the extent that comparison across languages is valid, it can be seen that Huygens' French text is more complex than Newton's English text, both from the point of view of number of words per sentence and that of number of finite verbs. It will also be noted that while the average number of words per

Table 3.6. Sentence complexity in Newton and Huygens.

	Words	Sentences	Words/Sent.	Fin.vbs	Fin.vbs/Sent
N1	1,459	35	41.7	105	3.0
N2	1,789	41	43.9	120	2.9
N3	1,493	40	37.3	116	2.9
Total	4,741	116	40.9	341	2.9
H1	1,806	42	43.0	168	4.0
H2	1,977	45	43.9	198	4.4
H3	2,048	41	50.0	185	4.5
Total	5,831	128	45.6	551	4.3

sentence varies from section to section for both writers, the average number of finite verbs per sentence is remarkably stable in Newton's case, but not in Huygens', where there are rather less in the first extract than in the other two. It seems reasonable then to say that Huygens' sentence structure is more complex than Newton's. However, in the absence of any comparative studies of seventeenth-century English and French, it is impossible to say whether this simply reflects the general language use of the period. Brunot and Bruneau (1969) describe the sentence of seventeenth-century French as being long, sometimes heavy, but at the same time, clear, precise, and solid. It is also difficult to know how this compares with the English sentence of the time, where in general it was evidently longer than that of present-day English, though perhaps not as long as that of the Victorian period (Banks 2007). Moreover, we know that education in this period was extensively influenced by classical studies, and the favoured sentence structure of the time was based on a classical model. As Rissanen points out:

> Classical ideals no doubt exercised an important influence on stylistic developments in Renaissance English writing, and this increased the popularity of certain constructions particularly those related to the formation of complex sentences with various types of subordination, non-finite clauses, etc. (Rissanen 1999: 189)

The use of passives has been one of the most extensively discussed features of scientific writing, so it is of interest to see to what extent they were used by these two writers. Table 3.7 gives the distribution of finite passives; non-finite passives have not been considered, and they are in any case rare in both the French and English texts. The Newton extracts have a total of eight infinitives, some of which might be thought of as adjectival (e.g. *to be a little*

Table 3.7. Passives in Newton and Huygens.

	Passives	*As percentage of finite verbs*
N1	21	20.0
N2	17	14.2
N3	6	5.2
Total	44	12.9
H1	13	7.7
H2	20	10.1
H3	8	4.3
Total	41	7.4

tinged), and two participles. Non-finite passives are virtually absent from the Huygens extracts, where there are three participles and no infinitives.

Given the differences between the two languages, it is unsurprising that Newton in general uses more passives than Huygens. Indeed the percentage rate in H2 is comparatively high for French, and almost double the rate of N3, which is surprisingly low, being almost four times less than N1. However, it remains true that in no individual section does Huygens attain the overall rate of the Newton extracts. The following may give some idea of the use of passives in the two authors:

Whence if that Proportion **be known** in any one Inclination of the incident Ray, '**tis known** in all the Inclinations, and thereby the Refraction in all cases of Incidence on the same refracting Body **may be determined**. (N1)

For let EG represent the Window-shut, F the hole made therein through which a beam of the Sun's Light **was transmitted** into the darkened Chamber, and ABC a Triangular Imaginary Plane whereby the prism **is feigned** to be cut transversely through the middle of the light. (N2)

Les démonstrations qui concernent l'Optique, ainsi qu'il arrive dans toutes les sciences où la Géométrie **est appliquée** à la matière, **sont fondées** sur des vérités tirées de l'expérience; telles que sont que les rayons de lumière s'étendent en droite ligne; que les angles de réflexion et d'incidence sont égaux: et que dans les réfractions le rayon **est rompu** suivant la règle des Sinus, désormais si connue, et qui n'est pas moins certaine que les précédentes. (H1)
[Demonstrations concerning optics, just as in any science where geometry is applied to matter, are based on truths drawn from experience; such as that rays of light are emitted in a straight line; that the angles of reflection and incidence are equal; and that in refraction, the ray is bent according

to the sine rule, now well known and no less certain than the previous examples.]

Laquelle pourtant on peut résoudre en disant que le mouvement très violent et rapide de la matière subtile qui rend l'eau liquide, en ébranlant les particules dont elle **est composée**, maintient cette liquidité malgré la pression que jusqu'ici on se **soit avisé** d'y appliquer. (H2)
[However, it can be resolved by saying that the rapid violent motion of the subtle matter which makes water liquid, by exciting the particles which form it, maintain its liquid state, despite the pressure which, thus far, it would have been necessary to apply.]

When passives are looked at in terms of the process types involved, some differences become apparent. The percentages of passives are almost the same for Mental process, 27 per cent (12 examples) for Newton and 24 per cent (10) for Huygens, but Newton passivises Material processes more frequently than Huygens does. These account for 68 per cent (30) of Newton's passives, but only 56 per cent (23) of Huygens'. This is compensated for by a rather higher proportion of Verbal processes among Huygens' passives, 20 per cent (8) compared with only 5 per cent (2) for Newton. These differences can be ascribed to the more experimental nature of Newton's text. Since Newton is describing what he did as an experimenter, he does not need to repeat himself as agent of the processes, even if he does so more frequently than is common nowadays, and it can be supposed that this leads to an increased use of Material process passives. The higher rate of Verbal process passives in Huygens' text might be thought of as resulting from the more philosophical bent of his book. Hence these differences, even though the figures are small, can be seen as consistent with the idea that Newton's text reflects his empirical philosophy, while Huygens' reflects his Cartesian stance.

Since the passive is often considered to be a way of avoiding mentioning the agent, it is worthwhile looking at the use of personal pronouns in subject position, as a sort of obverse of the use of the passive. Newton uses both *I* and, rarely, *you* in subject position, and there are ellipted cases of both. The details are given in Table 3.8.

Table 3.8. Personal pronoun Subjects in Newton.

	I	*Ellipted I*	*you*	*Ellipted you*	*my*
N1	16	—	2	2	—
N2	20	5	—	—	—
N3	15	3	1	—	1
Total	51	8	3	2	1

The following are typical examples:

About the axis **I turned** the Prism and **saw** the refracted Light on the Wall, or coloured Image of the Sun, first to descend, and then to ascend. (N2)

For it is manifest that Light consists of Parts, both Successive and Contemporary; because in the same place **you may stop** that which comes one moment, and **let pass** that which comes presently after; and in the same time **you may stop** it in any one place, and **let it pass** in any other. (N1)

Huygens uses *je* (first person singular), *nous* (first person plural), and *on*, including its variant *l'on* (impersonal third person singular). The details are given in Table 3.9.

Typical examples are:

En quoi ayant avancé des choses ingénieuses, mais non pas telles pourtant que les plus intelligents ne souhaitent des explications qui leur satisfassent d'avantage, **je** veux proposer ici ce que **j'ai** médité sur ce sujet, pour contribuer autant que **je** puis à l'éclaircissement de cette partie de la Science naturelle, qui non sans raison en est réputée une des plus difficiles. (H1)

[In which, after putting forward ingenious proposals, but not such, however, that the more intelligent will not desire explanations which satisfy them even more, I want to present here, the results of my reflection on the question, to contribute, as far as I can, to the elucidation of this part of natural science, which is supposed, not without reason, to be one of the most difficult.]

La rareté des corps transparents étant donc telle que **nous** avons dit, **l'on** conçoit aisément que les ondes puissent être continuées dans la matière éthérée qui emplit les interstices des particules. (H2)

[The density of transparent bodies being such as we have described, it is easy to suppose that waves can continue in the etherised matter which fills the interstices of the particles.]

Table 3.9. Personal pronoun Subjects in Huygens.

	je	*nous*	*on*
H1	16	6	12
H2	7	5	18
H3	4	6	15
Total	27	17	45

Derechef, si l'on suppose le point B infiniment loin, au lieu de notre première ovale, **nous** trouverons que CDE est la véritable Hyperbole; qui fera que les rayons, qui viennent du point A, deviendront parallèles. (H3) [Again, if point B is assumed to be infinitely distant, instead of our first oval, we find that CDE is a genuine hyperbola. This means that the rays, which come from point A, become parallel.]

If the frequencies of these pronouns are now calculated in terms of frequency per 1,000 words, and frequency per 100 finite verbs, the results are as shown in Table 3.10. In the case of Newton, ellipted and non-ellipted cases have been combined.

Newton's personal pronoun Subjects are almost restricted to *I*, the number of examples of *you* being small. Huygens uses the impersonal pronoun *on* more frequently than *je*. There is also some assimilation of *on* and *nous*, since he sometimes passes from one to the other, as in the above examples. Huygens uses personal pronoun Subjects slightly more frequently than Newton in terms of numbers of words, but slightly less in terms of numbers of finite verbs. However, more significant is the fact that whereas Newton's personal pronouns are predominantly first person singular (92 per cent), less than a third (30 per cent) of Huygens' fall into this category. Over half (51 per cent) of Huygens' personal pronouns are impersonal (since we are including the impersonal pronoun *on* in the category of personal pronouns), and the remainder (19 per cent) are second person plural. This is probably a result of the more highly personalised nature of Newton's text, where he is himself involved in carrying out the experiments, whereas Huygens' text is more abstract due to the Cartesian nature of his discourse, where there is no description of experiments carried out personally, and the argument is based on information presented as generally accepted fact.

If these pronouns are considered in terms of the process types with which they occur, then the results given in Table 3.11 are found.

Table 3.10. Frequencies of personal pronoun Subjects in Newton and Huygens.

Newton	*I*	*you*	*Total*	
Number	59	5	64	
Per 1,000 words	12.4	1.1	13.5	
Per 100 finite verbs	17.3	1.5	18.8	
Huygens	*je*	*nous*	*on*	*Total*
Number	27	17	45	89
Per 1,000 words	4.6	2.9	7.7	15.3
Per 100 finite verbs	4.9	3.1	8.2	16.2

Table 3.11. Personal pronouns and process types in Newton and Huygens.

Newton – *(I)*

	Material	Mental	Relational	Verbal
N1	—	8	—	8
N2	13	5	2	—
N3	2	10	—	3
N Tot.	15	23	2	11

Huygens – *(je)*

	Material	Mental	Relational	Verbal
H1	—	6	2	8
H2	1	2	—	4
H3	—	1	—	3
Total	1	9	2	15

Huygens – *(nous)*

	Material	Mental	Relational	Verbal
H1	—	3	1	—
H2	—	2	—	3
H3	—	2	—	4
Total	—	7	1	7

Huygens – *(on)*

	Material	Mental	Relational	Verbal
H1	—	9	3	—
H2	3	5	9	1
H3	—	10	2	3
Total	3	24	14	4

Newton uses the first person singular most frequently with Mental processes, and to a significant extent with Material processes. He uses it to a lesser extent with Verbal processes, but hardly at all with Relational processes. Huygens also uses personal pronouns mainly with Mental processes, but hardly at all with Material processes. He uses *je* and *nous* to a significant extent with Verbal processes, but hardly at all with Relational processes; on the other hand, he uses *on* with Relational processes, but rarely with Verbal processes. If these figures are reduced to overall percentages, which makes comparison easier, the results in Table 3.12 are found.

Table 3.12. Percentages of personal pronouns with process types.

	Material	Mental	Relational	Verbal
Newton	29 per cent	45 per cent	4 per cent	22 per cent
Huygens	5 per cent	46 per cent	20 per cent	30 per cent

Here it is seen that Newton and Huygens use personal pronoun Subjects with Mental processes extensively and to virtually the same extent. Newton, however, uses them fairly extensively with Material processes, while Huygens does so only rarely. On the other hand, Newton uses them rarely with Relational processes, while the inverse is true of Huygens. Both use personal pronoun Subjects to some extent with Verbal processes, but Huygens does so rather more than Newton. This means that while the personal pronoun Subjects of these authors are most frequently the Subjects of Mental process verbs, Newton's *I* is also secondarily the Subject of Material process verbs, and to a reasonable extent of Verbal process verbs. In the case of Huygens' *je, nous,* and *on,* it is Verbal process verbs which come in second place, followed by Relational process verbs. Huygens' pronouns occur only rarely with Material process verbs. Once again, this seems to stem from the differing natures of the two texts. While both are involved in cognitive activity, only Newton's *I* is described as doing physical actions, that is, carrying out experiments. The preponderance of Relational processes with Huygens' pronouns indicates the more abstract nature of his text, simply describing what is the case. Newton is experimental and inductive. Huygens is observational and deductive.

In this analysis I have followed what I said in Banks 2003a, and considered that the finite modal verbs of French should be analysed as examples of Relational process. It is perhaps worthwhile pointing out that had these cases been analysed as complex verb groups with the process being determined by the following infinitive, they would have been mainly examples of Mental process, with a few cases of Verbal process. If anything, this would strengthen the above analysis.

Nominalised processes are also a feature frequently cited as being typical of scientific text, and this is also the feature which Halliday isolates as being Newton's greatest contribution to the development of scientific writing (Halliday 1988[1]). Details of nominalized process in these two texts are given in Table 3.13.

In terms of overall frequency, both authors use nominalised processes to a similar extent, with Newton using them slightly more often, with 30 per 1,000 words, compared to 27 for Huygens. However, the token/type ratio shows that Newton reuses his nominalisations more than Huygens; this is

Table 3.13. Nominalised processes in Newton and Huygens.

Newton

	Material	*Mental*	*Relational*	*Verbal*	*Total*
Tokens	123	9	8	3	143
Types	26	7	6	3	42
Per cent tokens	86 per cent	6 per cent	6 per cent	2 per cent	
Per cent types	63 per cent	17 per cent	14 per cent	7 per cent	
Token/type	4.7	1.3	1.3	1.0	3.4
Tokens/1,000 words	26	2	2	—	30

Huygens

	Material	*Mental*	*Relational*	*Verbal*	*Total*
Tokens	116	36	8	1	161
Types	31	18	8	1	58
Per cent tokens	72 per cent	22 per cent	5 per cent	1 per cent	
Per cent Types	53 per cent	31 per cent	14 per cent	2 per cent	
Token/type	3.7	2.0	1.0	1.0	2.8
Tokens/1,000 words	20	6	1	—	27

3.4 for Newton and 2.8 for Huygens. This may be an indication of Newton using nominalisation as a method of building up a technical terminology. Both use nominalisation of Material process to a great extent, though Newton does so even more than Huygens; this accounts for 86 per cent of Newton's tokens and 72 per cent of Huygens. The nominalisation of Verbal and Relational processes is fairly marginal in both cases, accounting for 8 per cent of the tokens in Newton's case and 6 per cent in Huygens'. It is in Mental process that the most significant difference appears. nominalisation remains fairly marginal here in the case of Newton, 6 per cent, but 22 per cent of Huygens' tokens are cases of Mental process. Hence Newton is nominalising Material processes which are usually the experimental processes or the physical phenomena he is studying. While this is also true of Huygens to a certain degree, he is not describing experiments *per se*. However, unlike Newton, he nominalises Mental processes to a significant extent, so that it is the process of rationalisation itself which is put forward and concretised. Once again, the different stances of these two writers would appear to account for the differences found.

The situation of context of these two texts, in terms of field, tenor and mode, is virtually the same. The field is that of scientific activity in late-seventeenth-century Europe, and more specifically the study of light. The tenor is that of communication between members of the discourse community of practising scientists in late seventeenth-century Europe. The mode is that of book form, hence written, and intended to be read silently and linearly. The factors then which produce the differences in these two texts are not at the level of context but rather at the level of ideology. That is, Newton's position as a Baconian empirical scientist, working within an inductive method, as opposed to Huygens' stance as a Cartesian deductive thinker, creates differences in their respective ideologies, which ultimately are visible in their writing. From this point of view, ideology is something which is ethically neutral, and all discourses are informed by some ideology or other. It is therefore to be distinguished from a view, such as that of Fairclough (2003), which sees ideology as necessarily reprehensible. From the point of view presented here, there is no such thing as ideology-free discourse.

It was to take about half a century before Newton's empiricism was to fully take over from Cartesianism as the basis for science or natural philosophy on the European continent. A first timid attempt was made by Maupertuis, but, according to Le Ru (2005), it was left to Voltaire to be the prime mover in promoting Newton's ideas, primarily in his *Eléments de la philosophie de Newton*, published in 1738.

Part 2
THE INTERVENING CENTURIES

4   A way forward

Two centuries of increasing nominalisation

Previous studies (Banks 1999, 2001a, 2005a) suggest that although the features of the scientific journal article can be traced from the late seventeenth century to the present day, the rate at which features were introduced and developed differs for different types of scientific activity. We can distinguish roughly between the physical and the biological sciences, or the 'ultra-hard' and the 'not-so-hard' sciences, as I have sometimes called them (Banks 1998). It was shown in a previous chapter that in a 1660 extract from Robert Boyle, nominalisation of processes was used at a rate of one per 42 words of running text. Boyle's work falls clearly into the physical camp, and to compare this with something from the biological camp, extracts from Henry Power's *Experimental Philosophy*, and Hooke's *Micrographia* were taken. There it was found that these authors use hardly any nominalisation at all: one in 126 words of running text in the case of Power, one in 118 words in the case of Hooke. The examples which do occur are almost all material processes. It was also pointed out that although their work is obviously scientific, and they are quite evidently putting into practice the experimental philosophy of Bacon and the Royal Society, their writing frequently remains anecdotal, and bears the hallmarks of the *virtuoso* style of wonder at the beauty of nature. In discussing the flea, Power says:

> One would wonder at the great strength lodged in so small a Receptacle, and that he is not able onley to carry his whole armour about him, but will frisk and curvet so nimbly with it. Stick a large brass pin through his tayle and he will readily drag it away. I have seen a chain of gold (at *Tredescants* famous reconditory of Novelties) of three hundred links, though not about an inch long, both fastned to and drawn away by a Flea … Yea we have heard it credibly reported, saith [*Muffet*], that a Flea hath not onely drawn a gold Chain, but a golden Charriot also with all its harness and accoutrements fixed to it, which did excellently set forth the Artifice of the Maker, and Strength of the Drawer; so great is the mechanick power

which Providence has immur'd within these living walls of Jet. (Vickers
1987: 90)

A little more than a hundred years later, Joseph Banks left England with
Captain Cook on board the *Endeavour*, on a voyage of circumnavigation,
which was to last from 1768 to 1771. The official objective of the voyage was
to observe the transit of Venus, in the hope of improving the accuracy of the
calculations necessary for navigation. From a scientific point of view, the
ultimate importance of the voyage was to reside in the botanical and zoological
work carried out by Banks and his collaborators. Banks later established Kew
Gardens, and at the comparatively early age of 35, he became the President of
the Royal Society. He was to remain in this post for 42 years, during which he
directed the Royal Society in autocratic fashion, thus stamping the mark of
his personality on the scientific activity of the period (Cameron 1952; O'Brian
1987; Gascoigne 1994; Fara 2003).

Banks wrote virtually nothing that could be called a research article. The
plans to publish the results of the *Endeavour* voyage came to nothing. His
main contribution to writing is his *Journal* of the *Endeavour* voyage, which
itself was not published until the twentieth century (Banks 1768–71 [1962]).
Although this is not a scientific text *per se*, it is quite easy to see three subgenres within it, one of which might be categorised as scientific. These three
genres are simple diary entries, which give notes on tasks accomplished, and
on the weather, state of the sea, and so on; narrative passages which recount
events which occurred; and descriptions of plants and animals. It is this
latter type which falls into the scientific area. Nominalisation however does
not appear to be a significant feature of Banks' scientific writing. Study of
relevant extracts shows that the incidence of nominalisation is virtually the
same in the narrative and scientific sections; they occur at a rate of one per six
finite verbs in the former, and one per five finite verbs in the latter. Perrot
(1998) (using different extracts) measured the rate of nominalisation as one
per 150 words of running text. Perrot (1998) also considers Darwin's *Voyage
of the Beagle* (Darwin 1839 [1989]) which was published in 1839, and which,
like Banks' *Journal*, is the account of a voyage incorporating scientific sections
in the form of biological description. It is shown that in extracts from the
scientific sections totalling 6,349 words, there are 106 nominalised processes,
giving a rate of one per 60 words of running text. Thus Darwin is here using
nominalisation to a greater extent than Power or Banks, but still less than
Boyle almost two centuries earlier.

Faraday was working in the physical sciences at the same time as Darwin
in the biological. Faraday's article 'Experimental researches in electricity –
Thirteenth series' appeared in the *Philosophical Transactions of the Royal*

Society in 1838 (Faraday 1838).9 In an extract of 2980 words there are 61 cases of nominalised processes, a rate of one per 49 words of running text. Thus, if these extracts are typical, the gap between the physical and biological sectors has closed, but the physical sector is still nominalising to a greater degree than the biological sector; at the same time the frequency rate in the Faraday extract is no greater (in fact slightly less) than that in the Boyle extract.

Two articles from the early twentieth century were also looked at; these were Millikan (1910) for the physical sector, and Thompson (1913) for the biological sector. It is interesting that the address given for Thompson includes the line *Biochemical Department*, (i.e. not 'biological') and even a cursory reading of this article shows that it is experimental in nature, unlike the descriptive texts which previously appeared in our biological sample. Thompson's article has 2,810 words and 128 examples of nominalised processes, a rate of one per 22 words. Millikan's article, from the physical sector, has 6,530 words and 283 examples of nominalised processes, a rate of one per 23 words. Thus these two articles have virtually the same frequency rate, with the notable difference that the biological sector is no longer represented by a purely descriptive text, but by one that is now in the experimental camp.

To bring things up to date, three articles from the late twentieth century were considered. These are Sleigh *et al.* (1996) and Krieger and Sigler (1996), both from the biological sector, and Lindsay *et al.* 1996, for the physical sector. Kreiger and Sigler, for the biological field, has 2,930 words and 237 cases of nominalised processes, a rate of one per 12 words of running text, while Lindsay *et al.*, for the physical sciences, has 3,870 words and 253 nominalized processes, a rate of one per 15 words. Thus the general trend seems to be towards greater concentration of nominalized processes. However, Sleigh *et al.*, from the biological sciences, does not conform to this trend. It has 2,810 words and 83 examples of nominalised processes, a rate of one per 34 words, a lower frequency than Thompson and Millikan almost a century earlier.

The general picture given by this enables us to establish a hypothesis that there has been increasing use of nominalised processes from the late seventeenth century onwards, but at different rates in the physical and biological sciences. Initially the physical sciences developed rapidly and then remained fairly static for a period. The biological sciences developed more slowly in this respect and the gap between the two did not disappear until the end of the nineteenth century, when the biological sciences changed from being a descriptive to an experimental science. I would now like to see to what extent this hypothesis can be justified on the basis of a rather larger and more structured corpus. In this corpus I will consider not only nominalised processes, but also the use of passives, since this is frequently considered to be a distinctive feature of scientific discourse, and since passives are frequently said to be used to avoid mentioning the agent, that is the author/experimenter, I shall look at the use of first person pronoun Subjects. In addition, I shall look at the important feature of thematic structure, since, if as is commonly believed, the use of the passive voice is a significant feature of scientific writing, it is arguable that the motivation for this, rather than the oft-cited avoidance of agents, is to be found in thematic structure.

The corpus

In an attempt to determine more clearly the evolution of the scientific journal article, a corpus has been selected from the *Philosophical Transactions of the Royal Society*. Two articles, one from the physical and one from the biological sciences were selected at 20 year intervals, i.e. two articles for the year 1700, two for 1720, two for 1740, etc. up to and including the year 1980. The articles were selected and classed as physical or biological on the basis of their title as it appears in the Contents page of the relevant issue. I am using 'biological' in a fairly wide sense, so that this includes, for example, medicine and palaeontology. In the earlier part of the period, despite the fact that the epistolary form was the basis of the early issues, the selection of letters as such was avoided. In the latter part of the period covered, an attempt was made to avoid articles that were over-long. On a principle of diminishing returns it was considered that a 30-page article was probably already well beyond the length at which relevant features are simply being repeated. Other than this, the selection was arbitrary, if not technically random. The selection of texts thus provided will be referred to as the 'Philosophical Transactions Corpus'. This contains 30 articles. These are listed in Table 4.1, where they are quantified in terms of number of words and numbers of finite verbs. The first article for each date is the physical sciences article, the second is the biological. Full references are given in Appendix 2.

The corpus thus has a total of 126,555 words comprising 9,680 finite verbs. The count of words includes all of the main text. Excluded are those parts which are not part of the text as such, contents, legends and explanations to tables, and other forms of graphic presentation, titles and subtitles, and abstracts where this is clearly a separate section. None of the articles have a section which is labelled Abstract, but the later articles have what clearly is

Table 4.1. The Philosophical Transactions Corpus and size of articles.

Date	Article	Words	Finite verbs
1700	Povey, Thomas: The Method, Manner and Order of the Transmutation of Copper in Brass &c.	508	42
	Lafage Mr.: An Account of an Extraordinary Aneuisma of the Arteria Aorta near to the Basis of the Heart, with the Symptoms thereof.	445	44
1720	Desaguliers, J. T.: An Account of an Experiment made on *Thursday* the last day of *June, 1720.* before the *R. Society*, to shew by a new proof, that Bodies of the same bulk do not contain equal quantities of Matter, and therefore that there is an interspers'd Vacuum.	324	29
	Blair, Patrick: A Discourse concerning a Method of discovering the Virtues of Plants by their external Structure.	2,228	172
1740	Smith, Caleb: A new Method of improving and perfecting *Catadioptrical Telescopes*, by forming the *Speculums* of *Glass* instead of *Metal*.	3,414	238
	Baker, Henry: The Discovery of a perfect Plant *in Semine*.	1,504	134
1760	Wilson, Benjamin: Farther Experiments in Electricity.	2,779	215
	Edwards, George: An Account of the Frog-fish of *Surinam*.	1,127	91
1780	Cavallo, Tiberius: An Account of some new Experiments in Electricity, with the Description and Use of two new Electrical Instruments.	3,030	240
	Hunter; John: Account of an extraordinary Pheasant.	1,778	161
1800	Herschel, William: Experiments on the Refrangibility of the invisible Rays of the Sun.	2,054	165
	Home, Everard: Some Observations on the Head of the *Ornithorhynchus paradoxcus*.	1,240	116
1820	Davy, Edmund: On some combinations of Platinum.	4,583	397
	Knight, Thomas Andrew: Upon the different qualities of the alburnum of spring and winter-felled oak trees.	824	53
1840	Gassiot, John P.: An account of Experiments made with the view of ascertaining the possibility of obtaining a Spark *before* the Circuit of the Voltaic Battery is completed.	4,654	332
	Barry, Martin: On the Corpuscles of the Blood.	5,320	423

Date	Article	Words	Finite verbs
1860	Matthiessen, A. and M. Holzmann: On the Effect of the presence of Metals and Metalloids upon the Electric Conducting power of Pure Copper.	1,764	154
	De la Rue, Warren and Hugo Müller: On the Resin of *Ficus rubiginosa*, and a new Homologue of Benzylic Alcohol.	6,383	536
1880	Glazebrook, R.T.: Double Refraction and Disperson in Iceland Spar: an Experimental Investigation, with a comparison with HUYGEN'S Construction for the Extraodinary Wave.	5,067	355
	Owen, Prof.:On the Ova of the *Echidna Hystrix*.	1,228	76
1900	Townsend, John S.: The Diffusion of Ions into Gases.	10,135	867
	Dawson, Maria: 'Nitragin' and the Nodules of Leguminous Plants.	10,844	837
1920	Duffield, W. G., Thos. H. Burnham and A. H. Davis: The Pressure upon the Poles of the electric Arc.	6,582	490
	Mummery, J. Howard: The Epithelial Sheath of Hertwig in the Teeth of Man, with notes on the Follicle and Nasmyth's Membrane.	5,764	437
1940	Hartree, D. R., W. Hartree and Bertha Swirles: Self-consistent field, including exchange and superposition of configurations, with some results for oxygen.	5,042	281
	Lawrence, William John Cooper, James Robert Price, Gertrude Maud Robinson and Robert Robinson: The distribution of anthocyanins in flowers, fruits and leaves.	4,110	323
1960	Axford, W. I.: Ionization fronts in interstellar gas: the structure of ionization fronts.	10,700	892
	Joysey, K. A.: A study of variation and relative growth in the blastoid *Orbitremites*.	9,393	711
1980	Horai, K., J. L. Winkler Jr., S. J. Keihm, M. G. Langseth, J. A. Fountain and E. A. West: Thermal conduction in a composite circular cylinder: a new technique for thermal conductivity measurements of lunar core samples.	7,141	405
	Miller, J. and E. N. K. Clarkson: The post-ecdysial development of the cuticle and the eye of the Devonian trilobite *Phacops rana milleri* Stewart 1927.	6,590	464

an abstract, printed in smaller type than the main text of the article. Articles will be referred to by the name of the author (first-named author where there is more than one) and date, e.g. Povey (1700), Horai (1980), etc. I shall now discuss briefly each of the articles in turn, before going on to discuss the development of the genre over time. Thus what follows are notes on each of the items in the corpus, intended to give an overall view of it; this will be followed by detailed and more systematic consideration of the relevant features. The indication phys. or biol. is to show which of the two sub-corpora the article was selected for.

Povey (1700) (phys.) is a short article, only two pages in the original, which some might consider to be technical rather than strictly scientific, since it is concerned with smelting processes. It contains 508 words and 42 finite verbs, of which 21 (50 per cent) occur in the passive. This includes those cases which are passive, but elliptical:

> It **is burnt** or **calcined** in a Kiln or Oven made red hot, then **ground** to powder and **sifted** into the fineness of Flower, then **mixt** with ground Charcoal, because the *Calamine* is apt to be clammy and to clod, and not so apt or capable of incorporation; . . . (Povey 1700: 474)

The passive forms therefore occur at a rate of one per 24 words of running text. These passives are virtually exclusively (20 out of 21) cases of Material process. There is only one first person pronoun Subject, an inclusive **we**, which begins the article:

> **We** have in the North parts of *England* much Copper, which places, tho as they now lye, are barren and poor, might be rendred rich and useful, were sufficient encouragement given to the digging and raising thereof ... (Povey 1700: 474)

There are 14 cases of nominalised processes, a rate of one per 36 words of running text, and like the passives these are predominantly (12 out of 14) Material processes.

There may be some doubt as to whether Lafage is actually the author of Lafage (1700) (biol.). The article is written in the third person, so there are no first person pronoun Subjects. The full heading is as follows:

> An Account of an Extraordinary Aneurisma of the Arteria aorta near to the Basis of the Heart, with the symptoms thereof; Dissected by Mr *Lafage*, Surgeon, on the *10*th of *April, 1700.*

Hence it may be the case that this is an anonymous report of Lafage's dissection. Since this is a question of human post-mortem dissection, it falls into the area of human physiology. Again, it is short, less than two pages, with 445 words and 44 finite verbs. There are very few passives, only three in the whole text giving a rate of one per 148 words, or 7 per cent of the finite verbs. There are eight cases of nominalisation, six of which are Material processes, the two remaining being Mental.

Desaguliers (1720) (phys.) is a short report of a physical experiment, with 324 words and 29 finite verbs. There are four passives, a rate of one per 81 words, and these account for 14 per cent of the finite verbs. Three of these are Material, with one case of Mental process. There are four personal pronoun Subjects, all *I*, and these all occur with Material processes. Strangely, the personal pronoun Subjects all occur in the first 150 words of the text, where there are no passives. The passives occur in the second part of the text, from the 150th word onwards, where there are no personal pronouns. There are only two nominalisations, a rate of one per 162 words.

From the same year, Blair (1720) (biol.) is considerably longer at 2,228 words and 172 finite verbs. This article is concerned with the classification of plants according to their medicinal value. There are 24 passives, 14 per cent of the finite verbs, a rate of one per 93 words of text. The process distribution of these is:

Mat.: 54 per cent, Ment.: 25 per cent, Verb.: 13 per cent, Rel.: 8 per cent

There are 17 personal pronoun Subjects, of which 17 are singular, *I*, and three are inclusive plural **we**. These never occur with Material processes; Verbal process is the most common, with nine examples, while there are six Mental, and two Relational processes. There are 71 cases of nominalisation, a rate of one per 31 words. These are predominantly (75 per cent) Material processes, with 14 per cent Mental and 11 per cent Verbal.

Smith 1740 (phys.) is again perhaps more technical than physical, dealing with methods of producing better telescopes, but includes a certain amount of mathematical demonstration. It has 3414 words, which includes an extensive quote of 166 words from Newton in English, and a rather shorter one of 30 words in Latin. There are 234 finite verbs, of which four are in the Latin quote and 18 in the English. There are 56 passives, a rate of one per 61 words, and 24 per cent of the finite verbs. Of these, five are in the Newton quote. The process distribution of the passives is:

Mat.: 68 per cent, Ment.: 25 per cent, Verb.: 2 per cent, Rel.: 5 per cent

There are 24 first person pronoun Subjects; of these the vast majority (22 out of 24) are *we*. However, Smith frequently uses *we* as a singular, that is, where it can refer only to himself. Although some cases may be ambiguous, there are at least 16 examples of *we* which are clearly singular:

> Seeing therefore it is possible, and *we* believe also practicable, to remedy the imperfections of this kind of Speculums, (from whatever Cause they arise) by the Method *we* have here proposed; . . . (Smith 1740, 332)

The two examples of *I* which occur, do so with the verb *say* in sections of mathematical demonstration. As with Blair (1720), the first person pronouns never occur in Material processes. There are 15 with Mental processes, seven with Verbal and two with Relational. There are 112 cases of nominalised processes, a rate of one per 30 words of text. The vast majority (86 per cent) are Material processes, the remainder being 9 per cent Mental, 4 per cent Verbal and 2 per cent Relational.

Baker (1740) (biol.) has 1504 words, excluding the doggerel poem with which his contribution ends! The article argues that the seed of a plant is the plant itself in miniature. The text comprises 134 finite verbs. Of these 21 are passives, a rate of one per 72 words, and accounting for 16 per cent of the finite verbs. The majority, 13 (61 per cent), are Material processes, with six Mental and two Verbal. There are 27 examples of first person pronoun Subjects, 25 of which are singular, and two inclusive plural. The largest category is Mental process, with 13 (48 per cent), while there are nine (33 per cent) Material, three Verbal and two Relational. The passive forms occur mainly in the first half of the article, and the first person pronouns mainly in the second. There are 56 examples of nominalisation, over half of which, 31 (55 per cent) are Material processes; a further third, 19 (34 per cent) are Mental processes, with three Verbal, two Relational and one Existential process.

Although it is not evident from the title or contents entry, Wilson (1760) (phys.) is in fact cast in epistolary form. However, this affects the parameter which we are considering only to a marginal extent, in that it introduces one extra nominalized process:

> And here, with your Lordship's **leave**, I shall set down some farther experiments, most of which have been made with a view to shew, that a *plus* electricity may be produced by means of a *minus* electricity. (Wilson 1760: 899)

The article, which is concerned with static electricity, has 2,779 words including 53 words in a French quote, and 37 in an English quote from one of his own previous articles. There are 215 finite verbs, of which five are in the French quote. Fifty-eight of the verbs are passive, a rate of one per 48 words, and 27 per cent of the finite verbs. The vast majority of these, 53 (91 per cent), are Material processes, the others being three Mental and two Verbal. There are 24 personal pronoun Subjects, all singular, fairly evenly distributed between Material, seven, Mental, six and Verbal, eight, processes, with the three remaining being Relational processes. The article contains 95 nominalisations, of which over two-thirds are Material processes. The process distribution is:

Mat.: 69 per cent, Ment.: 16 per cent, Verb.: 1 per cent, Rel.: 14 per cent

Edwards (1760) (biol.) is concerned with the classification of a strange creature reportedly from Surinam. It is an article of 1127 words, of which 111 are in a quotation. There are 15 passive forms, of which five are within the quote. This means that passives occur at a rate of one per 75 words of running text, or one per 112 words if the quote is discounted. Similarly, the passive forms account for 14 per cent of the finite verbs, or 10 per cent if the quote is discounted. There are nine personal pronoun Subjects, of which eight are singular. None of these are cases of Material process; seven are Mental, while Verbal and Relational processes have one each. There are 20 cases of nominalisation, a rate of one per 56 words. The commonest process represented is Material, with 12 examples (60 per cent); three (15 per cent) are Mental and five (25 per cent) Verbal.

Cavallo (1780) (phys.), like the physical article of 20 years earlier, is concerned with static electricity. It has 3,030 words and 240 finite verbs. Of these verbs, 27 per cent are passives, occurring at a rate of one per 47 words of running text. Eighty-one per cent of the passive forms are cases of Material process. There are 25 first person pronoun Subjects, a rate of one per 121 words. Of these, 12 are Material process and nine Mental process, the remainder being Verbal, three examples, or Relational, one example. There are 63 examples of nominalized process, Material process being the most common. The process distribution is:

Mat.: 57 per cent, Ment.: 11 per cent, Verb.: 22 per cent, Rel.: 10 per cent

Hunter (1780) (biol.) describes a hermaphrodite pheasant. The article has 1,778 words and 161 finite verbs. 19 per cent of the finite verbs are passives, which thus occur at a rate of one per 59 words. There are more cases of Mental process among these passives, 14 (47 per cent), than Material process, nine (30 per cent), the rest being Verbal, six (20 per cent), with one case of Relational process. There are 16 personal pronoun Subjects, a rate of one per 111 words, none of which are in Material processes. They are fairly evenly divided into Mental processes, seven (44 per cent), Verbal five (31 per cent), and Relational, four (25 per cent). There are 43 nominalisations, a rate of one per 41 words, and almost three quarters (74 per cent) of these are Material processes.

Herschel (1800) (phys.) discusses the refraction of solar rays outside the visible spectrum. It has 2,054 words and 165 finite verbs. There are 38 passive forms, that is, 23 per cent of the finite verbs; the passives therefore occur at a rate of one per 54 words of running text. Of these 17 (45 per cent) are Material process, the others being fairly evenly distributed between Mental, seven (18 per cent), Verbal, six (16 per cent), and Relational, eight (21 per cent). There are 35 first person pronoun Subjects. Most of these are singular in form, but they do include seven examples of *we*, which all occur in the last 700 words of the text, where they are more frequent than *I*. Although some of the examples of *we* might be interpreted as inclusive, some seem more appropriate to a singular reading:

> **We** have traced these calorific rays throughout the whole extent of the prismatic spectrum; and found their power increasing, while their refrangibilty was lessened, as far as to the confines of red-coloured light. But their diminishing refrangibility, and increasing power, did not stop here; for **we** have pursued them a considerable way beyond the *prismatic spectrum*, into an invisible state, still exerting their increasing energy, with a decrease of refrangibility up to the maximum of their power; ... (Herschel 1800: 291–2)

The majority, 22 (63 per cent), of these pronouns occur with Material processes, the others being Mental, four, Verbal, five, or Relational, four. There are 70 cases of nominalisation in this article, of which 47 (67 per cent) are Material processes, the others being Mental, five, Verbal, eight, or Relational, ten.

Home 1800 (biol.) is concerned with the description and classification of an exotic zoological species. It has 1240 words and 116 finite verbs. There are 35 passives, that is, 30 per cent of the finite verbs, occurring at a rate of one per 35 words of running text. Of these 16 (45 per cent) are Material process, and 12 (34 per cent) Relational, the others being Mental, three, and Verbal, four. Home uses very few personal pronoun Subjects; there are two cases of *I*, and one of (inclusive) *we*. These occur in Verbal or Mental process. The (infrequent) rate is thus one per 413 words. There are 15 nominalisations, which are more frequent towards the beginning, the first 300 words or so, of the article, than later. Of these, six are Material processes, and six Verbal, with one case of Mental and two of Relational.

With Davy 1820 (phys.) we are in the field of chemistry, as the article deals with the chemical properties of platinum. There are 141 passive forms, 36 per cent of the finite verbs, which thus occur at a rate of one per 33 words of text. The vast majority of these, 123 (87 per cent) are Material processes, the remainder being either Mental, 14 (10 per cent), or Verbal, four (3 per cent). There are 43 examples of first person pronoun Subjects, which thus occur at a rate of one per 107 words. The largest number of these, 18 (42 per cent) are in Mental processes, but almost as many, 16 (37 per cent) are Material. The remainder are Verbal, eight (19 per cent), with a single example of Relational process. There are 128 nominalisations, a rate of one per 36 words. Almost three-quarters of these, 94 (73 per cent) are Material processes, and the process distribution is:

> Mat.: 73 per cent, Ment.: 8 per cent, Verb.: 6 per cent, Rel.: 13 per cent

The object of Knight 1820 (biol.) is to test the commonly held belief that the quality of the alburnum (or sapwood) of oak trees felled in winter is better than that of trees felled in spring. It is the first article in the biological sub-sample to describe itself as experimental, and the word experiment occurs five times in the course of this comparatively short three-page article.

> … and I was, consequently, led to make a few **experiments** (with the result of which I now take the liberty to trouble the Royal Society) with the hope of discovering the cause of this supposed superiority in the quality of the wood of winter-felled trees. (Knight 1820: 156)

> Many **experiments**, similar to the preceding, were made upon the heart wood, in which I found the disposition to absorb moisture, somewhat greater in that of spring-felled, than in that of the winter-felled tree; … (Knight 1820: 158)

The article has 824 words and 53 finite verbs. There are 27 passives, 51 per cent of the finite verbs, occurring at a rate of one per 31 words of text. These are all either Material process, 22 examples, or Mental, five. There are 11 first person pronoun Subjects, a rate of one per 75 words. Of these, six are with Mental processes, with one Material, three Verbal and one Relational. There are 19 nominalisations, a rate of one per 43 words. Of these 11 are Material, five Mental, and three Verbal.

With Gassiot 1840 (phys.) we are again in the area of electricity, though by now we have moved beyond the stage of purely static electricity. The article has 4654 words and 332 finite verbs. There are 148 passives, which account for 46 per cent of the finite verbs, and occur at a rate of one per 31 words. Virtually three-quarters of these, 110 (74 per cent) are Material processes, and the process distribution is:

> Mat.: 74 per cent, Ment.: 14 per cent, Verb.: 11 per cent, Rel.: 1 per cent

There are 64 examples of first person pronoun Subjects, a rate of one per 73 words. The largest process represented is Material, with 23 occurrences (36 per cent), but there are non-negligible numbers of the other processes, 16 (25 per cent) Mental, 15 (23 per cent) and ten (16 per cent) Relational. There are 161 nominalisations, the vast majority, 130 (81 per cent), of which are

Material, the others being Mental, 13 (8 per cent), Verbal 14 (9 per cent), and Relational, four (2 per cent).

Barry 1840 (biol.) is in the area of animal physiology, the blood of the rabbit being his object of study. The article has 5320 words, including two fairly extensive quotes, and 423 finite verbs. There are 101 passives, which thus account for 24 per cent of the finite verbs and occur at a rate of one per 53 words. Half, 51 (50 per cent), of these are Mental processes, and the process distribution is:

Mat.: 27 per cent, Ment.: 50 per cent, Verb.: 15 per cent, Rel.: 8 per cent

There are 45 first person pronoun Subjects, a rate of one per 118 words, of which 31 (69 per cent) are in Material processes, ten (22 per cent) in Mental processes, and four (9 per cent) Relational. There are 214 cases of nominalisation, a rate of one per 25 words, the most frequent rate we have seen so far. Over half (58 per cent) of these are Material, and the process distribution is:

Mat.: 58 per cent, Ment.: 11 per cent, Verb.: 15 per cent, Rel.: 15 per cent

And there is a single case of Existential process.

In 1860 we find the first cases in our sample of multiple authorship. Matthiessen 1860 (phys.) has two co-authors; it is an article of 1764 words and 154 finite verbs. It again deals with electricity, and more specifically, the conductivity of copper. There are 58 passives, which thus account for 38 per cent of the finite verbs, and occur at a rate of one per 30 words of text. The vast majority 51 (88 per cent) are Material processes, with three Mental, and four Verbal processes. There are 29 first person pronoun Subjects, which, since there are two co-authors, are exclusively *we*. They occur at a rate of one per 61 words of text, and are mainly in Material, 12 (41 per cent), or Mental, ten (34 per cent) processes; there are also four cases of Verbal, and three cases of Relational process. There are 55 cases of nominalisation, a rate of one per 32 words. Roughly three-quarters, 42 (76 per cent) are Material process, with four cases of Mental, two of Verbal, and seven of Relational process.

The other 1860 article, De la Rue 1860 (biol.) also has two co-authors. This deals with the chemical classification of a natural resin. The article has 6383 words and 536 finite verbs. There are 158 passive forms, which thus account for 29 per cent of the finite verbs, and occur at a rate of one per 40 words. The vast majority, 133 (84 per cent), are Material processes, with 18 examples (11 per cent) of Mental processes. It might be noted that a cluster of these Mental process passives occur towards the end of the article, seven examples in the final 400 words. The other examples are five Verbal and two Relational. There are 53 first person pronoun Subjects, exclusively *we* for obvious reasons, a rate of one per 120 words, and these tend to occur in clusters; 23 of them occur in Material processes, 14 in Mental, 11 in Verbal, and five in Relational. nominalisations, of which there are 193, occur at a rate of one per 33 words. The process distribution of these is:

Mat.: 69 per cent, Ment.: 15 per cent, Verb.: 4 per cent, Rel.: 12 per cent

The nominalized Mental processes are more frequent at the beginning of the article than later.

With Glazebrook 1880 (phys.) we are in the field of optics, with the subject of double refraction. The article contains numerous tables and considerable sections of mathematical calculation and demonstration. It has 5067 words and 355 finite verbs. There are 64 examples of passive forms; this is 18 per cent of the finite verbs, and a passive rate of one per 79 words of running text. 31 (48 per cent) of these are Material process, and 23 (36 per cent) are Mental, with five each of Verbal and Relational process. There are 76 first person pronoun Subjects, a rate of one per 67 words. Roughly two-thirds of these, 45 (67 per cent), are in Mental processes, with a further 22 (33 per cent) in Relational processes; there are also seven cases of Material process and two of Verbal. The plural form, *we*, is more frequent than *I*, occurring 55 times, whereas there are only 21 examples of *I*. The form *we* is particularly frequent in the mathematical sections, whereas *I* tends to occur in the experimental sections. nominalisations are comparatively frequent with 263 examples, a rate of one per 19 words. Roughly two-thirds of these, 173 (66 per cent), are Material processes. In addition, there are 48 examples (18 per cent) of Mental processes, and 40 (15 per cent) of Relational processes; the two remaining cases are of Verbal process.

Owen 1880 (biol.), from the field of zoology, is comparatively short with only three pages of text. This has 1228 words and 76 finite verbs. This however includes a 148-word quote from a letter, which is generically different to the rest of the text. There are 20 passive forms, of which four are in the letter quote. Overall this is 26 per cent of the finite verbs, and a frequency rate of one per 61 words of text. Of these 10 (53 per cent) are Material, four each of Mental and Verbal, with two Relational. There are 17 first person pronoun Subjects, but ten of these occur in the 148-word quote. This means that the overall rate is one per 72 words, but only one per 154 words if the quote is excluded. The process distribution of all 17 cases is five Material, six Mental, two Verbal and four Relational, but the seven that occur outside of the quote give two each for Mental, Verbal and Relational, with one case of Material. There are 37 nominalisations, of which two occur in the quote. Most of these 24 (65 per cent) are Material processes, with five Mental, and four each of Verbal and Relational.

We arrive in the twentieth century with Townsend (1900) (phys.), one of the longer items in the sample, being one of only three that run to a five-figure word count. In fact this precursor of particle physics, dealing with ions, has 10,135 words and 867 finite verbs. It contains a fair deal of mathematical calculation and demonstration. There are 270 passive forms which thus account for 31 per cent of the finite verbs and occur at a rate of one per 38 words of running text. The process distribution of these is:

Mat.: 56 per cent, Ment.: 34 per cent, Verb.: 7 per cent, Rel.: 4 per cent

There are 76 first person pronoun Subjects, a rate of one per 133 words of text. These are *we* throughout, except two cases of *I* which occur in the acknowledgements. Over three-quarters, 59 (78 per cent), are in Mental processes, there are only two examples of Material processes, with seven Verbal and eight Relational. In the mathematical section of the paper, passives are less frequent, and personal pronoun Subjects more frequent, than elsewhere. There are 375 cases of nominalisation, a rate of one per 27 words of text. The majority of these, 300 (80 per cent), are Material processes, the process distribution being:

Mat.: 80 per cent, Ment.: 13 per cent, Verb.: 2 per cent, Rel.: 5 per cent

Dawson (1900) (biol.) is the first article written by a woman to appear in the sample. At 10,844 words and 837 finite verbs, it is the longest article in the corpus. This article is in the area of plant biology. There are 200 passives, which therefore account for 24 per cent of the finite verbs, and occur at a rate of one per 54 words of text. The process distribution of these is:

Mat.:72 per cent, Ment.: 13 per cent, Verb.: 13 per cent, Rel 3 per cent

There are 123 examples of first person pronoun Subjects, which are usually *I*, only eight being examples of *we*. These thus occur at a rate of one per 88 words of text. The largest number, 77 (63 per cent), are Material, and the process distribution is:

Mat.: 63 per cent, Ment.: 26 per cent, Verb.: 7 per cent, Rel.: 5 per cent

This article includes an extensive literature review, and other researchers are referred to throughout the article. It may be that the frequency of personal pronoun Subjects, comparable with some nineteenth century items, but higher than those that follow in the twentieth, reflects a desire to contrast the work of the writer with that of other researchers. There are 530 cases of nominalisation, a rate of one per 20 words. Three-quarters of these, 396 (75 per cent) are Material processes, and the process distribution is:

Mat.: 75 per cent, Ment.: 14 per cent, Verb.: 6 per cent, Rel.: 4 per cent, Exist.: 1 per cent

Duffield (1920) (phys.) deals with electromagnetic effects, and has three co-authors. However, some tables and observations are attributed to individual authors, and Part II, which accounts for the final seven pages of this 28-page article is separately attributed to the first named author. The paper as a whole has 6,582 words and 490 finite verbs. There are 152 passives, which therefore occur at a rate of one per 43 words of text, and account for 31 per cent of the finite verbs. Their process distribution is:

Mat.: 58 per cent, Ment.: 22 per cent, Verb.: 16 per cent, Rel.: 5 per cent

There are no personal pronouns in the first 1,800 words of the article, which is basically the experimental part, so that personal pronouns tend to start occurring with the introduction of mathematical calculations. There are 32 personal pronoun Subjects, which thus occur at a rate of one per 206 words. These are mainly *we*, though *I* occurs four times in Part II, attributed only to Duffield himself. None of these personal pronouns occur in Material processes, and 63 per cent are in Mental processes. There are 479 examples of nominalised processes, a rate of one per 14 words of text. The vast majority of these (82 per cent) are Material processes, and the process distribution is:

Mat.: 82 per cent, Ment.: 12 per cent, Verb.: 2 per cent, Rel.: 3 per cent, Exist.: 1 per cent

Mummery (1920) (biol.) deals with the physiology of the human tooth. It is an article of 5,764 words including 437 finite verbs. There are 148 passive forms, which thus occur at a rate of one per 39 words and account for 34 per cent of the finite verbs. Half of these are Material processes and the process distribution is:

Mat.: 51 per cent, Ment.: 32 per cent, Verb.: 12 per cent, Rel.: 5 per cent

There are comparatively few personal pronoun Subjects, only 12 in the whole article, a rate of one per 480 words. These are almost evenly divided between Material processes (six examples) and Mental processes (five examples) with one example of Relational processes. There are 201 nominalised processes, a rate of one per 29 words. These also are predominantly Material processes, and the distribution is:

Mat.: 81 per cent, Ment.: 7 per cent, Verb.: 4 per cent, Rel.: 8 per cent

With Hartree (1940) (phys.) we are in the area of particle physics, and the use of configurations in the calculation of particle energy values. The 5,042-word article includes extensive mathematical sections, and there are 281 finite verbs. Of these, 105 are passives, a rate of one per 48 words, and accounting for 37 per cent of the finite verbs. There are virtually no Material process passives, and three-quarters are Mental processes. The process distribution is:

Mat.: 1 per cent, Ment.: 76 per cent, Verb.: 16 per cent, Rel.: 7 per cent

There are only 16 personal pronoun Subjects, a rate of one per 315 words. None of these are Material processes, and more than half (nine out of 16) are Mental processes. On the other hand nominalised processes are particularly frequent; there are 469 examples, a rate of one per 11 words of running text, the highest rate in the corpus. Half of these are Material processes, and just over a third are Mental. The distribution is:

Mat.: 50 per cent, Ment.: 36 per cent, Verb.: 2 per cent, Rel.: 11 per cent

Lawrence (1940) (biol.) is in the area of plant biochemistry, and deals with the distribution of certain sugars in different plant forms. The article, which includes extensive tables, has 4,110 words and 323 finite verbs. There are 104 passive forms, which therefore occur at a rate of one per 40 words of text, and account for 32 per cent of the finite verbs. The process distribution is:

Mat.: 44 per cent, Ment.: 30 per cent, Verb.: 17 per cent, Rel.: 9 per cent

There are very few personal pronoun Subjects, only six in the whole article, a rate of one per 685 words. Of these, four occur in Mental processes. There are 202 examples of nominalised processes, a rate of one per 20 words. The process distribution of these is:

Mat.: 60 per cent, Ment.: 20 per cent, Verb.: 8 per cent, Rel.: 9 per cent, Exist.: 2 per cent

At 10,700 words, Axford (1960) (phys.) is the second longest article in the sample and has 892 finite verbs. With this article we enter the area of astrophysics, and the properties of interstellar gas. There is a high degree of mathematicisation, but this leads to a grey area where there is little distinction between the mathematical model *per se*, and what the model is intended to represent. There are 267 passive forms in the article, so these occur at a rate of one per 40 words, and account for 30 per cent of the finite verbs. Roughly two-thirds of these are Mental processes, and the process distribution is:

Mat.: 10 per cent, Ment.: 67 per cent, Verb.: 19 per cent, Rel.: 3 per cent

There are virtually no personal pronoun Subjects in this article. The only two examples which occur do so in the acknowledgements, which is peripheral to the main text. These are in a Mental and a Relational process. The author does refer to himself as *the author* on two occasions, one of which is an example functioning as Subject in a Verbal process:

> **The author** suggests that some success may possibly be obtained by mixing the combustible gases with a fog of a neutral liquid.

There are 787 nominalised processes, which hence occur at a rate of one per 14 words. Three-quarters of these are Material processes, and the distribution is:

> Mat.: 76 per cent, Ment.: 15 per cent, Verb.: 5 per cent, Rel.: 4 per cent

Joysey (1960) (biol.) is in the area of palaeontology, and deals with an analysis of fossil forms. It has 9,393 words and 711 finite verbs. Of these 234 are passives, which occur at a rate of one per 40 words, and account for 33 per cent of the finite verbs. Over half are Material processes, which is the largest process type. The process distribution is:

> Mat.: 58 per cent, Ment.: 16 per cent, Verb.: 12 per cent, Rel.: 5 per cent

There are few personal pronoun Subjects. There are ten examples in total, three of which occur in the acknowledgements. The rate of frequency is therefore one per 939 words. The three occurrences in the acknowledgements are examples of *I*, whereas, Joysey uses *we* elsewhere in the text. They are fairly evenly divided between Mental process (six examples) and Relational process (four examples). There are 428 nominalised processes, a rate of one per 22 words. Two-thirds of these are Material processes. The process distribution is:

> Mat.: 66 per cent, Ment.: 14 per cent, Verb.: 5 per cent, Rel.: 15 per cent

Horai (1980) (phys.) is again in the area of astrophysics (if one considers studies relating to the moon to be 'astro-'), since it deals with the analysis of lunar core samples. The article, of 7,141 words, has 405 finite verbs, of which 188 are passives. This gives a rate of one per 38 words, accounting for 46 per cent of the finite verbs. The process distribution of these is:

> Mat.: 48 per cent, Ment.: 39 per cent, Verb.: 9 per cent, Rel.: 4 per cent

There are 14 examples of first person pronoun Subjects, a rate of one per 510 words. Only one of these is in a Material process, the others being Mental (nine examples) or Verbal (four examples). There are 499 nominalised processes, a rate of one per 14 words of text. Three-quarters of these are Material processes. The process distribution is:

> Mat.: 77 per cent, Ment.: 17 per cent, Verb.: 2 per cent, Rel.: 3 per cent

Miller (1980) (biol.) is another palaeontological article, dealing with the eye of a fossil species; it has 6,590 words and 464 finite verbs. There are 138 passive forms, which occur at a rate of one per 48 words, and account for 30 per cent of the finite verbs. Just over two-thirds of these are Material processes; the distribution is:

Mat.: 68 per cent, Ment.: 17 per cent, Verb.: 14 per cent, Rel.: 1 per cent

There are only nine personal pronoun Subjects, a rate of one per 732 words. Of these, four are in Mental processes, two each in Verbal and Relational and one Material. There are 285 nominalised processes, a rate of one per 23 words. The vast majority, 83 per cent of these are Material processes, and the distribution is:

Mat.: 83 per cent, Ment.: 5 per cent, Verb.: 6 per cent, Rel.: 6 per cent

Some may feel uneasy at the inclusion in the corpus of authors who may not be native speakers of English. It may therefore be useful at this point to include some notes on those authors who do not have typically anglophone names.

Lafage (1700). I have no information on Lafage himself, but in any case, as has been pointed out, it is not evident that this contribution was drafted by Lafage himself. It is written in the third person, and may well be a report by some anonymous author.

Desaguliers (1720). Although described by the Encyclopaedia Britannica as a 'British inventor', John Theophilus Desaguliers (1683–1744) was born in France, but brought to England as a Huguenot refugee at the age of 11. He was therefore 37 at the time this article was published.

Cavallo (1780). Tiberius Cavallo was born in Naples in 1749, and died in London in 1809. He lived in England from 1771, so was then 22, and would have been 31 at the time the article was published.

Herschel (1800). Sir Frederick William Herschel, was born as Friedrich Wilhelm Herschel at Hanover in 1738. He came to England in 1757 at the age of 19, and would have been 62 by the time this article was published. He died at Slough in 1822. He was perfectly integrated into British society, as the fact that he was knighted shows.

Gassiot (1840). John Peter Gassiot, wine merchant and scientist, lived from 1779 to 1877. As his forenames imply, he was an Englishman.

Matthiessen (1860). Augustus Matthiessen was born in London in 1831 and died there in 1870. His co-author for this article is M. Holzman.

De la Rue (1860). Warren De la Rue was born in the Channel Islands, on Guernsey, in 1815, and died in London in 1889. The co-author of this article is Hugo Müller.

Horai (1980). K. Horai is one of six co-authors, the others being J. L. Winkler Jr., S. J. Keihm, M. G. Langseth, J. A. Fountain and E. A. West. All have institutional addresses in the USA.

So, out of 30 articles, only three can be said to have authors who were born in a non-anglophone country. However, even these three, Desaguliers, Cavallo and Herschel, were permanent immigrants to England, one of them from the age of 11, and all had been living there for a considerable time when these articles were published. Thus, any possible non-native influence must be fairly minimal.

I shall now go on to consider each of the relevant features, passives, first person pronoun subjects, nominalisation, and thematic structure, in more detail.

5 Passives

Increasing use of passives

The figures from the corpus can now be considered as a whole, showing developments over the period 1700–1980. Table 5.1 gives the extent of passive use in terms of frequency and percentage of finite verbs. It will be remembered that frequency is here measured as the average number of words of running text for a single example of the phenomenon; hence the smaller the figure the more frequent the occurrence. For those who prefer frequency measured in terms of numbers of occurrences per 1,000 words, a rough guide is that a frequency of one per 50 words corresponds to 20 examples per 1000 words. In Table 5.1 the results have been arbitrarily divided into centuries.

The earliest articles in the sample, Povey (1700) in the physical section and Lafage (1700) in the biological, both seem to be outriders, Povey using a comparatively high percentage of passives, and Lafage using by far the lowest proportion. Otherwise, within each subsection the figures seem fairly consistent. In the physical section the numbers are fairly stable, particularly from 1740 onwards when the percentage of passive finite verbs is consistently in the mid-20s. Similarly for the biological articles where from 1720 onwards the percentage of passive finite verbs is in the range 14 per cent–20 per cent. It is noticeable however that the percentage in the biological section is systematically lower than in the physical section. None of the biological articles has a rate of more than 19 per cent, whereas only one of the physical articles, Desaguliers (1720), has a rate which is less than this figure, the others being well over 20 per cent. Hence it seems reasonable to say that in the eighteenth century the use of passives is more extensive in physical articles than in biological articles.

The rate of passives for the physical section is carried over into the nineteenth century, where Herschel (1800), with 23 per cent, also falls into the same range as those in the latter part of the seventeenth century. Thereafter, passive use increases, though fairly erratically. The average rate for the last four articles in the nineteenth century is 34.5 per cent, and indeed two of the

Table 5.1. Passive use in the *Philosophical Transactions* Corpus.

1700–80

	Physical			Biological	
	Frequency	Per cent fin vbs		Frequency	Per cent fin vbs
Povey, 1700	24	50	Lafage, 1700	148	7
Desaguliers, 1720	81	14	Blair, 1720	93	14
Smith, 1740	61	24	Baker, 1740	72	16
Wilson, 1760	48	27	Edwards, 1760	75	14
Cavallo, 1780	47	27	Hunter,1780	59	19

1800–80

	Physical			Biological	
	Frequency	Per cent fin vbs		Frequency	Per cent fin vbs
Herschel, 1800	54	23	Home, 1800	35	30
Davy, 1820	33	36	Knight, 1820	31	51
Gassiot, 1840	31	46	Barry, 1840	53	24
Matthiessen, 1860	30	38	De la Rue, 1860	40	29
Glazebrook, 1880	79	18	Owen, 1880	65	25

1900–80

	Physical			Biological	
	Frequency	Per cent fin vbs		Frequency	Per cent fin vbs
Townsend, 1900	38	31	Dawson, 1900	54	24
Duffield, 1920	43	31	Mummer, 1920	39	34
Hartree, 1940	48	37	Lawrence, 1940	40	32
Axford, 1960	40	30	Joysey, 1960	40	33
Horai 1980	38	46	Miller, 1980	48	30

four, Davy (1820) and Matthiessen (1860), are within a few points of this figure. In this context, the figure of 18 per cent for Glazebrook (1880) is surprisingly low. The percentages for the biological sector show a marked increase over those for the eighteenth century; all of the figures are higher than the highest of the previous century. Although there is a certain degree of instability at the beginning of the century, this seems to settle, with figures in the mid-20s, from 1840 onwards. Although taken year by year, for three articles out of five, the biological article has a higher percentage than the corresponding physical article, it is nevertheless possible to see a general tendency to a higher rate in the physical articles. Here, Glazebrook (1880) notwithstanding, the trend seems to be towards the mid-30s, with a range of 36 per cent–46 per cent for the period 1820–60. On the other hand we have just seen that the trend for the biological sector is towards the mid-20s, with a range of 24 per cent–29 per cent for the period 1840–80.

As we move into the twentieth century, what seemed a fairly erratic movement towards the mid-30s in the physical sector, becomes fairly well established at over 30 per cent. The final article in the series, Horai (1980), shows a jump to 46 per cent. However, an earlier study (Banks, 1994a), based on a small corpus of 11 articles from the hybrid science of oceanography all published in 1982, showed an average of 31 per cent for this corpus with a range of 24 per cent–42 per cent, and a median of 34 per cent. Hence it is likely that the figure for Horai 1980 is simply at the top end of the range, rather than indication of a sudden surge in passive use. On the biological front the percentage of something in the mid-20s is carried over from the nineteenth- into the twentieth century, but from 1920 onwards that figure rises to the low-30s, and becomes stable at that point. Thus, it is only from the early twentieth century onwards that there is correspondence between the physical and biological sectors. Since the general trend has been one of increasing use, this can be thought of as the biological sector lagging behind developments in the physical sector and only catching up in the early twentieth century.

Passives and process types

I shall now consider passive use in terms of the process types which are passivised. For the sake of convenience, I shall again do this century by century, though, as was said above, the century break is an arbitrary one. Table 5.2 shows the figures for the eighteenth century. The *n* column indicates the actual number of examples.

It will be seen that where passives are used, there is a strong tendency to do so in Material processes. This tendency is even stronger in the physical sector than in the biological. In the physical articles, only two articles have a percentage of less than 80 per cent, and one of these, Desaguliers (1720), provides so few examples that it is difficult to say anything about it, other than that passives are rare in this short article, where one example constitutes

Table 5.2. Process distribution of percentages of passive verbs, 1700–80.

	Physical				
	Material	*Mental*	*Verbal*	*Relational*	*n*
Povey, 1700	95	—	5	—	21
Desaguliers, 1720	75	25	—	—	4
Smith, 1740	68	25	2	5	56
Wilson, 1760	91	5	3	—	58
Cavallo. 1780	81	9	8	2	64

	Biological				
	Material	*Mental*	*Verbal*	*Relational*	*n*
Lafage, 1700	100	—	—	—	3
Blair, 1720	54	25	13	8	24
Baker, 1740	61	29	2	—	21
Edwards, 1760	53	7	40	—	15
Hunter, 1789	30	47	20	3	30

25 per cent. The other is Smith (1740) where 25 per cent of the 56 examples are of Mental processes. The majority of these are of the cognitive type:

> The Telescope **is** deservedly **reckoned** one of the most excellent of all the Inventions of the Moderns ... (Smith, 1740)

> The first of these Defects only, **was known** to the Writers of Dioptrics, before Sir *Isaac Newton* ... (Smith, 1740)

In general however, the passive is used in the description of technical or, increasingly as the century moves on, experimental activity, and hence in Material process:

> The ivory **was supported** horizontally by a stand made of the prepared wood. When the glass **was made** a little warmer than the external air, my finger rubbed that side thereof which was farthest from, and opposite to, the ivory. (Wilson, 1760)

> The upper part of the tube CDMN **is shaped** tapering to a smaller extremity, which **is** entirely **covered** with sealing wax melted by heat, and not dissolved in spirits. Into this tapering part a small tube **is cemented**, which, with its under extremity, touches the flat piece of Ivory H, fastened to the tube by means of cork. (Cavallo, 1780)

Although Material process is still the process type predominantly passivised in the biological sector, that dominance is less marked than for the physical sector. With the exception of Lafage (1700), which has only three examples, the highest percentage of Material process passives in the biological sector (61 per cent) is lower than the lowest (68 per cent) in the physical sector. Moreover in one case, Hunter (1780), the percentage of Mental processes is greater than that of Material. This would seem to indicate that the experimental process is much less marked here than in the physical articles. Here, rather than describing experiments which have been carried out, procedures are described in general terms, or the passive is used in observational passages:

> It is here to be noted, that I have not inserted any Plant in this Table, but such as are indigenals in *Britain*, or such as **are Cultivated** in *British Gardens*; and to render it still the more useful, I have added such particular Parts as **are used** in the Shops ... (Blair, 1720)

> But, say they, in Animals, either the finest Part of the *Semen* **is taken** in by the Vessels of the *Vagina* and *Uterus*, **circulated** with the Fluids, and **carried** into the *Ovaria*, and even into the Ova, by the Vessels that run thither; or else, Fecundation **is occasioned** by a *subtile Spirit* in the *Semen masculinum* ... (Baker 1740)

This is a reflection of the fact that at this period the biological sciences were observational, and much of the work done was that of classification. It is noticeable that in Hunter 1780, where it is the Mental process passives which form the largest category, these are predominantly of the perception type:

> This, however, does not appear to be a principle the action of which takes place at the first formation of the animal, so as to grow up with it, but appears to be one of those actions which take place, perhaps, at certain periods of life, similar to many common and natural phenomena; like to what **is observed** of the horns of the stag, which differ at different ages; or to the mane of the lion, which does not grow till after his fifth year, &c.

> This change **has been observed** in some of the bird tribe, but principally in the common pheasant. (Hunter, 1780)

Of the relatively small number of passives in Edwards (1760), a comparatively high proportion are of Verbal processes:

> I Have now the honour to lay before this Royal Society an animal not to be found in the British Museum, nor in any other collection that I have seen in England, and which, perhaps, deserves attention, in regard to what **is said** of its strange metamorphoses, as much as any part of natural history whatever. (Edwards, 1760)

However, some of these are for visual rather than verbal communication:

> I find the four toes to stand, three of them in the form of fingers, and one opposite to them, which serves as a thumb, which **is not expressed** in Marian's figure. The general shape of it **is expressed** by the figures F. G, in my print. (Edwards, 1760)

The corresponding details for the nineteenth century are given in Table 5.3.

In the physical sector, the use of the passive in nineteenth century articles is, as it was in the previous century, predominantly a question of Material process, in that, for each author in the sample Material process produces the highest percentage of examples. However, the range is wider, since while three are within the same range as the eighteenth-century articles, two are rather lower. Where Material process passives are used this is largely a case of involvement in the experimental procedure. Thus the pattern that was developing in the eighteenth century is established in the nineteenth. The passives may be used to describe the actions of the researcher or the effects produced on the experimental materials:

> When the powder **is boiled** in alcohol, it **is** partially **decomposed**, and assumes a lighter colour ... (Davy, 1820)

> When arsenic **is thrown** upon melted copper the greater part of it **is absorbed**, whilst a part volatilizes; and on re-fusing the alloy formed, if a

Table 5.3. Process distribution of percentages of passive verbs, 1800–80.

	Physical				
	Material	*Mental*	*Verbal*	*Relational*	*n*
Herschel, 1800	45	18	16	21	38
Davy, 1820	87	14	4	—	141
Gassiot, 1840	74	14	11	1	148
Matthiessen, 1860	88	5	7	—	58
Glazebrook, 1880	48	36	8	8	64

	Biological				
	Material	*Mental*	*Verbal*	*Relational*	*n*
Home, 1800	46	9	11	34	35
Knight, 1820	81	19	—	—	27
Barry, 1840	27	50	15	8	101
De la Rue, 1860	84	11	3	1	158
Owen, 1880	50	20	20	10	20

large quantity of arsenic **has been used**, it has a dingy grey colour, and is very hard and brittle. (Matthiessen, 1860)

For the prisms **were** so **placed** that by turning the table on which they rested without altering the position of the collimator, either face of the prism **could be made** a face of incidence. (Glazebrook, 1880)

In the case of Herschel (1800), with a smaller percentage of Material passives, the second most common category is that of Relational process. These tend to occur in description and many of the examples can be assimilated to the possessive type:

It being now evident that there was a refraction of rays coming from the sun, which, though not fit for vision, **were** yet highly **invested** with a power of occasioning heat, I proceeded to examine its extent as follows. (Herschel, 1800)

The four last experiments prove, that the maximum of the heating power **is vested** among the invisible rays; and is probably not less than half an inch beyond the last visible ones, when projected in the manner before mentioned. (Herschel, 1800)

The other article in this group, which has a comparatively low percentage of Material passives, is Glazebrook (1880). The second largest category in his case is that of Mental process, which accounts for 36 per cent of his passives. This is due to the fact that mathematical calculation and demonstration play a large part in his article. The processes of mathematical calculation are necessarily of a cerebral type and hence fall into the category of Mental process. A considerable number of these verbs are passivised:

For prisms I., III., and IV., the value of θ **is given** by formulæ of the form ... (Glazebrook 1880)

Hence ψ is unchanged, ψ' **is increased**.

The value of μ **will** therefore in all cases **be decreased**. (Glazebrook, 1880)

They, however, **were determined** from observations at nearly grazing incidence. (Glazebrook, 1880)

It will be noted that for the period 1700–1860, with the single exception of Herschel (1860), there is no article in which Material process accounts for less than 68 per cent of the passive forms, and in five of the nine the rate is over 80 per cent. So in physical articles of this period, passive use tends strongly towards Material process, and this is largely due to the experimental nature of the activity being described.

When this is compared with the biological articles from the same period, it is seen that, as in the preceding century, with one exception, Material process accounts for the highest percentage of finite passive forms. However, although the general level is lower than that of the physical articles, an average of 58 per cent compared with 68 per cent for the physical sector, two of these biological articles have a percentage of over 80 per cent of their passive forms in the Material category. This is due to experimental procedures being described in these articles:

> In the spring of 1817, two oak trees, of nearly the same age, and growing contiguously in the same soil, **were selected**, each being somewhat less than a century old. The one **was deprived** of its bark, to as great an extent as the inexperience of my workmen permitted me to have done without danger to them, and it **was** then **suffered** to remain standing. The other tree **was felled**, and, in the usual manner, immediately **stript** of its bark; and the trunk **was** then **removed** to a situation in which it **was** securely **protected** from the sun and rain. (Knight, 1820)

> At common temperatures no reaction took place, but when the temperature **was elevated** to about 60°C. [140° F], hydrochloric acid **was given off**, and the pentacholoride gradually disappeared. After the disengagement of hydrocholoric acid had ceased, the liquid **was removed** from the remaining pentachloride and **washed** with water, and afterwards with an alkaline solution. After the benzol **had been got** rid of by keeping the liquid for some time in a warm place, a viscid residue **was obtained**, which was soluble with great difficulty in alcohol, but easily soluble in ether or chloroform. (De la Rue, 1860)

This feature is an indication that experiment is playing in increasingly important part in the biological sector, so that observational and classificatory studies are now supplemented by experiment in certain cases. It will be noted however that this sample gives us Barry (1840), inserted between Knight (1820) and De la Rue (1860), and this article has a comparatively low rate of Material process passives. The Mental process passives are also twice as numerous as the Material, and this is due to the presence of a large number of passives of a perception type:

> Long before separate muscular fibres **are perceived**, the globules of the primitive mass **are seen** arranged in longitudinal lines. (Barry, 1840)

Like its 1800 physical counterpart, Home (1800) has a comparatively high proportion (34 per cent) of Relational process passives. They are similar to those found in Herschel (1800) in that they are involved in description and can be assimilated to a possessive type, though frequently an abstract form of possession:

But, in this animal, the two thin plates of bone are in the centre; and the parts which surround them **are composed** of skin and membrane, in which a muscular structure probably **is inclosed**. (Home, 1800)

The corresponding details for the twentieth century are given in Table 5.4.

As we move into the twentieth century, there is a noticeable change. In the physical sector the proportion of passives in the Material process category falls while that in the Mental category rises. The average rate of Material processes falls from 68 per cent for the nineteenth century to 54 per cent for the twentieth, with a corresponding rise from an average of 17 per cent to 48 per cent for Mental process passives. It will be noted that while there is a general trend of this type, Hartree (1940) and Axford (1960) are extreme examples of the movement. It would also seem that this movement starts in the late nineteenth century rather than the beginning of the twentieth, as Glazebrook (1880), seems to foreshadow the change, in that his article too has a lower rate of Material process passives and a higher rate of Mental process passives than the articles earlier in the nineteenth century. Where Material process passives are used, this is again largely linked to experimental activity and its description:

A stirrup **was suspended** by a torsion fibre, or sometimes by two fibres, F, as in the illustration, in this **was placed** a copper rod, E, to whose extremity **was fixed** at right angles a short carbon rod, C, which **was balanced** by a

Table 5.4. Process distribution of percentages of passive verbs, 1900–80.

| | *Physical* | | | | |
	Material	*Mental*	*Verbal*	*Relational*	*n*
Townsend, 1900	56	34	7	4	270
Duffield, 1920	58	22	16	5	152
Hartree, 1940	1	76	16	7	105
Axford, 1960	10	67	19	3	267
Horai, 1980	48	39	9	4	188
	Biological				
	Material	*Mental*	*Verbal*	*Relational*	*n*
Dawson, 1900	72	13	13	3	200
Mummery, 1920	51	32	12	5	148
Lawrence, 1940	44	30	17	9	104
Joysey, 1960	58	26	12	5	234
Miller, 1980	68	17	14	1	138

counterpoise, W, at the other end. The arc **was formed** between this carbon rod and another, D, fixed either as shown in the figure or in some other manner to be described later. (Duffield, 1920)

Before the temperature measurements, the experimental heater and core-tube system **was installed** in a vacuum chamber and the atmospheric pressure within the chamber **reduced** to 10^{-4}Pa. This is to suppress gaseous convective motion which, if operative, will interfere with the radiative heat transfer. The heating element **is energized** by a constant d.c. voltage, either 25.0 or 27.5V, for 60 min. (Horai, 1980)

The change that is apparent in the move towards Mental process passives is due to the same reason that was already apparent in Glazebrook (1880), that is, the mathematisation of the physical domain, with a resulting increase in the use of mathematical Mental processes. This phenomenon is present in all the twentieth-century physical articles, but is most noticeable in Hartree (1940) and Axford (1960). In Hartree (1940) Material process passives have been virtually eliminated, with only a single example in the whole article, leaving the examples dealing with mathematical calculation and demonstration as the dominant feature:

Those in column (c) are to be regarded as the most accurate, as both exchange and superposition of configurations **have been included** in the calculation both of the radial wave functions and of the energy from those wave functions. The energy values in columns (a) and (b) **have been calculated** from the wave functions obtained by the solution of Fock's equations with exchange but without the superposition of configurations, which **has** also **been omitted** in the energy formula in obtaining the results in column (a), but **included**, in the energy formula *only*, in obtaining the results in column (b). (Hartree, 1940)

There is a further problem in these articles, which is particularly evident in the case of Axford (1960), where the situation is compounded by the fact that since the mathematical model represents physical phenomena relating to ions in interstellar gas, there is a grey area in which examples are ambiguous between a reading which relates them to the phenomenon, and one which relates them to the model. The analysis has been made here on the basis of the most likely reading, but it is evident that there is room for disagreement in individual cases. It is also probably the case that for some of these examples there is no single reading and that both are permissible:

Shocks **can be inserted** in both the channel and the ionization front to alter the flow from supersonic to subsonic, but there is no mechanism whereby this change, or its reverse, **can be made** smoothly. Thus, if heat **is** always **added** to the flow in the channel, or if the process involved in the ionization front is purely exothermic, the Chapman-Jouguet hypothesis **is obeyed**. (Axford, 1960)

Thus in the course of the twentieth century, a change which probably started in the late nineteenth century is confirmed as a general rule. The increasing mathematisation of the physical articles results in a change in the process distribution of the passives which are used. There is a smaller percentage of Material process passives than previously, compensated for by an increased percentage of Mental process passives, mainly of a mathematical type.

This change is not evident in the articles from the biological sector. Here the overall distribution remains largely what it was in the nineteenth century. For the nineteenth century the average percentage for Material process passives is 58 per cent, and it is virtually the same at 59 per cent in the twentieth century. For Mental processes the average percentage is 22 per cent in the nineteenth and 24 per cent in the twentieth century. On the other hand the range is each case is much more restricted. In the case of the physical sector this is 27 per cent–84 per cent in the nineteenth century, but 44 per cent–72 per cent in the twentieth, and for the biological sector, it is 9 per cent–50 per cent in the nineteenth, and 13 per cent–30 per cent in the twentieth century. So although there is still a fairly high degree of spread, it is less than it was, and so is to some extent more restricted round the overall average. As before, the Material process passives are frequently concerned with experimental procedure:

> From this solution they **are transferred** to the dye, which **is prepared** by mixing an alcoholic solution of aniline blue with orseillin, drop by drop, until a violet solution **is obtained**. This mixture **is acidulated** with a few drops of glacial acetic acid. The sections remain in the stain for about two hours, and **are** then **transferred** directly to dilute glycerine, and finally **mounted** in glycerine. (Dawson, 1900)

> In order to clean the specimens, they **were boiled** for some hours in a saturated solution of potassium hydroxide to destroy organic material. Constant washing in water for several days was necessary to remove the alkali, and then each specimen **was** thoroughly **brushed** with a medium-grade nylon tooth-brush, to remove the softened dirt. (Joysey, 1960)

But they are also used, also fairly frequently for descriptive purposes:

> These cells **are elongated** and **flattened** and **arranged** in many layers. (Mummery, 1920)

> The remaining 356 specimens, which showed no distortion, were by no means perfect. Of these, 186 **were fractured** or badly **weathered**. (Joysey, 1960)

So although experiment becomes a significant factor in the use of passives in biological articles in the course of the nineteenth century, the observational and classificatory roles of these articles are still evident in the late twentieth century. The observational nature of these biological articles is evident in many of the Mental process passives used, which are of a perception type:

> In the lower part of the follicle opposite the point of the forming root, large accumulations of epithelial cells **are** sometimes **seen**, resembling those in the coronal portion of the follicle. Scattered groups of epithelial cells **are** also **seen** within the connective tissue to the outside of Hertwig's sheath, both here and at the lateral margins of the tooth. (Mummery, 1920)

> Where the cornea is translucent the embryonic upper unit of the lens **can be seen** through the transparent cornea as a clear, small, dark circle, 150μm across the centre of the lens. (Miller, 1980)

However, the cognitive type also plays a significant role:

> These $C_6.C_3$ compounds **are known** and **are characterized** by orientation of hyroxyl groups similar to those obtaining in the unfused benzene ring of the anthocycanins. (Lawrence, 1940)

> In a study of the Cretaceous echinoid *Micraster*, Kermack (1954) found that a pair of characters, which **would** both **be regarded** as advanced in the evolutionary sense, **were** often negatively **correlated** with one another in the individual (Joysey, 1960)

The general picture which emerges is the following. In the physical sector, the use of the passive is established as a discursive strategy from the beginning of the period under study, with something of the order of 25 per cent of finite verbs being passivised in the eighteenth century articles. These are most frequently examples of Material process, and this is due to the experimental nature of the enterprise being described and reported. The use of the passive continues into the eighteenth century where its frequency extends to a figure in the low 30s, in percentage terms, a figure which is continued to the end of the period under consideration, that is, the end of the twentieth century. Material processes continue to be used mainly for the reporting of experimental activity, but from the late nineteenth century onwards the increasing use of mathematics leads to a reduction in percentage terms of Material process passives, in favour of Mental process passives, which represent the cognitive nature of mathematical calculation and demonstration.

In the early years of the period covered, the biological articles use passives, but not to the same extent as the physical articles, the difference being up to ten percentage points. In the course of the nineteenth century the gap narrows, but it is only in the twentieth century that the rate of use in the biological articles is of the same order as that in the physical articles. Material process is the most common process type, but here again, not to the same extent as in the physical articles, and the rate of Mental process is correspondingly higher. This is due to the fact that the biological sector remains largely observational until the late nineteenth century. In the twentieth century, the process distribution in the biological sector is comparable with that of the nineteenth century for the physical sector. This is accounted for by the fact that the biological sector has recourse to mathematical explanation to nothing like the same extent as the physical sector.

It will be noted that the use of passives, and the type of process which is passivised, is related to the nature of the activity of which the language production constitutes a part. So, when Material process passives in the physical sector give way partially to Mental process passives, this is due to the changing nature of the activity going on; cerebral activity is to some extent replacing physical activity. When the process distribution for twentieth century biological articles resembles that for nineteenth-century physical articles, it is because there is something similar about the respective activities in these two areas. In other words the situation has a causal role in determining the language used. Since this feature is directly related to the nature of the ongoing activity, in terms of field, tenor and mode, we are here concerned with field. So field is intimately concerned in the way this feature is used. This is an excellent example of the way in which the situation and the lexicogrammar produced within it are intimately linked, so that ultimately one cannot be considered in isolation from the other.

In a later section, I will attempt to show that the use of the passive is intimately related to thematic structure, which I would claim is the driving force behind passive use.

6 First person pronoun Subjects

A rare phenomenon

Since the use of the passive removes the need to express agents, and since the activity of the researcher is an important ingredient in this type of text, it is of interest to see to what extent first person pronouns continue to be used in these articles. Table 6.1 gives the number and frequency (average number of words of running text for one pronoun) of first person pronoun Subjects.

The first thing that needs to be said is that in none of the articles are the numbers of first person pronouns particularly high, and many are extremely small. Consequently any remarks made on the basis of these figures are naturally qualified by the paucity of those numbers. This should be taken as a global hedge for the remarks that follow. It will be noted that in the eighteenth century, with the exception of Povey (1700) which has only one example, and Lafage (1700) which has none at all, but which may be an anonymous third person report, the frequency seems fairly stable at round about one per 110 words of running text, with little difference between the physical and biological sectors. The range is 81 to 142 in the physical sector, and 56 to 131 in the biological sector; and if Desaguliers and Baker, which have by far the highest frequencies, are excluded, the ranges become 116 to 142 and 111 to 131 respectively, lowering the average frequency by something of the order of 15 words. In the following century first person pronoun Subjects become more frequent in the physical sector, but less frequent in the biological sector. Once into the twentieth century however, frequency drops significantly, so that these pronouns become rare in the physical sector, and exceedingly rare in the biological sector, and indeed in one physical article, Axford (1960), they virtually disappear altogether, the only examples, and only two of them, being found in the acknowledgements.

Table 6.1. *First person pronoun Subjects in the* Philosophical Transactions *corpus.*

1700–1780

	Physical			*Biological*	
	No.	*Frequency*		*No.*	*Frequency*
Povey, 1700	1	508	Lafage, 1700	—	—
Desaguliers, 1720	4	81	Blair, 1720	17	131
Smith, 1740	24	142	Baker, 1740	27	56
Wilson, 1760	24	116	Edwards, 1760	9	125
Cavallo, 1780	25	121	Hunter, 1780	16	111

1800–1880

	Physical			*Biological*	
	No.	*Frequency*		*No.*	*Frequency*
Herschel, 1800	35	57	Home, 1800	3	413
Davy, 1820	43	107	Knight, 1820	11	75
Gassiot, 1840	64	73	Barry, 1840	45	118
Matthiessen, 1860	29	61	De la Rue, 1860	53	120
Glazebrook, 1880	76	67	Owen, 1880	7	154

1900–1980

	Physical			*Biological*	
	No.	*Frequency*		*No.*	*Frequency*
Townsend, 1900	76	133	Dawson, 1900	123	88
Darfield, 1920	32	206	Mummery, 1920	12	480
Hartree. 1940	16	315	Lawrence, 1940	6	685
Axford, 1960	2	5350	Joysey, 1960	10	939
Horai, 1980	14	510	Miller, 1980	9	732

The eighteenth century situation

Since the numbers are already small, giving a process distribution is obviously delicate; nevertheless this is worth doing for comparative purposes. Table 6.2 gives the distribution for the eighteenth century articles.

Although the numbers are small, it will be noticed that while three of the physical articles have examples of first person pronouns in Material process, only one of the biological articles does so. Those that appear in the

Table 6.2. Process distribution of first person pronoun Subjects 1700–80.

| | *Physical* | | | | |
	Material	*Mental*	*Verbal*	*Relational*	*n*
Povey, 1700	—	—	—	100	1
Desaguliers, 1720	100	—	—	—	4
Smith, 1740	—	63	29	8	24
Wilson, 1760	29	25	33	13	24
Cavallo, 1780	48	36	12	4	25

| | *Biological* | | | | |
	Material	*Mental*	*Verbal*	*Relational*	*n*
Lafage, 1700	—	—	—	—	—
Blair, 1720	—	35	53	12	17
Baker, 1740	33	48	11	7	27
Edwards, 1760	—	78	11	11	9
Hunter, 1780	—	44	31	25	16

physical articles are processes that are involved with the carrying out of experiments:

> After the Fluids in the Flasks had receiv'd a sufficient degree of heat from the Water, which was round the Flasks, for the Space of five Minutes, I **took** the Flasks out of the hot Water, and putting that which held the Water into a Cylindrick Vessel that had three pints of cold Water in it, I **did** at the same time **plunge** the Flask with *Mercury* into another Cylindrick Vessel containing also three Pints of cold Water, and observ'd which of the cold Waters was most heated in the following manner. (Desaguliers, 1720)

> In order to that, I **tied** a stick of sealing wax to a silk string about a yard long, and after having excited it very powerfully with flannel, I **plunged** it in a tin vessel full of water, and immediately drawing it out, brought a very accurate electrometer near it, and observed, that at first it shewed no sign of electricity; but in about half a minute's time it manifested a small but very sensible degree of negative electricity. (Cavallo, 1780)

On the other hand, in Baker (1740), the only biological article in this century with any first person pronouns in Material processes, the actions carried out are simply aids to observation:

> I **stuck** the Point of the Lancet into it, with no other Design than to take it up, and place it in the Microscope to see what it might be ... (Baker, 1740)

Mental process also plays a proportionately significant role. In the physical articles, particularly those of Smith (1740) and Wilson (1760), though less so in the case of Cavallo (1780), these are mainly of the cognitive type:

> ... and in Practice **we judge** it will be most convenient, that the Radii of the Sheres to which the concave and convex Sides of the Speculum are ground, be nearly in the Ratio of 6 to 5 ... (Smith, 1740)

> **I chose** the lower part thereof, for no other reason, than to have the poker out of the reach of any effect that might happen from the conducting-wire, which communicated with the machine, and the inside coating of the bottle. (Wilson, 1760)

In the biological sector, the Mental processes that occur with personal pronoun Subjects tend, like their physical counterparts, to be of a cognitive type:

> This was a Sight **I** little **expected** to meet with; and being aware how much Imagination has frequently had to do with microscopical Observations, **I distrusted** my own Eyes ... (Baker, 1740)

> **I think**, however, that our assent to such an opinion may reasonably be suspended, till **we are confirmed** in it by farther observations of the real fact ... (Edwards, 1760)

It is only in the last of the biological articles of this century that there seems to be a bias towards Mental processes of the perception type:

> In those orders of animals, which are composed of distinct sexes, **we may observe**, the genital organs not only subject to a mal-conformation, similar to a mal-conformation in any other part of the animal; but **we may** likewise sometimes **observe** an attempt to unite the two parts in one animal body, producing an animal called an unnatural hermaphrodite. (Hunter, 1780)

It will also be noted that there are a number of personal pronoun Subjects that occur with Verbal processes in this biological section. These might be considered to be of a metalinguistic type, in that the author is discussing one of his own publications:

> In this **I have not kept** to the Dispensatory Catalogue, but **have added** several Congeners, that **I might give** a Specimen of what is proposed concerning the Virtues and Characters. Thus **I have added** *Cuminum* and *Meum to Faeniculum* ... (Blair, 1720)

> That this is the distinct character of such animals is evident, for the castrated male and the spayed female have but one set of properties between them; and when **I treated** of the Free-martin, which is a monstrous hermaphrodite ... (Hunter, 1780)

Continuation in the nineteenth century

As was pointed out above, the numbers involved here are extremely small, and must hence be treated with circumspection. In passing from the eighteenth to the nineteenth century, the numbers remain small, though examples are considerably more numerous than in the previous century: two and a half times as many for the century as a whole. This is partly due to the fact that the articles are, in general, longer, but even taking this into account first person pronoun Subjects are rather more frequent in the nineteenth century than they had been in the eighteenth. The overall frequency for the eighteenth century is one per 117 words of running text, whereas in the nineteenth century the frequency is one per 97 words. The process distribution for the nineteenth century is given in Table 6.3.

The figures for Owen (1880) are for the text of his article excluding a quotation from a letter, which within its 148 words includes ten first person pronoun Subjects. Inclusion of this section would obviously have skewed the figures. There are some general trends that are evident in Table 6.3. That trend is that for the physical sector there is a bias towards Material process that is absent in the biological sector. In the physical sector, personal pronoun Subjects are most common in Material processes in three of the five articles, and in only one case does the proportion fall below a third. In the biological

Table 6.3. Process distribution of first person pronoun Subjects 1800–80.

	Physical				
	Material	*Mental*	*Verbal*	*Relational*	*n*
Herschel, 1800	63	11	14	11	35
Davy, 1820	37	42	19	2	43
Gassiot, 1840	36	25	23	16	64
Matthiessen, 1860	41	34	14	10	29
Glazebrook, 1880	10	67	3	33	76

	Biological				
	Material	*Mental*	*Verbal*	*Relational*	*n*
Home, 1800	—	67	33	—	3
Knight, 1820	9	55	27	9	11
Barry, 1849	—	69	22	9	45
De la Rue, 1860	43	26	21	9	53
Owen, 1880	14	29	29	29	7

sector, in only one article do the personal pronoun Subjects occur most frequently with Material processes. Two have none at all (though one with extremely small overall numbers), and it is only in the single case where the Material process category is the dominant one, that the rate rises above 15 per cent. In the physical sector the Mental process cases are the most frequent in one article, and the second most frequent in three others; in only one case does the rate fall below 25 per cent. In the biological area, however, the Mental process category is the most frequent in four of the five articles. It is also worth noting that Verbal process provides a considerable percentage of examples in the biological sector. All of the articles have 20 per cent or more. In the physical sector, however, in only one case do personal pronoun Subjects occur with Verbal processes at a rate of more than 20 per cent.

Where the first person pronoun Subject occurs in a Material process in the physical sector, this is most frequently in processes connected with experiments:

> In order to have a confirmation of this fact, **I cooled** the thermometer No. 1, and **placed** No. 2 in the room of it: I also **put** No. 3 in the place of No. 2, and No. 1 in that of No. 3 ... (Herschel, 1800)

> On two occasions I inadvertently **touched** both wires, the armature making three or four revolutions; the pain was so intense that **I suffered** from the effects for a considerable time afterwards; but as this effect, as is well known to all who have experimented with the secondary coil, is so much increased by the introduction of iron wires in the helix, **I repeated** the experiments under rather different circumstances, viz. by avoiding the use of the metal. (Gassiot, 1840)

This is also largely the case in the single biological article where there is more than one example of a first person pronoun Subject in a Material process:

> ... **we** nevertheless **repeated** subsequently these experiments on a somewhat larger scale, with the view, however, chiefly of studying the other products of decomposition which are formed. In order to eliminate as much as possible the effect of temperature, **we made** use of that powerful reagent, the so-called 'sodium-alcohol', which is obtained by dissolving sodium in absolute alcohol. (De la Rue, 1860)

When the pronoun occurs in Mental process, it does so most frequently in cognitive processes in both the physical and biological articles:

> Although **I must consider** that Professor DANIELL laboured under some such error when he describes the discharge passing in the form of a spark (8.) when the cells were approximated, yet **I cannot** but **feel** that it will be with the aid, and through the principles of this philosopher's scientific

apparatus, which he has so appropriately denominated the constant battery, that the true principles of voltaic action will be correctly ascertained. There is already one fact which was obtained with the 160 pairs (10.) which cannot, **I believe**, be satisfactorily accounted for by any of the existing theories. (Gassiot, 1840)

The product so obtained was washed and boiled with a dilute solution of potash, but after saturating this alkaline solution with an acid, no precipitate was formed, and it was altogether impossible to detect any acid; therefore **we must conclude** that this acid was not formed by this treatment. (De la Rue, 1860)

However, in the physical sector Davy (1820) has a number of occurrences of *found* which might be considered on the borderline between cognition and perception:

I afterwards **found** that the substance in question may be readily obtained by boiling the sulphate and alcohol together for a few minutes ... (Davy, 1820)

And in the biological sector, Barry, 1840, which has the highest rate of Mental processes, has a tendency to use the perception type:

I have seen these motions of the altered blood-discs when the latter were covered, – in some instances with glass, in others with mica, – and also when uncovered; and **I have observed** them as late as two hours and a half after death as in fig. 3. (Barry, 1840)

In the case of Glazebrook (1880), in the physical sector, the rate of first person pronoun Subjects in Mental process is affected by the extensive use of mathematics in this article:

We take then as the value of μ_1, 1.65441. (Glazebrook, 1880)

Where, mainly in the biological sector, first person pronouns occur in Verbal processes, they appear to have two main functions: either a metalinguistic function pointing to other parts of the text or other statements by the author, or a function of naming and defining:

I formerly **showed** that during the passage of the ovum through the Fallopian tube, there rises from the thick transparent membrane (*f*) a thinner membrane. The latter was traced from stage to stage up to the period when villi form upon it, and thus ascertained to be the incipient chorion.

In a later paper **I stated** that the thin membrane in question (the incipient chorion) is formed of cells ... (Barry, 1840)

In order to identify it hereafter, **we propose** to call this resin Sycoretin. (De la Rue, 1860)

The twentieth century: a radical change

The corresponding details for the period 1900–80 are given in Table 6.4.

When we pass into the twentieth century not only are the overall numbers of first person pronoun Subjects very low, particularly after 1920, but in addition one author, Axford (1960), can be said for practical purposes not to use them at all; as has been pointed out, the two that do occur in his article are in the acknowledgements. Moreover, in the physical sector, they virtually never occur in Material processes; there are only three examples in all five articles, two in Townsend (1900), and one in Horai (1980). In the biological sector, there seems to be continuing use of first person pronoun Subjects with Material processes until 1920, but from 1940 onwards this becomes almost as rare as in the physical sector. Throughout this century, where first person pronoun Subjects are used (albeit in small numbers), it is most frequently in Mental process, continuing a trend begun in 1880 for the physical sector, and from 1940 on for the biological sector.

Throughout the twentieth century, the few first person pronoun Subjects of these Mental processes are usually of the cognitive type:

Table 6.4. Process distribution of first person pronoun Subjects 1900–80.

| | *Physical* | | | | |
	Material	*Mental*	*Verbal*	*Relational*	*n*
Townsend, 1900	3	78	9	11	76
Duffield, 1920	—	63	22	16	32
Hartree, 1940	—	56	25	19	16
Axford, 1960	—	50	—	50	2
Horai, 1980	7	64	29	—	7

| | *Biological* | | | | |
	Material	*Mental*	*Verbal*	*Relational*	*n*
Dawson, 1900	63	26	7	5	123
Mummery, 1920	50	42	—	8	12
Lawrence, 1940	17	67	17	—	6
Joysey, 1960	—	60	—	40	10
Miller, 1980	11	44	22	22	9

Remembering that the effects of conversion currents have been underestimated, and therefore that the convexion current curve should have been rather lower, **we see** that it is probable that the corrected curve is linear, and that the reaction varies directly with the current; it is unfortunate that information is very difficult to obtain in the crucial part of the curve where the current is small; there is no evidence that the pressure when corrected for convexion ever becomes negative. It is clear therefore that, without much error, **we may take** the origin of the observed curve at the point at which the straight portion when produced backwards cuts the vertical or pressure axis. (Duffield, 1920)

... but **we know** nothing of changes in the force of mortality during the life history of a blastoid, subsequent to its metamorphosis. **We do not know** whether storms in the Carboniferous seas were more likely to break large or small blastoids from their anchorages, and **we do not know** whether disease took greater toll among the aged than among the young. (Joysey, 1960)

In the case of the physical articles, this is sometimes related to the use of mathematics, which plays a part, to varying extents, in all of them:

The second gas, B, has practically no motion in passing along a tube, except along the axis, which **we take** as coinciding with the axis of coordinates z. The notation can therefore be simplified, and in what follows **we shall let** n be the number of ions per cub. centim. ... (Townsend, 1900)

There are also examples of *we find, we obtain, we get,* etc. followed by mathematical formulae. This is not, however, the case in Joysey (1960), the only biological article to use mathematics to any extent.

In overall terms, the use of first person pronoun Subjects is far less frequent than the use of passives. In only two of the 30 articles in the sample, Baker (1749) and Glazebrook (1880), is the frequency of first person pronoun Subjects greater than that of passives, and in most cases it is considerably less. Where they are used, in the physical sector this is mainly with Material processes throughout the eighteenth century, and this continues until the late nineteenth century, from which point it drops dramatically to almost zero, and this remains the case throughout the twentieth century. From the late nineteenth century onwards there is increasing use with Mental processes, and this is partly due to the introduction of mathematics. In the biological sector, first person pronoun Subjects are associated with Mental processes throughout the eighteenth century and until after the mid-nineteenth century. Thereafter, there is increasing use with Material processes until the mid-twentieth century, when there is a return to use with Mental processes.

Throughout the whole of the period, Mental processes tend to be of the cognitive type.

Just as was the case with the passive, use of first person pronoun Subjects can be linked to the changing situation of scientific research. Here the field includes the fact that the physical sector is experimental from the beginning of the period, but becomes increasingly mathematised from the late nineteenth century onwards, whereas the biological sector is basically observational until the mid-nineteenth century but this approach is intermixed with experiment from then on. Observation and mathematics tend to be related to Mental process, and experiment usually leads to Material process. In terms of tenor, the fact that the first person is the scientist himself communicating with his peers is obviously relevant, and the restrained use of first person pronoun Subjects is obviously related to this fact. Once again, the lexicogrammar and the situation are intimately linked, and must be seen in terms of each other.

7 Nominalisation

Nominalising processes

If one considers that passive use is related to the possibility of not encoding the agent, the nominalisation of processes, which is a form of grammatical metaphor, must be considered in the same light. Whereas it is possible to give the agent of a passivised process as an agentive Adjunct, using the preposition *by*, the agent of a nominalised process can only be given as a possessive Modifier of the nominalised Head. This, as well as the change from verb to noun, makes the nominalisation of processes even more removed from notions of agentivity than the passive voice. The frequency of nominalised processes, in terms of the average number of words for one example of nominalisation, is given in Table 7.1.

Nominalised processes are comparatively frequent right from the start of the period under consideration. Desaguliers (1720) is the only article where they might be said to be virtually absent. In the physical sector, the rate seems to settle at something like one per 30 words from 1740 onwards, with only Cavallo (1780) having a rather less frequent rate. This lasts until 1920 when there appears to be a sudden increase in the uses of nominalisations, for the final four articles all have rates that are more frequent than one per 15 words. It is possible that Glazebrook (1880), at one per 19 words, is a forerunner of this trend. In the biological sector the figures seem more erratic until they too settle at something like one per 30 words in the mid-nineteenth century. This becomes more frequent from the beginning of the twentieth century, with figures in the low 20s, but never as frequent as the rates shown in the physical sector.

When nominalised processes are distributed according to the type of process they represent, those for the eighteenth century provide the figures given in Table 7.2.

Where processes are nominalised, they tend to be Material processes, and this tendency is even more marked in the physical sector than the biological. The average percentage for the century as a whole is 80 per cent for

Table 7.1. Frequency of nominalisation the *Philosophical Transactions* corpus.

1700–80			
Physical		*Biological*	
Povey, 1700	36	Lafage, 1700	56
Desaguliers, 1720	162	Blair, 1720	31
Smith, 1740	30	Baker, 1740	29
Wilson, 1760	29	Edwards, 1760	56
Cavallo, 1780	48	Hunter, 1780	41
1800–80			
Physical		*Biological*	
Herschel, 1800	29	Home, 1800	83
Davy, 1820	36	Knight, 1820	43
Gassiot, 1840	29	Barry, 1840	25
Matthiessen, 1860	32	De la Rue, 1860	33
Glazebrook, 1880	19	Owen, 1880	33
1900–80			
Physical		*Biological*	
Townsend, 1900	27	Dawson, 1900	20
Duffield, 1920	14	Mummery, 1920	29
Hartree, 1940	11	Lawrence, 1940	20
Axford, 1960	14	Joysey, 1960	22
Horai, 1980	14	Miller, 1980	23

the physical sector, and 68 per cent for the biological; or, if the figures for 1720 and 1740 are discounted as being too small to be reliable, the percentages for the final three articles is 71 per cent for the physical sector and 63 per cent for the biological. Where these nominalised Material processes are used they tend, in the biological sector and in the early physical articles, to be related to natural processes, that is, processes of which the researcher is not the agent:

> ... and the interval *QP* will be the greatest Aberration, or Error, occasioned by the **Separation**, or unequal **Refraction**, of the greatest and least refrangible Rays, after their **Emergence** from the concave surface *FED*. (Smith, 1740)

> The **Growth** of Animals and Vegetables seems to be nothing else but a gradual **Unfolding** and **Expansion** of their Vessels by a slow and

Table 7.2. Percentage process distribution of nominalisations, 1700–1780.

	Material	*Mental*	*Verbal*	*Relational*	*Existential*	*n*
			Physical			
Povey, 1700	86	—	14	—	—	14
Desaguliers, 1720	100	—	—	—	—	2
Smith, 1740	86	9	4	2	—	112
Wilson, 1760	69	16	1	14	—	95
Cavallo, 1780	57	11	22	10	—	63
			Biological			
	Material	*Mental*	*Verbal*	*Relational*	*Existential*	*n*
Lafage, 1700	75	25	—	—	—	8
Blair, 1720	75	14	11	—	—	71
Baker, 1740	55	34	5	4	2	56
Edwards, 1760	60	15	25	—	—	20
Hunter, 1780	74	14	7	5	—	43

> progressive **Insinuation** of Fluids adapted to their Diameters, until being stretched to the utmost Bounds allotted them by Providence at their **Formation** ... (Baker, 1740)

From 1760 on, however, they are used in the physical sector for experimental procedures:

> These opposite **effects**, occasioned by the different **applications** of the flat, or edge of the silver, seem to arise from an **alteration** made in the surface of the wax, by *destroying* the *polish* in one case, and not in the other ... (Wilson, 1760)

> ... if any electrified substance is brought near the cap EF, the corks of the electrometer by their **converging** or **diverging** more, will shew the species of that body's electricity. (Cavallo, 1780)

Wilson (1760) and Cavallo (1780) also use the word *experiment* extensively. This is also a nominalised process, though one that was probably lexicalised at an early date. I believe its use to be significant, and I shall return to this point below. In the biological sector, there is a significant degree of nominalisation of Mental processes. In the case of Blair (1720), there is a high proportion of the perception type of Mental processes:

> Thus *Apium* and *Petroselinum* have a **Taste** resembling to each other, therefore they are to be prescribed together. The Seeds of *Fœniculum*

and *Anisum* have much of the same **taste** and **smell**, and therefore both of them must be Carminative, or expellers of Wind, &c. (Blair, 1720)

In the later biological articles in this century the nominalised Mental processes tend to be of the cognitive type:

Amongst numberless Inquirers, whom the **Opinion** that every Seed includes a real Plant, has set at work to open all Kinds of Seeds, and try by Glasses to find evident **Proofs** thereof, I have not been the least industrious ... (Baker, 1740)

This lady for some time had bred pheasants, and had paid particular **attention** to them. (Hunter, 1780)

This also tends to be the case, where Mental processes occur, in the physical articles:

... which Quantity, or Error, thus obtained, (to abbreviate the **Calculation**) call ε ... (Smith, 1740)

... but thus much may be safely advanced, that we have learned to produce at **pleasure** the *plus* or *minus* electricity from the same bodies ... (Wilson, 1760)

Edwards (1760) also has a number of nominalised Verbal processes, which tend to express communication by others:

... and gives five figures to illustrate her **description**; the subjects whereof, she says, were then in the collection of Albert Seba at Amsterdam, from whom she also had her figures and **information**, as appears since by the **account** published by Mr. Seba of his curious cabinet of natural history, in two pompous folio volumes, a copy of which, finely illuminated, is now in the British Museum. (Edwards, 1760)

The pattern established by the end of the eighteenth century continues through the nineteenth. That is, the nominalisations are predominantly of Material processes, but even more so in the case of physical articles, where the average for the century is 73 per cent (i.e. the average percentage, not the overall average); for the biological articles, the average for the century is 58 per cent. In the biological sector there are also a certain number of nominalised Mental and Verbal processes, accounting for 15 per cent and 17 per cent respectively. The details are given in Table 7.3.

The nominalized Material processes which occur in the physical sector are mainly involved in the experimental processes, though not necessarily of an agentive type, that is not necessarily carried out by the scientists themselves; there are also a number of other non-agentive types,

Table 7.3. Percentage process distribution of nominalisations, 1800–80.

	Physical				
	Material	*Mental*	*Verbal*	*Relational*	*n*
Herschel, 1800	67	7	11	14	70
Davy, 1820	74	8	6	16	128
Gassiot, 1840	81	8	9	2	161
Matthiessen, 1860	76	7	4	7	55
Glazebrook, 1880	66	18	1	15	263
	Biological				
	Material	*Mental*	*Verbal*	*Relational*	*n*
Home, 1800	40	7	40	13	15
Knight, 1820	58	26	16	?	19
Barry, 1840	58	11	15	15	214
De la Rue, 1860	69	15	4	12	193
Owen, 1880	65	14	11	11	37

that is, things which happen, effects of natural forces in the course of the experiment:

> It seems to undergo no **change** by **exposure** to the air for some time. When it is gently heated, on a slip of platinum or paper, a hissing noise or a feeble **explosion** is produced, and this **effect** is accomplished by a **flash** of red light, and the platinum is reduced. (Davy, 1820)

> The **union** of the copper with the other metals was effected in the **manner** before described, which offers in this case the additional advantage, that by the constant **movement** caused by the hydrogen in the melted metals, the most intimate **combination** results. (Matthiessen, 1860)

In the case of the biological sector, where in any case the overall numbers are much smaller, the picture is less clear. Home (1800), which has very few examples, Barry (1840), and Owen (18800 all tend to be non-experimental:

> I have seen both in the Fallopian tube and on its fimbriated extremity, a curious network (fig. 22.), apparently formed by the **coalescence** of blood-corpuscles, which, like those entering into the **formation** of the chorion, seemed for this purpose to have sent out processes or arms. (Barry, 1840)

> Concomitantly with the more equal **development** of the right and left female organs in *Echidna*, as compared with *Ornithorhynchus*, is the evidence of an ovipont by the right ovarium shown by the **reception** of the impregnated ovum in the uterus of that side ... (Owen, 1880)

Knight (1820), albeit with very few examples, and De la Rue (1860) have a stronger experimental component:

> Cold alcohol of moderate strength dissolves the principal part of the original resin, forming a light brown solution, which on **precipitation** with water, or the **separation** of the alcohol by means of **distillation**, furnishes the sycoretin. The alcoholic solution of this resin is perfectly neutral, and scarcely any precipitate is caused in it on the **addition** of an alcoholic solution of acetate of lead or acetate of copper. (De la Rue, 1860)

Those nominalised Mental processes which occur in the biological sector tend to be of the cognitive type, though De la Rue has a number of other types too:

> This **supposition** was confirmed ... moreover, we were ultimately enabled to give the fullest **confirmation** to this theoretical **speculation**, by actually reforming the original substance in a manner suggested by this view. (De la Rue, 1860)

> I welcomed this satisfactory **confirmation** of the marsupial structure ... (Owen, 1880)

Of the biological articles, only Barry (1840) shows a predominance of the perception type:

> This however – from **observations** on the varying state of the interior of nuclei and the continual origin there of fresh objects, recorded in my 'Third Series' ... (Barry, 1840)

Glazebrook (1880), the only physical article to use nominalised Mental processes in any numbers, has examples of both types, but rather more of the cognitive type:

> I therefore completed the **calculations** for only about a third of the **observations**, giving a series of values of ì in direction inclined at angles of about 4° to each other, extending in an almost continuous arc from the optic axis to directions perpendicular to it. (Glazebrook, 1880)

Where, in the biological articles, Verbal processes are nominalised, this is more frequently for the author's pronouncements, than for the pronouncements of others:

> In the sixth month I have recently discerned on these fibres the first traces of transverse striæ, and hence (having now at **command** one of the best instruments of Plössl) must retract the **statement** I formerly made, that these transverse striæ are entirely absent from the embryo. (Barry, 1840)

I noted in **correspondence** with friends in localities frequented by the Echidnæ ... with **instructions** as to the parts to be preserved and transmitted, in alcohol ... (Owen, 1880)

It will however have been noted that the proportion of nominalised Material processes in the biological field tends to rise towards the figure for the physical sector. This is confirmed in the twentieth century, where the average percentage for both sectors is 73 per cent. The details for the twentieth century are given in Table 7.4.

There are two main types of nominalized Material processes: those that are related to the actions of the experimenter, and those that are related to the phenomena under study. Both are present in slightly different ways in the physical and biological subsamples. In the physical area although both occur there is an increase in the phenomenon type where the interest is more on modelling than experiment as such:

These **results** show that the mean rate of **diffusion** is only slightly altered by the presence of moisture, but a large **change** is produced in the ratio of the coefficients of **diffusion** of positive and negative ions. (Townsend, 1900)

When heat is added to the **flow** in such a channel, the Mach number becomes closer to unity whether the **flow** is supersonic or subsonic. When the Mach number is unity, no further **addition** of heat is possible without

Table 7.4. Percentage process distribution of nominalisations, 1900–80.

	Physical					
	Material	*Mental*	*Verbal*	*Relational*	*Existential*	*n*
Townsend, 1900	80	13	2	5	—	375
Duffield, 1920	82	12	2	3	1	497
Hartree, 1940	50	36	2	11	—	469
Axford, 1960	76	15	5	4	—	787
Horai, 1980	77	17	2	3	—	499

	Biological					
	Material	*Mental*	*Verbal*	*Relational*	*Existential*	*n*
Dawson, 1900	75	14	6	4	1	530
Mummery, 1920	81	14	4	8	—	201
Lawrence, 1940	60	20	8	9	5	202
Joysey, 1960	66	14	5	15	?	428
Miller, 1980	83	5	6	6	?	237

causing a **breakdown** of the **flow**. Exactly the same situation is found in **ionization** front structure when **cooling** and **recombination** are neglected and the **process** is therefore exothermic. (Axford, 1960)

In the biological articles there seems to be more of the experimental type where the article itself is experimental, but more of the phenomenon type where the article is observational:

> For the **preparation** of preserved material I tried various **methods** of **hardening**, such as a saturated solution of mercuric chloride … (Dawson, 1900)

> Its **function** would appear to be in man, as in other mammalia, the **limitation** of the **growth** of the dentine, and the **moulding** as it were of the apical foramen of the tooth, leaving open the space through which the nerves and blood-vessels enter the pulp, the **growth** of the dentine ceasing where it is not surrounded by the epithelial layer. (Mummery, 1920)

Just as was the case with use of the passive and first person pronoun Subjects, it is evident that use of nominalisation is rooted in the situation. The nature of the activity going on to some extent determines the form of the language used. Thus the inseparability of the language from its situation is again in evidence.

Experiment

From the above it will be seen that there are two watershed dates in the history of science which are important for their effect on scientific writing. The first of these occurs in the mid- to late nineteenth century. The physical sciences had been experimental since the late seventeenth century, but the biological sciences remained observational and classificatory until the middle of the nineteenth century. It was only at this point that an experimental element was introduced into the biological sciences, which then continued side by side with its observational and classificatory roles. This continues to the present day, where, for example, we are told that in the area of deep-sea studies numerous species remain to be discovered and classified. The second turning point is the early twentieth century, when the physical sciences turn towards mathematical modelling, which takes over part of the role previously played by physical experiment. The biological sciences do not yet (at least up to 1980) seem to have followed this path.

Since both of these turning points are, in different ways, related to experimentation, it is interesting to look at the use and frequency of the word *experiment* itself. This counts as a nominalised process, since it represents a process, or bundle of processes, and not an entity. It was however lexicalised at an early date. The *OED* gives examples dating from as early as the mid-fourteenth century, and the earliest citations of the verb *experiment* are from roughly the same date. The verb does occasionally occur in the corpus:

> That a spark does appear when the contact is made on completing the circuit of the voltaic battery, is well known to all who **have experimented** with that apparatus. (Gassiot, 1840)

> Professor DANIELL, in describing some very curious and important experiments made with his constant battery when excited with strong acid solutions, says, 'That a discharge may take place from the copper of one cell to the copper of the next, when the regular circle is interrupted between the two, I had many opportunities of observing with the powerful currents with which I **had been experimenting** ...' (Gassiot, 1840)

But this is rare, while there are numerous examples of the noun.

The word *trial* is also sometimes used with a sense very similar to that of *experiment*, particularly in early papers:

> Whoever shall think fit to put the Method here proposed in Execution, we dare venture (from a **Trial** that has been made) to assure him of Success ... (Smith, 1740)

> When the preceding experiments were first made, I was a little embarrassed with the uncertain appearances of a *plus* electricity at one time, and a *minus* electricity at another, in the same experiment: but by repeated **trials** and observations, I have found that a *plus* or *minus* electricity may be produced at pleasure ... (Wilson, 1760)

> In my first attempts to ascertain the nature of the black powder, I was limited to very minute quantities of it; and I made several **trials**, before I gained any satisfactory evidences of its constitution. (Davy, 1820)

However, in terms of numbers this was never a serious rival to *experiment*. The frequency of the use of this word can therefore be used to give some sort of qualitative picture of the extent of involvement in experimental science. Table 7.5 gives the frequency of the use of this nominalized process.

In the physical sector, the word *experiment* appears in these papers in significant numbers from the middle of the eighteenth century on. Throughout the nineteenth century it remains comparatively frequent, occurring roughly once for every 150–200 words of text. Use of the word continues in the early twentieth century, although it is less frequent, and the articles for 1940 and 1960 have no examples at all. In the biological sector, the term appears much less frequently than in the physical sector. Only six of the

Table 7.5. Numbers and frequency of the word *experiment*.

	Physical			*Biological*	
	No.	Frequency		No.	Frequency
Povey, 1700	—	—	Lafage, 1700	—	—
Desaguliers, 1720	1	324	Blair, 1720	3	573
Smith, 1740	1	3414	Baker, 1740	4	376
Wilson, 1760	20	139	Edwards, 1760	—	—
Cavallo, 1780	15	202	Hunter, 1780	—	—
Herschel, 1800	10	205	Home, 1800	—	—
Davy, 1820	23	199	Knight, 1820	4	206
Gassiot, 1840	27	172	Barry, 1840	—	—
Matthiessen, 1860	10	176	De la Rue, 1860	14	456
Glazebrook, 1880	32	158	Owen, 1880	—	—
Townsend, 1900	32	316	Dawson, 1900	23	471
Duffield, 1920	27	244	Mummery, 1920	—	—
Hartree, 1940	—	—	Lawrence, 1940	—	—
Axford, 1960	—	—	Joysey, 1960	1	9393
Horai, 1980	13	549	Miller, 1980	—	—

15 articles have any examples at all, and they only appear in any sort of numbers in the articles for 1860 and 1900. I would claim that the development of these frequencies is a reflection of the two major changes mentioned above. The use of the word *experiment* is constant from the end of the eighteenth century and throughout the nineteenth in the physical sector, but wanes as mathematical techniques begin to be used in the twentieth century, leading to some articles not using the word at all from the mid-twentieth century onwards. Indeed, Hartree (1940) and Axford (1960), the two articles in which there are no examples of the nominalised process *experiment*, both make extensive use of mathematics. In the biological sector the articles that use this word in any numbers occur after the middle of the nineteenth century, that is De la Rue (1860) and Dawson (1900). Both of these are experimental, while the other articles from this period, Barry (1840), Owen (1880) and Mummery (1920) are observational rather than experimental.

Nominalized processes as Modifiers

It is a general feature of contemporary English that words which are nominal in form can also function as Modifiers. This can also occur with nominalized processes, where the nominalised process functions as Modifier of a Head, which itself may be, but is not necessarily itself a nominalised process. In previous studies of a small corpus (Banks, 1999, 2001a, 2003b) I suggested that this was a twentieth-century development. The following is an example from the corpus then used:

> To determine the sampling capabilities of the trawl during retrieval, **catch** rates from six 'standard' **trawl** hauls were compared with **catch** rates from seven '**retrieval' trawl** hauls. (Krieger and Sigler 1999)

From a purely theoretical point of view, it would be possible to think of these as adjectivalised processes rather than as nominalised processes. However, since they are nominal in form, and it would seem that they function nominally before going on to function adjectivally, it seems reasonable to think of this as a double movement in terms of grammatical metaphor. That is, there is a movement from process (congruently verbal form), to noun, and thence to Modifier. Thus, my claim is that these are nominalised processes functioning as Modifiers. The suggestion that, in terms of the scientific journal article, this is a twentieth-century development that is borne out by the *Philosophical Transactions* corpus. There is only one single example of a nominalised process as Modifier earlier than 1900, and this occurs in De la Rue (1860):

> The existence of a volatile acid with the odour of acetic acid, was rendered evident by saturating the alkaline mother-liquor with phosphoric acid and distilling; the distillate was saturated with carbonate of barium and evaporated to the **crystallization** point, when prismatic crystals, of the characteristic form of acetate of barium, were obtained. (De la Rue, 1860)

Since many readers are likely to find this example banal, it is worth remembering that there are no examples of nominalized processes functioning as Modifiers earlier than this in the corpus. All other examples are 1900 or later. Table 7.6 gives the details from 1860 onwards. It gives the raw numbers, the frequency, and the feature as a percentage of the total number of nominalised processes.

This is evidently a phenomenon which starts with the twentieth century, and in the physical sector seems to be established by 1920. Its use then accelerates rapidly, and by 1960, as the case of Axford (1960) shows, can amount to 30 per cent of all nominalised processes, and occur at a rate of one per 45 words of running text. There may however be considerable difference between authors: the three 1996 articles studied in Banks (2003b) showed percentages ranging from 8 per cent to 27 per cent. In the biological sector too, the use of this feature seems to be established from 1900 onwards. However, its use remains at a fairly modest level throughout this period, never

Table 7.6. Nominalised processes as Modifiers, 1860–1980.

	Physical		
	No.	*Frequency*	*Per cent of nominalized processes*
Matthiessen, 1860	—	—	—
Glazebrook, 1880	—	—	—
Townsend, 1900	1	10,135	—
Duffield, 1920	35	188	7
Hartree, 1940	13	388	3
Axford, 1960	239	45	30
Horai, 1980	62	115	12
	Biological		
	No.	*Frequency*	*Per cent of nominalized processes*
De la Rue, 1860	1	6,383	1
Owen, 1880	—	—	—
Dawson, 1900	20	542	4
Mummer, 1920	2	2,882	1
Lawrence, 1940	1	4,110	—
Joysey, 1960	31	303	7
Miller, 1980	14	470	5

amounting to more than 7 per cent of the nominalised processes. On the other hand, the 1996 article by Krieger and Sigler used in Banks (2003b) is in the biological field, and this has a percentage of 27 per cent. Therefore it cannot be ruled out that there is a rapid increase in the biological sector after 1980, and that the field can thus be seen to be running about 30 years or so behind the physical field in terms of this development.

It can further be noted that where nominalised processes function as Modifiers they are almost exclusively cases of Material process:

> The dashed lines, C, are the loci of possible transitions, via an **ionization** front, from various points on the strong **shock** curve. (Axford, 1960)

> When it is necessary to fit a straight line to a **scatter** distribution, it is common practice to employ one of the **regression** lines. (Joysey, 1960)

> If the core-tube surface temperature is measured away from the middle of the heater, the component of heat flow, parallel to the direction of the core-tube's axis, will not be negligible, thereby invalidating the thermal

conductivity determination theory because it assumes a thermal conduction in a cylindrical system with its **flow** line confined within a plane perpendicular to the cylindrical axis. (Horai, 1980)

In the last example above, it will be noted that the word *conductivity* combines the features of a nominalised process and a grammatical metaphor of modality. Whereas for nominalised processes as a whole, the proportion which function as Material processes is about three-quarters, when it comes to nominalised processes as Modifiers they are virtually all, that is 98 per cent, Material process. Some of the remaining 2 per cent are Mental processes (two examples), analysed as such because of their mathematical nature, like *determination* above, or *transform* in the following:

Solution derivations by the Laplace **transform** method will be outlined briefly in appendix A. (Horai, 1980)

The remainder are Relational processes (six examples, of which five concern the word *equilibrium* in a single author, Axford (1960)):

The burnt gas in this case is in an **equilibrium** state and has a lower stagnation enthalpy than some of the gas ahead. Thus if the strength of the process is maintained by signals from the fluid which has the greatest stagnation enthalpy, the combustion zone can quite easily move supersonically relative to the fluid behind, as these signals are propagated at a speed greater than the **equilibrium** sound speed. (Axford, 1960)

Thus, although there has been rapid increase in the use of nominalised processes as Modifiers in the course of the twentieth century, for practical purposes, it can be said that so far this phenomenon is virtually restricted to Material process.

Part of the explanation of this phenomenon, and of its increasing use, seems to lie in the way it is used in the creation of technical vocabulary. Ormrod (2001, 2004) has shown that vocabulary can be created within the discourse, moving from clausal form to complex noun group. This is a specific instance of Halliday's remarks on the creation and uses of grammatical metaphor in scientific writing (Halliday, 1988, 1998, 2004b). However, it is probable that the vast majority of these terms are already established within the discourse community at the time of writing the article. This can be seen clearly in the case of Axford (1960). Of the 239 instances of nominalised processes functioning as Modifiers, 61 per cent concern the nominalisation *ionisation* in collocation with the Head *front*:

The 'signals' argument would be justified if **ionization fronts** were such that recombination and cooling could be neglected, for here the strong *D*-type **ionization front** has been proved impossible, and the weak

> *R*-type **ionization fronts** (which incidently, are shockless) can be said to occur only because the ionizing process is independent of any motion of the fluid. But what can be said in the case of **ionization fronts** with cooling and recombination included? Here strong *D*-type **ionization fronts,** and weak *R*-type **ionization fronts** with shocks in their structure, certainly occur, in addition to the shockless weak *R*-type, and it is not the ionizing mechanism but the presence of cooling and recombination which permits this. (Axford, 1960)

In a sense, this is not surprising insofar as this article is specifically about ionisation fronts, and the term already occurs in the title. It is however a striking illustration of the extent of the phenomenon. Moreover, the occurrences of the collocation *ionization front,* include a number of cases where this complex term itself functions as a complex Modifier of a further Head; this is the case in *ionization front speeds, ionization front transition,* and especially *ionization front structures,* which itself occurs 13 times.

> A strong R-type **ionization front structure** with one shock is the one which is most likely to occur. (Axford, 1960)

This also occurs to a lesser degree with the collocation *flow pattern,* of which there are 24 examples, and which occurs as a complex Modifier in the noun group *flow pattern solution.* In total, there are 32 types in Axford (1960) that have the form nominalised process + Head, and of these 15 occur more than once. These are given in Table 7.7.

Table 7.7. Nominalised process + Head in Axford (1960).

	Occurrences
Combustion process	2
Combustion waves	9
Combustion zone	2
Cooling effect	2
Deflagration branch	2
Flow pattern	24
Flow solution	3
Ionisation front	145
Ionisation process	2
Shock conditions	2
Shock curve	2
Shock position	2
Shock wave	4
Stagnation enthalpy	2
Transition lines	15

Although Axford (1960) is the most striking example of this phenomenon, it is certainly not isolated to this article. In Horai (1980), the collocation *conductivity measurement* accounts for 24 per cent of the 62 examples, and this includes its use as a complex Modifier in *conductivity measurement technique*; and *conductivity determination*, which accounts for 11 per cent, also appears in *conductivity determination theory*. There are also three examples each of *conduction equation*, and *test measurement*, and two examples each of *transmission characteristics*, and *pumping rate*. In Joysey (1960), from the biological field, 32 per cent of the 31 examples are accounted for by *growth curve*, and there are also four examples of *growth parameter*, three of *scatter diagram*, and two of *growth line*.

This indicates that these groups consisting of nominalised processes functioning as Modifiers in noun groups, once created, tend to become standard terms which can then be repeated as such. It has therefore an extremely important function in the creation of technical and specialised vocabulary.

8 Thematic structure

Motivation for the passive

As has been pointed out, the use of passive forms is a significant feature of scientific writing (Banks 1994a). The motivation for the use of the passive in scientific writing was, for many years, seen in terms of the supposed impersonality and objectivity of the genre. A fairly typical statement of several years ago is that of Cooray:

> The passive voice is frequent in scientific writing. The use of the passive voice here helps the writer to maintain an air of scientific impersonality. (Cooray 1967: 207)

In the same vein, Turner, although his main point is about non-agency, says:

> The impersonal manner of technology and the succinct, objective and orderly language of geometry both promoted the passive of suppressed agency. (Turner, 1972: 190)

Even the highly respected grammar of Quirk and his associates states that:

> The passive is generally more commonly used in informative than in imaginative writing, and is notably more frequent in the objective, impersonal style of scientific articles and news reporting. (Quirk *et al.*, 1985: 166)

This statement is taken virtually word for word from their earlier work (Quirk *et al.*, 1972). Carnet accepts the notion of impersonal style:

> ... l'énonciateur efface l'agent par un style impersonnel et objectif ... (Carnet, 1997: 511)
> [... the speaker evinces the agent with an impersonal, objective style ...]

but he later goes on to point out the importance of thematisation:

> ... la détermination passive correspond à une opération de thématisation. (Carnet, 1997: 514)
> [... the passive determination corresponds to an operation of thematisation.]

The importance of thematic structure in the rhetorical organisation of scientific text, as in other genres, is also pointed out by Gosden (1992).

It is easy to see what is meant by the notion of the impersonality of scientific writing, and the role that the passive might play in this strategy. Nevertheless, if it is admitted that thematic structure is a prime element in the rhetorical organisation of the text, then the passive can be seen as a major resource in that organisation. The passive can then be seen as a resource for placing an element other than the Actor in material process (and its analogue in other types of process) in theme position. Thus, the supposed impersonality produced by not mentioning the agent is the result of the process of thematisation. I do not think that the motivation is to produce impersonal text, and that as a result the thematic structure has non-agentive items in theme position; it is rather that the motivation is to place certain items in theme position, and that in some cases the resource for doing this is the use of the passive. So, the use of the passive is the result of a more extensive strategy of thematisation, not the other way round. It is for this reason that consideration of thematic structure in the *Philosophical Transactions* corpus seems in order.

The grammatical functions of topical themes

The function of Subject coincides with Theme in the majority of cases. It is the major form in all the articles from the nineteenth and twentieth centuries. In the eighteenth-century articles there are two cases where the percentage of ranking clauses with Subject as Theme is less than 50 per cent. This is the case in Smith (1740), where the percentage is 43 per cent, and in Baker (1740), where it is 49 per cent. In Desaguliers (1720) it is 50 per cent. However, percentages in these early articles must be treated with some caution due to the shortness of some of the articles. Of the eighteenth-century articles only Cavallo (1780) has more than 100 ranking clauses. Of the three mentioned above, Smith (1740) has 62, Baker (1740) only 37, and Desaguliers (1720) a mere ten. Where, the Theme is not Subject, it is usually an Adjunct. For the purposes of this study, subordinate clauses (â-clauses) in theme position were considered to be Adjuncts:

> **If the Focal Length of the Eye-glass be ¼ of an Inch**, the Telescope will magnify about 200 times. (Smith, 1740)

> **When the powder is mixed with flowers of sulphur, and heated**, a sulphuret of platinum is formed of a blue colour. (Davy, 1820)

> **If the quantity of moisture which is removed be found experimentally,** the coefficient of diffusion of water vapour into the gas can be deduced. (Townsend, 1900)

A small number of gerundive clauses were also assimilated to Adjuncts of the non-finite clause type:

> **Having electrified the inside of a large *Leyden* bottle plus, by means of a conducting-wire from an excited glass globe,** I set it upon a stand of prepared wood, and took away the conducting-wire; (Wilson, 1760)

> ... and **on refusing the alloy formed,** if a large quantity of arsenic has been used, it has a dingy grey colour, and is very hard and brittle. (Matthiessen, 1860)

> **In concluding this paper,** I wish to record my thanks to Professor MARSHALL WARD for allowing me to carry out this work in his laboratory, and for the constant advice and help which he has given me throughout. (Dawson, 1900)

Subject and Adjunct Themes together account for more than 90 per cent of Themes in all articles. The lowest percentage is 91 per cent in Smith (1740). There are small numbers of Complements, or sometimes part of the Complement where this is a rankshifted clause, functioning as Theme:

> ... **which Point, *R*, where a perfect Image of an Object infinitely distant will be formed,** we call the focus of the Telescope, to distinguish it from the Point, *P*, which we have before called the focus of the Speculum; (Smith, 1740)

> **The above-described condition of the blood-corpuscles during vital turgescence of the vessels,** I think deserving of consideration, in connection with many of the phenomena attending local accumulations of blood both in health and disease; and more especially with reference to increased pulsation, the exudation of colourless fluid, and the heat and redness of inflamed parts. (Barry, 1840)

> **The Bacteroids** he regards as the infecting organisms, (Dawson, 1900)

There are also a small number of Predicators functioning as Theme. There are one or two examples of inverted Predicators and Subjects in the early articles, but otherwise these tend to be imperatives, or, more occasionally, infinitives in extraposed structures (frequently referred to as cases of 'postposed subject' in Systemic Functional Linguistics (Halliday, 2004a)), where the extraposition matrix is a grammatical metaphor functioning as an interpersonal Theme:

insulate a metal plate upon an electric stand, (Cavallo, 1780)

It is necessary **to explain**, that, since making the experiments I am about to describe, my attention has been pointed to similar results obtained by Dr. Faraday in his Ninth Series; (Gassiot, 1840)

Consider now the structure of an ionization front, with the effects of cooling and recombination included. (Axford, 1960)

There are also a small number of extraposition matrices, other than those which are interpersonal grammatical metaphors, which function as topical Theme:

> **It is likewise a considerable Advantage in this Construction**, that the Reflection from the concave Side of the Speculum will do no sensible Prejudice; because the Image of any Object made thereby, is removed to so vast a Distance from the principal Image, formed by the convex Surface, as to create no manner of Confusion or Disturbance in the Vision; which necessarily happens, in some Degree, from the Vicinity of those Images, when the Glass is ground concave on one Side, and as much convex on the other; according to the Method propounded by Sir *Isaac Newton*, in his most excellent Book of *Optics*. (Smith, 1740)

> **It is still a question with some**, whether the blood-corpuscles in the embryo are formed out of granules of the yolk. (Barry, 1840)

> **It is concluded** that the trivial names *orbicularis*, *mccoyi* and *companulatus* describe shape variant and juvenile forms of the species *O. ellipticus* (Sowerby). (Joysey, 1960)

Table 8.1 gives the full details of the grammatical functions of topical Themes in the corpus.

In addition to the above there are very small numbers of cleft elements functioning in theme position. (In systemic Functional Linguistics, cleft sentences are referred to as cases of 'predicated theme' (Halliday, 2004a), or as 'enhanced theme' by those working within the framework of Cardiff Grammar (Fawcett and Huang, 1995; Fawcett, 2000)). There is a single example in the eighteenth century, none at all in the nineteenth, the few remaining being in the twentieth century:

> **It must have been a long Tract of Experience**, which enabled *Dioscorides* and *Theophrastus* to collect and receive from their wise Ancestors, such a lasting Catalogue of the Virtues of Plants as scarce any thing has been added to even to this day. (Blair, 1720)

> **It is only through the study of the post-ecdysial development of the lenses** that this has become clear (*q.v.*), for in the mature eye it is solely

Table 8.1. Percentages of grammatical forms functioning as topical Theme.

	Physical					*Biological*				
	S	*A*	*P*	*C*	*Extra*	*S*	*A*	*P*	*C*	*Extra*
1700	85	10	—	—	5	63	38	—	—	—
1720	50	50	—	—	—	72	22	1	2	1
1740	43	48	3	2	5	49	49	3	—	—
1760	57	40	1	—	2	78	17	5	—	—
1780	59	36	2	—	4	76	23	1	—	—
1800	70	28	—	—	3	81	19	—	—	2
1820	63	36	—	—	*	85	15	—	—	—
1840	58	37	1	1	3	72	23	1	1	3
1860	67	31	—	1	1	63	36	*	*	1
1880	68	31	*	*	*	65	33	*	1	*
1900	63	31	*	—	6	53	43	*	2	2
1920	70	26	—	—	4	72	21	*	—	6
1940	68	27	—	—	5	69	26	1	—	5
1960	66	28	2	—	4	69	26	—	—	5
1980	65	31	—	—	4	77	20	—	1	2

* = < 0.5 per cent

apparent in the real discontinuity of the laminae within and without the intrasceral membrane. (Miller, 1980)

In no instance do these exceed 0.5 per cent, except in Blair (1720) where a single example accounts for 1 per cent, due to the shortness of the article.

The figures for the eighteenth century show the widest variation; this is partly due to the small numbers involved, but it probably also shows that the genre of the scientific research article was, albeit no longer in a state of flux, at least still finding its norms, and not yet fully stabilized. In the physical sciences, the incidence of Subjects as Theme ranges from 43 per cent to 85 per cent, a difference of 42 percentage points, with an average percentage of 58 per cent. If, however, the exceptionally high 85 per cent of Povey 1700 is excluded the average drops to 52 per cent. The biological sciences are rather less varied with a range of 49 per cent to 78 per cent, and an average of 68 per cent. In the nineteenth century the incidence of Subjects as Theme tends to increase, and variability drops. In the physical sector, the range is from 58 per cent to 70 per cent, a difference of 12 points. The change in the biological sector is less marked, with a range of 63 per cent to 85 per cent, a difference of 22 points, the averages being 65 per cent for the physical sciences, and 73 per cent for the biological. In the twentieth century, the figures for the biological sector are comparable with those of the nineteenth century, with a range of 53 per cent to 77 per cent, a difference of 24 points, and an average of 68 per cent. The physical sector, however, seems much more standardised; the range is reduced to seven points, 63 per cent to 70 per cent, with an average of 66 per cent. If only the final four biological articles are considered then the figures are comparable with those for the twentieth-century physical articles: the average is 71 per cent, with a much reduced range of 69 per cent to 77 per cent, eight points.

The incidence of Adjuncts as Theme is virtually the mirror image of Subject as Theme, since together they account for more than 90 per cent of the topical Themes in all the articles of the corpus. In the eighteenth century there is a great deal of variation: 10 per cent to 50 per cent in the physical sector, a difference of 40 points and an average of 37 per cent; 17 per cent to 49 per cent in the biological sector, a difference of 32 points and an average of 30 per cent. In the nineteenth century, there is less variation, particularly in the physical sector where the range is 28 per cent to 37 per cent, a difference of nine points, with an average of 33 per cent. In the biological sector the range is 15 per cent to 36 per cent, a difference of 21 points, and an average of 25 per cent. In the twentieth century, the range for the physical sector is 26 per cent to 31 per cent, a difference of only five points, with an average of 29 per cent. In the biological sector, the range is 21 per cent to 43 per cent, a difference of 22 points with an average of 27 per cent; however, if, as before, Dawson (1900) is excluded and only the final four articles are considered, the range is reduced to 21 per cent to 26 per cent, a difference of five points with an average of 23 per cent.

Predicators functioning as Theme are rare. In the nineteenth and twentieth centuries, they occur in only half of the articles, and never exceed 2 per cent. They account for a larger percentage in the eighteenth century, where they occur in seven of the ten articles. However the apparently higher percentage is more the effect of short articles, rather than greater numbers. Even the 5 per cent of Edwards (1760), is in fact only two examples.

Complements as Theme are, if anything, even rarer. They occur in ten of the 30 articles in the corpus, and never exceed 2 per cent.

Extraposition matrices as Theme are fairly rare in the eighteenth century, occurring in four of the five physical articles, but in only one biological article. Although they can account for as much as 5 per cent, this is in fact only one instance in the case of Povey (1700), and two in Smith (1740). They are slightly more numerous in the nineteenth century, with examples occurring in nine of the ten articles, but never exceeding 3 per cent. In the twentieth century they appear in all the articles and account for 4 per cent to 6 per cent of the Themes in the physical sector, and 2 per cent to 6 per cent in the biological sector. It is therefore interesting to note, that although use of extraposition remains modest, it has nevertheless increased over time, and seems to have become a permanent, if minor, feature in the course of the twentieth century, a fact that will not be lost on those involved in the teaching of scientific writing to non-English speakers.

Textual Themes

Table 8.2 gives the incidence of textual Themes in the articles of the corpus. The incidence of textual Themes has been calculated as a percentage of the ranking clauses. Since the number of ranking clauses with more than one textual Theme is very small, this figure can be taken for practical purposes as being the same as the percentage of ranking clauses containing a textual Theme.

The vast majority of textual Themes which occur are simple single word Themes:

> ... **and** had it been pronounced impracticable to this Day, to make a reflecting Telescope that should equal or excel refracting ones of Ten times its length; though we now see, that most of these Artificers are capable of making them to such a Degree of Perfection as was formerly despaired of. (Smith, 1740)

Table 8.2. Textual Themes as a percentage of ranking clauses.

	Physical	*Biological*
1700	30	31
1720	40	40
1740	58	35
1760	40	19
1780	30	33
1800	37	27
1820	29	52
1840	29	17
1860	20	17
1880	21	7
1900	17	16
1920	18	25
1940	27	28
1960	29	31
1980	12	17

> **Thus** copper, chemically purified, was fused with borax and chloride of sodium (the flux not quite covering the surface of the melted copper). (Matthiessen, 1860)

> **However,** for D-type ionization fronts, all three parameters must be specified. (Axford, 1960)

Even where multiple-word textual Themes occur, these can hardly be said to be any more complex:

> **On the contrary,** I could heartily recommend another Method, hitherto much neglected, and which I am convinc'd would be of great Use, if accurately gone about; (Blair, 1720)

> **... or, in other words,** one thickness of a silk handkerchief interposed between the electrodes of such a powerful battery was sufficient to prevent any perceptible action. (Gassiot, 1840)

> **... for instance,** Mr HOWARD RYLAND (37) reports that with green peas, broad beans, and sweet peas, he has obtained favourable results, but that the effect produced upon French beans was very doubtful. (Dawson, 1900)

It will be noted that in the second of the above examples there are two textual Themes, the second of which, *in other words*, is multi-word. More peculiar examples are exceedingly rare, but the following with an extraposition matrix functioning as textual Theme might be considered an example:

> **It remains to add,** that the cells in question, delineated in that paper, not merely have the same appearance, but are identical with those in Plate XXIX. fig. 7, of the present memoir: in other words, that the chorion is formed of cells which are altered corpuscles of the blood. (Barry, 1840)

This is however an isolated example, and so does not alter the overall picture.

In the eighteenth-century articles, the average percentage of textual Themes in the physical sector is 40 per cent, ranging from 30 per cent to 58 per cent; in the biological sector the average percentage is slightly lower at 30 per cent, with a range of 19 per cent to 40 per cent. In the nineteenth century, the incidence of textual Themes is (even) lower. For the physical articles, the average percentage is 27 per cent, ranging from 20 per cent to 37 per cent, and for the biological articles, the average is 24 per cent, with a range of 7 per cent to 52 per cent. The range here is obviously very wide. In particular, the 7 per cent, which occurs in Owen (1880) seems exceptional. The average for the other four biological articles of the nineteenth century is virtually the same as that for the physical articles, 28 per cent. In the twentieth century, the incidence of textual Themes in the physical articles is lower again. The average percentage is 21 per cent, with a range of 12 per cent to 29 per cent. The reduction is less perceptible in the biological sector, where the average is 23 per cent, with a range of 16 per cent to 31 per cent. Even in the eighteenth century only a minority of ranking clauses have a textual Theme, and although there is a great deal of individual variation, it is possible to see a general tendency over time to an ever lower incidence of textual Themes. Thus from the eighteenth century, where textual Themes occur roughly in one out of three ranking clauses, there is a reduction to a rate of something approaching one in five ranking clauses in the twentieth century. This shows that the genre is one which increasingly allows textual links to remain implicit. This finding again has pedagogical implications for the training of scientists whose native language is not English, particularly those whose mother tongue is a language which requires rather more explicit textual links than is the case in English.

Interpersonal Themes

In view of the common perception of scientific writing as being impersonal, interpersonal Themes take on a particular interest. They are much less frequent than textual Themes. Table 8.3 gives interpersonal Themes as a percentage of ranking clauses.

Table 8.3. Interpersonal Themes as a percentage of ranking clauses.

	Physical	*Biological*
1700	—	—
1720	—	2
1740	13	—
1760	5	7
1780	1	15
1800	—	2
1820	4	—
1840	3	5
1860	2	2
1880	7	2
1900	5	4
1920	5	2
1940	3	5
1960	4	6
1980	2	3

If one takes the average percentage, there seems to be very little change. For the physical sector this is 4 per cent in the eighteenth and twentieth centuries, and 3 per cent in the nineteenth; in the biological sector, it is 5 per cent in the eighteenth century, 2 per cent in the nineteenth, and 4 per cent in the twentieth. However, this masks the fact that, particularly in the eighteenth century there is a great deal of variation. Only six of the ten articles in that century have any examples at all, and of the 29 examples which occur, 17, or almost 60 per cent occur in just two of the articles; there are eight instances in Smith (1740), and 11 in Hunter (1780). In the nineteenth century eight of the ten articles use this resource, and the range is a more modest 2 per cent to 7 per cent. In the twentieth century all of the articles have some interpersonal Themes, with a range similar to that of the nineteenth century, 2 per cent to 6 per cent. Hence, I would claim that use of interpersonal Themes has become more widespread and uniform, even if in terms of raw numbers it is hardly any more frequent. Nevertheless, it must be remembered that interpersonal Themes remain comparatively rare; apart from two articles in the eighteenth century, it never occurs in more than 7 per cent of the ranking clauses.

There are 208 interpersonal Themes in the corpus as a whole. By far the most common means used to encode interpersonal Themes is that of an extraposition matrix functioning as a grammatical metaphor of modality. These account for 89, or 43 per cent, of the total number of interpersonal Themes:

> From hence **it might be supposed**, that the female character contains more truely the specific properties of the animal than the male; (Hunter, 1780)

> but **it is certainly not unimportant** that there exists so perfect a resemblance, in appearance, between two objects, the nature of which has been ascertained. (Barry, 1840)

> **It is at once clear from the above results** that the success or failure of infection does not depend upon the passage of the organism through the soil ... (Dawson, 1900)

Of the 30 articles in the corpus, 20 use this resource on at least one occasion. This includes all of the twentieth-century articles. Joysey (1960) uses it relatively frequently having 14 examples. Moreover, in Lawrence (1940), all eight examples of interpersonal Theme are of this type, as are all eight examples in Duffield (1920), one of these being combined with another preceding interpersonal Theme (and where the extraposed Subject is a cleft structure):

... **indeed, it may be** that it is the undiminished momentum of the electron as it leaves the atom which has been measured. (Duffield, 1920)

This obviously relates to the well-documented question of hedging in scientific writing (Hyland, 1998; Banks, 1994a, 1994b; Salager-Meyer, 1994, 1998; Salager-Meyer and Defives, 1998; Salager-Meyer *et al.*, 1996), whereby the scientific author reduces the force of what he wishes to say in order to avoid possible confrontation or criticism. There are, in addition, a dozen examples of clausal items functioning as interpersonal Theme, which therefore are also grammatical metaphors of modality:

> **It seems** they have narrowly considered their *Facies externa*, and thus concluded; If such a Plant partake of such Virtues, such another so very like to it, must be endow'd with the same ... (Blair, 1720)

> ... but **what was more important to me for the object I had in view**, I proved the correct action of my instrument; (Gassiot, 1840)

> **There is thus no doubt** that the structural elements observed in the visual apparatus, as well as finer architectural details such as lamination were originally present and are not artefacts produced either by diagenesis or preparation. (Miller, 1980)

These examples function in a way not dissimilar to the extraposition type.

Markers which indicate the mood of a clause function as interpersonal Themes when they are in initial position in the clause. This is notably the case of *let*, as an indicator of directive (or imperative) mood. There are 45 examples of this in the corpus, that is, 22 per cent of the interpersonal Themes. Although this feature occurs throughout the period, with eight examples in the eighteenth-century articles, 17 in the nineteenth, and 20 in the twentieth, they tend to be concentrated in a small number of articles. Indeed, 40 of the 45 examples occur in just three articles, Smith (1740) (six examples), Glazebrook (1880) (16 examples), and Townsend (1900) (20 examples). Moreover in these three articles the examples occur almost exclusively in a mathematical context. In Smith (1780) this is basically geometrical with reference to a geometrical figure:

> ... **let** *HP* the given Distance of the Point in the Axis *H*, from the Focal Point *P*, be called *d*; (Smith, 1780)

The examples in Glazebrook (1880) and Townsend (1900) are even more clearly mathematical in nature, relating to modelling or calculation:

> **Let** $PR_1 = \theta_1$ (Glazebrook, 1880)

> **Let** θ_n and $\theta_{n'}$ be such values of θ as will make φ_n and $\varphi_{n'}$ vanish at the surface S of the region throughout which the above volume integral is taken. (Townsend, 1900)

Examples which are unconnected with mathematics do occur, but these are comparatively rare, and none of this type are used in the twentieth century articles, where all the examples are related to mathematics:

> **Let** a slender brass, or iron wire, five or six inches long, and finely pointed at each end, be fitted in the middle, with a brass cap, void of angles; then **let** half an inch at each extremity be bent in opposite directions, till they are perpendicular to the rest of the wire, and in such a manner, that when the wire is suspended, by means of its cap, on a point of metal, it may lie in a plane parallel to the horizon. (Wilson, 1760)

> **Let** us now examine the results obtained by the experiments detailed in this paper; (Gassiot, 1840)

It will be noted that the example from Wilson (1760) has two examples in consecutive clauses, but these are the only examples in the article.

A Finite can also function as an interpersonal Theme, the most obvious example being the standard interrogative form, with Finite followed by Subject. As one might expect this is extremely rare in the scientific journal article. Finites as interpersonal Theme occur in only four articles in the corpus and the total number of examples is seven. In the two earliest of the articles concerned (Hunter, 1780 and Davy, 1820 with a total of three examples), it is not a question of interrogative form, but the thematisation of the negative conjunction *nor*, which induces the corresponding thematisation of the Finite:

> ... **nor is** the ignited metal extinguished by exposure to the atmosphere, or by blowing the breath on it; (Davy, 1820)

In the two later articles (Barry, 1840 and Dawson, 1900) it is a question of the interrogative, and of the four examples, three occur in consecutive clauses in Dawson 1900:

> **Is** it a case of chemiotaxis, depending upon certain variations in the composition of the excreta from the root-hairs; or **does** it result from the production by the invading organism itself of some form of ferment capable of dissolving the cell-wall; or again, **is** it a question of some special state of external conditions, which react either upon the organism or upon the roots, such as the chemical composition of the air surrounding the root-hairs, its degree of humidity, temperature, and so forth? (Dawson, 1900)

At all events, it is evident that Finites as interpersonal Themes are extremely rare in this corpus, and, one may presume in the scientific research article in general.

Modal and attitudinal adverbs are probably most people's prototypical interpersonal Themes. In this corpus however they are less frequent than extraposition matrices and than cases of *let* functioning as interpersonal Theme. There are 23 examples of modal adverbs functioning as interpersonal Themes in the corpus; they thus account for 11 per cent of the interpersonal Themes. Moreover they are not evenly distributed across the corpus. There are no examples in the eighteenth-century articles, and only four in the nineteenth-century articles. The majority (19 examples occur in the twentieth-century articles, but even here they are not evenly distributed, only six of the ten articles have any examples, and Axford (1960) has seven, more than a third of the twentieth century sample. No lexical item occurs more than three times, and only five lexical items occur more than once; these are: *certainly, clearly, fortunately, normally* and *probably*.

> ... **probably** it is common air, as the oxide appears to undergo no change by being kept for some weeks in ammonia. (Davy, 1820)

> **Certainly**, were the calcite composition of both bowl and core different in this way, this might give the required shift in refractive index to enable them to function as correcting elements as discussed on page 478. (Miller, 1980)

Those which occur only once are: *actually, apparently, evidently, generally, obviously, personally, possibly, presumably, similarly, undoubtedly,* and *usually*.

Other modal phrases functioning as interpersonal Theme are extremely rare: four examples in the whole of the corpus, of which three are the phrase *in general:*

> **In general**, it is difficult to attribute a zoological meaning to the values of the slope and intercept of a straight line which has been fitted to an arithmetical plot of a growth curve. (Joysey, 1960)

There are a small number of words or phrases which operate as interpersonal intensifiers, functioning as Theme. There are 17 examples of these, so they account for 8 per cent of the interpersonal Themes. Of these 17, eight are *in fact*, and *indeed* occurs six times; the others with one occurrence each are *in any case, in particular,* and *of course*. Here again, the few examples are concentrated in the twentieth century:

> **Indeed**, this cooling may be so strong that the overall effect of the ionization process is to reduce the total energy of the fluid, rather than to add to it. (Axford, 1960)

There is only one example for the eighteenth century and three for the nineteenth.

There remain a couple of anomalous phrases, in early articles, which function as interpersonal Themes, and which I add here for interest:

> Therefore, **in my humble opinion**, a most proper Means to find out the Virtues of Plants, is to have recourse to the proper *Menstruums*. (Blair, 1720)

> And here, **with your Lordship's leave**, I shall set down some farther experiments, most of which have been made with a view to shew, that a *plus* electricity may be produced by means of a *minus* electricity. (Wilson, 1760)

Thus, while interpersonal Themes are never numerous, where they do occur they tend to take the form of extraposition matrices, the mood marker *let*, or modal adverbs, in that order. Other forms are so infrequent that they cannot be considered features of this genre, though in some cases one might argue that their absence might constitute a feature.

Thematic progression

The notion of thematic progression was originally developed within the Prague School framework (Firbas, 1992; Carter-Thomas, 2000). This has been taken over by numerous linguistic approaches, and I think that two of the forms of progression proposed are particularly important (Banks, 2005c). These are those where the Theme is derived from the Rheme of a previous clause, though not necessarily the immediately preceding clause, and those where the Theme is derived from the Theme of a previous clause, though, again, not necessarily the immediately preceding clause. The first of these is linear Theme, and the second, constant Theme. The third type of theme usually referred to, hypertheme, it seems to me, is not of the same order, indicating rather the topic or general subject matter of a stretch of text; it will frequently be present in a given clause in addition to constant and linear thematic progression. Although the relationship between genre and type of progression is complex (McCabe, 2004; Crompton, 2004), there does seem to be some tendency for explanatory or expository texts to use linear progression, and for descriptive texts to use constant progression. According to Bloor and Bloor (1995) constant progression:

> is common in short passages of biographical information … and sometimes in narratives which focus on the behaviour of one person. It is also

frequently found in textbooks and descriptions of factual information focusing on a particular thing or concept. (Bloor and Bloor, 1995: 90)

Halliday (1988[1], 1994[3]) points out the importance of linear progression in scientific writing, where he specifically relates it to the creation of grammatical metaphor.

There is therefore an expectancy that scientific writing, particularly the research article, will use linear progression rather more than constant progression. In order to see to what extent this is true over time, the *Philosophical Transactions* corpus has been analysed for constant and linear thematic progression. The situation is obviously complex, and as in any text, long stretches with the same type of progression are rare. However these do occasionally occur. In the following thematic structure analysis of a short extract from Dawson (1900), the progression is systematically made up of links of the linear type:

Th1 → Rh1	Accordingly I		allowed pea seed to to germinate between layers of cotton wool, until the radicles were about one inch long
	Th:txt	Th:top	Rh
↙ Th2 → Rh2	These		I then dropped with sterile forceps into tubes containing well wetted plugs of cotton wool, the tubes having of course been very thoroughly sterilised beforehand
		Th:top	Rh
↙ Th3 → Rh3	In these		the seedlings were steamed in a water bath for ten to fifteen minutes, in order to kill the roots
		Th:top	Rh
↙ Th4 → Rh4	After cooling		I infected the roots with drops of water contain ing nitragin, and then kept the tubes in the dark
		Th:top	Rh
↙ Th5 → Rh5	In about ten days		a good growth was obvious along the radicles
		Th:top	Rh
↙ Th6 → Rh6	and	upon examination	the organism present appeared to be the one for which I was seeking
	Th:txt	Th:top	Rh
↙ Th7 → Rh7	I		consequently tried to separate it in a pure state by means of plate cultures
		Th:top	Rh
↙ Th8 → Rh8	but		all my attempts failed owing to a rapid liquefying of the gelatine solution
	Th:txt	Th:top	

Although some of these links may seem more tenuous than others, they provide a reasonably good example of a short stretch of text displaying linear progression.

In a similar way, short stretches of text displaying constant Theme occur. This tends to occur where an individual researcher is ascribed a series of actions, or in descriptive passages, as in the following comparatively simple example from Davy (1820). The sequence is broken by a single linear link between Rheme 3 and Theme 4, due to the nature of the coordinate clause:

Th1 → Rh1   The oxide thus prepared   exhibits the following characteristics
            Th:top   Rh
            It   has the metallic lustre

Th2 → Rh2   Th:top   Rh
            It   is sufficiently hard to cut brass, which it polishes

Th3 → Rh3   Th:top   Rh
     ↙   and   when the polished surface is   a delicate coating of

Th4 → Rh4   rubbed a little with the oxide,   platinum remains
            Th:txt   Th:top   Rh
    (from Th3)

Th5 → Rh5   It   does not touch steel
                 Th:top   Rh
            It   is not affected by cold or hot water, nor by the nitrous,

Th6 → Rh6   sulphuric; or phosphoric acid at a boiling heat
            Th:top   Rh
            It   is insoluble in nitro-muriatic acid, and in cold muriatic

Th7 → Rh7   acid
            Th:top   Rh
            but   it   slowly dissolves in this last acid by the assis

Th8 → Rh8   tance of heat.
            Th:txt   Th:top   Rh
            It   is not acted upon by a strong solution of the fixed alkalies

Th9 → Rh9   Th:top   Rh
                 When the oxide is put   minute globules of air are evolved

Th10 → Rh10   into liquid ammonia,   from it
              Th:top   Rh

Table 8.4 gives instances of linear and constant progression as a percentage of the number of ranking clauses for each of the articles in the corpus. There are in each article a number of cases where a theme cannot be analysed as either linear or constant, notably where a new theme is introduced. These do not appear in the table, but their incidence can be seen from the difference of the sum of the two percentages for each article and 100 per cent.

This is an admittedly blunt instrument, as the simple identification of linear and constant links masks a myriad of more sophisticated strategies of

Table 8.4. Linear and constant progression as a percentage of ranking clauses.

1700–1780						
	Physical			*Biological*		
	Ranking n	*Linear per cent*	*Constant per cent*	*Ranking n*	*Linear per cent*	*Constant per cent*
1700	20	30	25	16	44	31
1720	10	30	40	85	33	46
1740	62	48	15	37	43	19
1760	88	25	17	41	32	32
1780	106	35	22	75	55	27

1800–1880						
	Physical			*Biological*		
	Ranking n	*Linear per cent*	*Constant per cent*	*Ranking n*	*Linear per cent*	*Constant per cent*
1800	71	61	24	59	39	44
1820	221	43	47	27	33	52
1840	156	42	40	208	43	41
1860	81	51	36	289	53	36
1880	256	59	25	46	46	35

1900–1980						
	Physical			*Biological*		
	Ranking n	*Linear per cent*	*Constant per cent*	*Ranking n*	*Linear per cent*	*Constant per cent*
1900	431	55	26	452	62	26
1920	279	39	42	203	47	38
1940	175	59	23	176	53	26
1960	503	57	31	433	46	39
1980	278	57	32	295	51	37

discourse construction, and development of argumentation. It nevertheless gives a general picture of the overall working of thematic progression in these texts.

The hypothesis that linear progression is more frequent than constant progression is shown to be generally true. Of the 30 articles in the corpus, on only six occasions is constant progression more frequent than linear progression. In the physical sector, this occurs once in each century (Desaguliers, 1720; Davy, 1820; Duffield, 1920). In the biological sector, this also occurs on three occasions, once in the eighteenth and twice in the nineteenth century (Blair, 1720; Home, 1800; Knight, 1820); this means that there are no examples in the biological sample from 1840 onwards. Looking at these individually, Desaguliers (1720) is, in any case, very short (the shortest in the corpus) with only ten ranking clauses. The constant links tend to occur in the straightforward narrating of his experiment:

> **A little Thermometer being held in the first Vessel of cold Water so as to have its Ball cover'd with the Water**, upon the putting in the Flask of warm Water, the Spirit rose 2 degrees; **then putting the Thermometer into the Water where the Flask that has the *Mercury* was**, the Spirit rose three degrees higher. **The Thermometer** being again put into the first Vessel fell 4 degrees, and afterwards again into the last it rose almost 3 degrees. (Desaguliers, 1720)

Davy (1820) describes a series of chemical experiments, and many of the constant links occur in descriptions of the substances produced. An example is given in the thematic analysis above, and this is a further example:

> **The substance** is of a black colour, and in small lumps, which are soft to the touch, and easily reduced to an impalpable powder. **It** readily soils the fingers or paper. **It** is destitute of lustre. **It** is tasteless and apparently unaffected either by cold or hot water. **It** has a peculiar ethereal smell that is not easily removed, and probably arises from the presence of a little inflammable matter occasioned by the action of the alcohol. **It** seems to undergo no change by exposure to the air for some time. **When it is gently heated, on a slip of platinum or paper**, a hissing noise or a feeble explosion is produced ... (Davy, 1820)

The description of electrical experiments play an important part in Duffield (1920), and this is where many of his constant links occur:

> **The deflection corrected for convexion** is therefore 47 degrees, corresponding to 1.22 dynes. **The couple due to convexion** is in this experiment approximately 36 per cent of the ideal couple upon the poles, **and it** corresponds to a negative pressure of −0.44 dyne. (Duffield, 1920)

Turning to the biological examples, Blair (1720) is attempting to show that the medicinal virtues of plants are indicated by their form. Some of his constant links occur in descriptive sections, while others occur where the Themes are members of a list:

> **The Corymbiferous kind**, are either Stomachicks, Hystericks, and Vermifuges. The Gentian Bitters, Stomachicks, Hystericks, and Febrifuges. **The *Pomiseræ Scandentes*, as Cucumbers, Melons, &c.** are Coolers; **but some** are Cathartick, as *Cucumis sylvestris*, and *Colocynthis*. **The Convolvulvi, as *Mechoacanna*, &c.** are Purgative; (Blair, 1720)

Home (1800) is describing an unusual zoological specimen, and it is precisely in descriptive passages that the constant links tend to occur:

> **The tongue** is extremely short, not half an inch long; and the moveable portion not more than a quarter of an inch; **the papillæ on its surface** are long, and of a conical form. **When the tongue is drawn in**, it can be brought intirely into the mouth; **and, when extended**, can be projected about a quarter of an inch into the beak. (Home, 1800)

Knight (1820) is again a comparatively short article, the shortest after the eighteenth century, with only 27 ranking clauses. It describes an experiment carried out on oak trees. Constant links occur, again, in the narration of the experiment carried out:

> **The one** was deprived of its bark, to as great an extent as the inexperience of my workmen permitted me to have done without danger to them, **and it** was then suffered to remain standing. **The other tree** was felled, and, in the usual manner, immediately stript of its bark; **and the trunk** was then removed to a situation in which it was securely protected from the sun and rain. (Knight, 1820)

Thus, although this is not systematically the case, the two features which seem to favour the use of constant progression are description of substances or specimens, and narration of the experiment. This does not mean that description and narration will invariably be in this form, far from it, but where constant progression is used it is frequently in these contexts. In the case of the narration of experiments, it is where the experiment is related as a simple sequence of actions.

In the physical sector, linear progression accounts for roughly a third of the ranking clauses in the eighteenth century, but with a fair degree of variation, 25 per cent–48 per cent. In the nineteenth century, this rises to about a half, and in the twentieth century, this remains at about the same rate. If there is a difference between the nineteenth and twentieth centuries, it is that in the twentieth century the figures become more stable. In the nineteenth century there is still considerable variation, 42 per cent–61 per cent, whereas, in the twentieth century, if one excludes the exceptional Duffield (1920), all the values are in the narrow range of 55 per cent–57 per cent. In the biological sector, the values for the eighteenth and nineteenth centuries are similar, with an average of just over 40 per cent, and a range from the low 30s to the low 50s. In the twentieth century however, linear progression occurs at a rate similar to that for the physical sector, just over 50 per cent, but with rather more variation, 47 per cent–62 per cent. Use of constant links is more common in the biological than the physical sector. In the physical sector, it accounts on average for 24 per cent of the ranking clauses in the eighteenth century, whereas the corresponding figure for the biological sector is 31 per cent. However the variation in each case is fairly wide, from 15 per cent to 40 per cent for the physical articles, and 19 per cent to 46 per cent for the biological articles. On average, use of constant links rises in the nineteenth century, to 34 per cent in the physical sector and 42 per cent in the biological sector, with about the same variation in the physical sector, 24 per cent to 47 per cent, but rather less in the biological sector, 35 per cent to 52 per cent. The average rates remain similar, in fact a slight fall, for the twentieth century, 31 per cent for the physical sector and 38 per cent for the biological sector, but with reduced variation; this is 23 per cent to 42 per cent for the physical sector, but only 26 per cent to 32 per cent if Duffield (1920) is discounted, and 26 per cent to 39 per cent in the biological articles. Thus over time there seems to have been a tendency for the use of linear and constant thematic links to stabilise at something just over 50 per cent for linear links, and round about a third for constant links, in both the physical and biological fields.

9   The semantic nature of Themes

A typology of Themes

In order to attempt to see what sort of items are selected as (topical) Theme, and thus taken as the speaker's starting point in the presentation of clauses, the Themes have been classified in terms of 14 categories. These, with examples, are as follows:

1.   The object of study or observation (Obj):

The Calamine is digged out of certain Mines, of which there are several in the West of *England*, (as about *Mendip*, &c.) which lye about 20 Foot deep, as coals do, thence brought up by Sea. (Povey, 1700)

The moulting process in trilobites has twofold significance for palaeontology. (Miller, 1980)

2.   The experiment and the experimental process (Exp); these can be expected to be less frequent in the biological articles, particular in the earlier period:

The double-arc method was adopted because it eliminated the electromagnetic effects upon the movable parts of the circuit due to the earth's field and to the rest of the circuit; (Duffield, 1920)

The plots chosen had been previously employed for the cultivation of peas and beans, but had never before been planted with Lucerne or clover. (Dawson, 1900)

3.   The equipment used in the experiment, or more occasionally in the observation process (Equip):

The upper part of the tube CDMN is shaped tapering to a smaller extremity, which is entirely covered with sealing wax melted by the heat, and not dissolved in spirits. (Cavallo, 1780)

These tubes were also wider and longer than those employed in the former series of experiments. (Dawson, 1900)

4.   Observation and the process of observation (Obs). This obviously relates mainly to the biological sector, only occurring marginally in one physical article:

When I first observed these phenomena, I thought that there was no apparent reason why the powder of rosin should be attracted by those parts of the electrophorus, which are in a positive state of electricity, and not by those that are negative. (Cavallo, 1780)

In the course of the individual examination of this large number of blastoids, several abnormal specimens of *O. derbiensis* were found, some of which are worthy of special note, as the syndrome is present in more than one individual. (Joysey, 1960)

5.   References to the author himself or to a group to which he belongs, including (in fact, mainly) first person pronouns (Auth):

I provided a small stand, with four short legs, and covered it with white paper. (Herschel, 1800)

… and **I** found that each substance permanently retained moisture nearly in the same proportion that it absorbed it. (Knight, 1820)

6.   References to persons other than the author (Oth); usually, but not exclusively other scientists:

Kahn gave equations representing the conversion of mass, momentum and energy across the ionization front, and showed that there is a close analogy between combustion waves and ionization fronts. (Axford, 1960)

Lady Tynte had a favourite pyed pea-hen, which had produced chickens eight several times; (Hunter, 1780)

7.   Metalinguistic references, or references to other parts of the text (Meta):

Table VII gives the results of these calculations. (Glazebrook, 1880)

… and **the following points** indicate that it is not: (Lawrence, 1940)

8.   References to other texts (Inter):

… **in GMELIN's 'Chemistry'** it is also stated that copper which contains even 0.1 percent. of lead cannot either be drawn into fine wire or rolled into thin sheets. (Matthiessen, 1860)

A series of papers has been published which are concerned with the investigation of the nature of the anthocyanins present in a variety of plants and in various organs, including flowers, fruits and leaves (Robinson and Robinson 1931, 1932*a*, 1933, 1934; Lawrence, Price Robinson and Robinson 1938; Price and Sturgess 1938). (Lawrence, 1940)

9. Existential clauses (Exist). This is restricted to existential *there* functioning as Theme:

There were two main modifications based on the experience of work subsequent to that on Be; (Hartress, 1940)

There is no sex of any animal whatever that has any peculiarity in shape when born, or when young; (Hunter, 1780)

10. Field of study (Field). This is in fact very rare but has been used for a very small number of cases that could not otherwise be categorised:

The chemical history of platinum, is far from being complete. (Davy, 1820)

The second field where moulting is of importance is that of trilobite biology. (Miller, 1980)

11. References to mental processes and argumentation, including the argument structure of the article itself (Ment). This includes some examples which are in the form of an extraposition matrix, and some which are imperative Predicators:

It is to be observed here, that the plus appearance in the poker was caused by that portion of the fluid; which was driven off from the outside of the bottle, by the repulsive force of the fluid conveyed into the bottle. (Wilson, 1760)

. . . but before any conclusions can be drawn, two assumptions must be made: (Lawrence, 1940)

12. Expressions indicating time (Time):

Later, the same experiment was repeated with a glass tube of the same length and inner diameter as the lunar core-tube to visually examine the artificial strata for possible disturbances. (Horai, 1980)

Fifteen years ago, one *John Potin, French-man*, the Servant to my Lord *Culpeper*, got a fall, which caused him a heavy pain in the Breast for a while. (Lafage, 1700)

13. Expressions of radical modality, known as 'modulation' in Halliday's terminology (Halliday, 2004a), (Rad). These are mainly in the form of extraposition matrices:

It will now be easy to draw the results of these observations into a very narrow compass. (Herschel, 1800)

... but **it has been possible** to trace only one sample with additional locality data (Joysey, 1960)

14. Mathematical expressions and references to mathematical calculation (Math). These occur mainly in the later articles:

The partial differential equations which describe the development of an ionized region around a star have been given by Goldsworthy (1960). (Axford 1960)

... and hence *a* and *b* are the slope and intercept of the growth line when *x* and *y* are plotted on a double logarithmic scale. (Joysey, 1960)

The details for the articles in the corpus are given in Table 9.1. For ease of comparison, these are given in terms of percentages per article, despite the small numbers involved in some cases.

I would not wish to claim that these categories are watertight. Some of the categories have significant grey areas at their boundaries. The object of study is closely involved in the experiment in the physical domain or the observation in the biological domain, and hence there is a certain fluidity between these categories. In the same way, the equipment used is part of the experiment, hence there is a degree of overlap at this point. There is also an area where references to others and references to other texts come together, since the texts are obviously written by others, and some cases may be ambiguous between the writer and his text. Nevertheless, these figures provide an interesting picture of the way in which the scientific author selects clausal starting points in the logogenesis of his discourse.

Minor types of Theme

Some of the categories are only of marginal interest. This is notably the case for the field of study which only appears in three of the articles in the sample, and even then in very small numbers, never accounting for more than 1 per cent of the Themes in the articles concerned. Also fairly marginal in overall terms is the case of radical modality. This appears in three eighteenth-century articles, four nineteenth-century articles, and six twentieth-century articles. There seems, then, to be an increase in the use of this type of Theme over time, appearing in over half of the twentieth-century articles, and three of the four articles from 1960 onwards. It has therefore a certain significance for

Table 9.1. Percentages per article of semantic categories of Themes.

	Physical				
	1700	*1720*	*1740*	*1760*	*1780*
Obj	55	—	52	5	7
Exp	15	90	11	69	55
Equip	—	—	—	—	16
Obs	—	—	—	—	1
Auth	5	10	5	9	5
Oth	20	—	6	7	2
Meta	—	—	8	—	5
Inter	—	—	—	2	—
Exist	—	—	3	1	—
Field	—	—	—	—	—
Ment	—	—	11	7	7
Time	—	—	—	—	3
Rad	5	—	2	—	3
Math	—	—	2	—	—

	Biological				
	1700	*1720*	*1740*	*1760*	*1780*
Obj	50	54	32	68	60
Exp	—	7	5	—	—
Equip	—	—	3	—	—
Obs	—	10	16	5	1
Auth	13	7	8	5	13
Oth	—	10	5	5	4
Meta	—	1	5	5	4
Inter	—	7	5	7	3
Exist	—	1	—	2	7
Field	—	—	—	—	—
Ment	6	1	16	2	3
Time	31	—	3	—	5
Rad	—	—	—	—	—
Math	—	—	—	—	—

	Physical				
	1700	*1720*	*1740*	*1760*	*1780*
Obj	6	21	5	28	14
Exp	62	59	47	38	18
Equip	3	1	10	4	3

Obs	—	—	—	—	—
Auth	14	7	10	15	12
Oth	—	3	8	2	1
Meta	—	*	6	1	9
Inter	1	*	1	—	1
Exist	1	*	1	—	1
Field	—	*	—	—	—
Ment	10	3	8	2	8
Time	—	4	1	—	—
Rad	1	—	—	1	—
Math	—	—	—	2	34

Biological

	1700	1720	1740	1760	1780
Obj	92	48	50	44	63
Exp	—	15	1	43	2
Equip	—	—	—	—	—
Obs	2	—	6	1	9
Auth	—	19	10	4	4
Oth	2	—	3	*	4
Meta	—	—	9	—	2
Inter	—	—	8	—	4
Exist	3	—	3	1	4
Field	—	—	—	—	—
Ment	—	11	7	6	4
Time	—	7	2	1	2
Rad	2	—	1	—	—
Math	—	—	—	—	—

Physical

	1700	1720	1740	1760	1780
Obj	17	20	25	30	24
Exp	25	39	—	2	22
Equip	8	7	—	*	11
Obs	—	—	—	—	—
Auth	5	6	4	1	2
Oth	2	3	1	5	1
Meta	1	7	6	3	4
Inter	1	*	1	1	—
Exist	*	2	3	2	*
Field	—	—	—	—	—
Ment	5	11	6	12	5

Time	—	*	—	1	1
Rad	1	—	2	—	2
Math	34	2	51	43	27

	Biological				
	1700	*1720*	*1740*	*1760*	*1780*
Obj	31	61	65	53	74
Exp	30	—	2	—	—
Equip	2	—	—	1	*
Obs	3	3	—	11	7
Auth	7	3	2	2	2
Oth	9	17	1	5	6
Meta	2	4	7	1	2
Inter	2	3	3	3	1
Exist	—	2	3	3	2
Field	—	—	1	—	*
Ment	7	5	15	7	3
Time	7	*	—	2	*
Rad	*	—	—	2	1
Math	—	—	—	9	—

* < 0.5

the contemporary article in that it tends to be present though only in small numbers. Moreover, as has already been noted, its most common formal feature by far is that of extraposition, where the modality involved is that of dynamic possibility or necessity:

> **It has, unfortunately, not proved possible** to count accurately the number of lens files on the intaglio of AMNH 29282 owing to considerable flattening and distortion of the eyes. (Miller, 1980)

> Thus **it is not necessary** to extract the sample from the core-tube to make the measurements. (Horai, 1980)

Those interested in formal features will note that in these cases the extraposed Subject is most frequently an infinitive clause. An extraposed *that*-clause usually occurs in cases where the extraposition matrix is functioning as an interpersonal Theme, being a grammatical metaphor of (epistemic) modality.

Existential Themes also occur in modest proportions. These occur in five of the eighteenth-century articles, eight of the nineteenth-century articles, and nine of the twentieth-century articles. Hence, although it is not particularly prevalent in the eighteenth century, it is a small but standard feature from the beginning of the nineteenth century. It also seems to be slightly more frequent in the biological articles, where it accounts for 3 per cent or 4 per cent in five articles in the two later centuries, whereas it only reaches 3 per cent in one physical article of the same period. These two features, themes of radical modality and existential Themes, although occurring in small numbers, are significant for those involved in the teaching of scientific discourse to non-anglophone speakers (Banks, 1994c, 1995).

Time is also a minor feature which increases over time. Temporal Themes occur in four of the eighteenth-century articles, six of those in the nineteenth, and seven of those in the twentieth century. In each case they occur in more biological than physical articles. It may be the nature of biological, as opposed to physical, research that needs to be placed within a thematised temporal framework. Moreover, while in most cases temporal Themes account for no more than 1 per cent or 2 per cent, and rise to no more than a maximum of 4 per cent in the physical field (in Davy, 1820), there are individual cases in the biological field where the rate is much higher: even allowing for the anomalous 31 per cent of Lafage (1700), there is 7 per cent in the case of Dawson (1900), and 7 per cent in the case of Knight (1820). Dawson (1920) includes an extensive literature review, which, in fact becomes a history of the area of study into which her own work fits. Thus the work of others is frequently framed as a temporal narrative:

> **Also during 1897** ZINSLER (18) working in Leipzig upon the conditions of infection with Rhizobium made use of silicic acid jelly, which was introduced by WINOGRADSKY for the isolation of nitrifying bacteria. (Dawson, 1900)

It is within the time framework thus established that her own work is then placed, though in terms of number of occurrences this is much less frequent:

> In October, 1897, I began the study of this subject by the microscopic examination of nodules of different ages from the roots of different genera and species of the Leguminosæ, amongst which were *Vickie hirsute, V. Faber, V. saliva, Possum stadium, Hippocratic multisiliquosa, Trifolium maritimum, Lathyrus aphaca, L. Chymenium, Lupinus albus, L. luteus, Phaseolus multiflorus.* (Dawson, 1900)

Knight (1820) deals with an experiment on the wood of oak trees. Since this article is relatively short, there are only a few actual examples, but where these occur, it is the fairly long time span of the procedure which requires the thematising of the time frame:

The following winter, in December, the other tree (which still retained life) was felled, and its trunk immediately placed in the same situation with that of the other tree; (Knight, 1820)

Features of the experiment

At the other end of the scale the object of study is a virtually omnipresent Theme. Only one early article, Desaguliers (1720), does not display this type of Theme. The proportion of Themes that relate to the object of study is particularly high in the biological sector, ranging from 32 per cent to 68 per cent in the eighteenth century, 44 per cent to 92 per cent in the nineteenth, and 31 per cent to 74 per cent in the twentieth. Hence there seems to have been little change from this point of view over the period covered, with perhaps a tendency towards the upper end of the scale in the more recent articles, in the sense that no biological article has had a rate of less than 50 per cent since 1900. In the physical sector, this type of Theme is always present (with the single exception of Desaguliers (1720)) but in rather smaller proportions. In the eighteenth century the variation is wide, two articles having small percentages (5 per cent and 7 per cent), and two having over 50 per cent (55 per cent and 52 per cent). In the nineteenth century the range is 5 per cent to 28 per cent, and in the twentieth 17 per cent to 30 per cent. If the first half of the eighteenth century is discounted, there seems to be a tendency to rise over time, though the proportions never reach the high levels exhibited in the biological sector. Thus it would seem to be reasonable to say that the authors of biological articles take their object of study as thematic starting point more frequently than the authors of physical articles do.

The fact that the authors of physical articles thematise the object of study less frequently than the authors of biological articles has to be balanced against their respective use of the experiment itself as Theme. In the physical sector, the experiment appears as Theme in all but one (Hartree, 1940) of the articles. In the biological sector, it appears in two of the eighteenth-century articles, four of the nineteenth-century articles, and two of the twentieth-century articles. Moreover, only two of the physical articles, Hartree (1940), already mentioned, and Axford (1960), have less than 18 per cent, whereas only three of the biological articles have more than 10 per cent. Hence the authors of physical articles thematise the experiment itself much more than the authors of biological articles. This has a great deal to do with the fact that the biological sciences in general did not become experimental until the mid-nineteenth century, but it will be noted that this does not have a significant effect on the thematisation patterns, which are higher in some individual cases, but not in general. Although this type of Theme is used extensively in the physical sector, its importance dwindles over time. In the eighteenth century, its rate of use is comparatively high, though with wide variation, from 11 per cent to 90 per cent, the average being 48 per cent. In the nineteenth century, the average falls to 34 per cent, though this is mainly due to the comparatively low 18 per cent for Glazebrook (1880), which seems to foreshadow the lower figures of the twentieth century. The average for 1800–1860 is 52 per cent. The range for the nineteenth century as a whole is 18 per cent to 62 per cent. The lower proportion of Glazebrook (1880) is continued in the twentieth century with an average of 18 per cent, ranging from none to 39 per cent. Hence although the physical sciences are basically experimental, in terms of thematisation, interest is turning to other features (or one particular other feature, as we shall see below) from the late nineteenth century on. In the biological sector, as we have said, only eight of the 15 articles use experiment as Theme, and this is in very small numbers, with three exceptions, Knight (1820), De la Rue (1860) and Dawson (1900). Knight (1820), as we have seen, seems to be a forerunner of experimental technique in the biological field. However, his experiments are not laboratory experiments for they concern the wood of oak trees:

> But **efforts** have been made, and supposed to be successful, to obtain the advantages of both seasons of felling, by taking off the bark in spring, and suffering the tree to stand till the ensuing winter. (Knight, 1820)

After the mid-nineteenth century watershed, De la Rue (1860) has 43 per cent of its Themes dealing with the experimental process. The article describes a series of experiments of chemical analysis, whose object is to discover the chemical properties of a gum or resin from a species of *Ficus:*

> **By the addition of a little water** a small quantity of syncoretin was then thrown down, in order to carry down the last traces of the less soluble crystalline compound, in case any were still present. (De La Rue, 1860)

Dawson (1900) is trying to establish the properties of a substance known commercially as nitragin. This question had apparently been a subject of controversy in the recent past. She presents a series of experiments with the object of analysing this substance:

> **With this method** I obtained very promising results, (Dawson, 1900)

So from the mid-nineteenth century on, the more observational nature of the biological articles is disturbed by the inclusion of experimentally orientated articles; in our sample this occurs in two out of seven articles.

The equipment used is evidently closely connected to the experiment, and the equipment appears as Theme, as one would expect, more frequently in the physical than in the biological articles. However this does not apply to the eighteenth century where equipment as Theme only occurs in one article from the physical sector and one article from the biological sector. Nevertheless, from 1780 onwards it is a permanent feature of the physical articles, with the exception of Hartree (1940). Otherwise its incidence varies from a trace (less than 0.5 per cent) to 11 per cent. In the biological sector, it appears in none of the nineteenth century articles, and three of the twentieth century articles, where it never accounts for more than 2 per cent.

The process of observation is to the biological sector what, in many ways the process of experimentation is to the physical sector. They can be thought of almost as mirror images of each other. Thus, observation as Theme is rare in the physical sector, but virtually systematic in the biological sector. Indeed in the physical sector it only accounts for 1 per cent of the Themes in one of the articles in the sample. In the biological sector, on the other hand, it appears in four of the five articles in each century. There is little variation from century to century, in that in those articles in which it is present it accounts for 1 per cent to 16 per cent in the eighteenth century, 1 per cent to 9 per cent in the nineteenth, and 3 per cent to 11 per cent in the twentieth.

These four categories, that is, the object of study, the experimental process, the equipment, and the process of observation, together represent everything that concerns the experiment or observation. It is therefore interesting to see to what extent, as a whole they account for the Themes of the articles concerned. This is given in Table 9.2.

In the physical sector for the eighteenth century these Themes account for about three-quarters of the Themes in the articles, with a range from 63 per cent to 90 per cent. In the biological sector the rate is only slightly less, at about two-thirds, with a range of 50 per cent to 73 per cent. In the nineteenth century, it is the physical sector which has rates of about two-thirds, although it is rather higher if Glazebrook (1880) is discounted, the overall range (including Glazebrook, 1880) being 35 per cent to 80 per cent. In the biological sector the rate is about three-quarters, with a range of 57 per cent to 94 per cent. These rates are maintained in the biological sector in the twentieth century, with about three-quarters, and a range of 64 per cent to 81 per cent. However, if Miller (1980) is discounted, this rate drops to about two-thirds and the range is a fairly narrow one of 64 per cent to 67 per cent. In the physical sector however there is a considerable fall, with Glazebrook's position as forerunner confirmed. Three of the five articles for this century have 50 per cent or less of their Themes from this group, and in the case of Hartree (1940)

Table 9.2. Overall percentages for Obj + Exp + Equip + Obs.

	Physical	*Biological*
1700	70	50
1720	90	71
1740	63	56
1760	74	73
1780	79	71
1800	68	94
1820	80	63
1840	52	57
1860	66	88
1880	35	74
1900	50	66
1920	68	64
1940	25	67
1960	32	65
1980	57	81

it is only 25 per cent. This confirms the fact that in the physical sector another feature is claiming attention from 1880 onwards. But before turning to this question, it is appropriate to compare what has been found for the experimental section with Themes covering the human element.

The human element

The author, or a group to which he belongs, virtually always serves as Theme in these articles. There is a single exception to this: Home (1800). Home (1800) is the description of the head of an unusual animal, and the description is so strongly centred on the animal that the object of study is the overwhelming Theme used: 92 per cent of Home's Themes are of this type, to the total exclusion of author Themes. In other cases the author is always present as Theme, but in fairly modest proportions. In the eighteenth century physical articles, these Themes never account for more than 10 per cent, and in three of the articles the rate is 5 per cent. The biological articles for this century have rather more, with rates ranging from 5 per cent to 13 per cent. In the nineteenth century physical articles, the proportion rises to around 12 per cent, with a range of 7 per cent to 15 per cent; in the biological articles however, the rate remains fairly low, but with a wide range of 4 per cent to 19 per cent, and none in Home (1800). The rate falls in the twentieth century, with a range of 1 per cent to 6 per cent in the physical sector, and 2 per cent to 7 per cent in the biological sector. If anything it tails off towards the end of the century, for the rate does not rise above 2 per cent in the second half of the twentieth century (i.e. in the last two articles). Hence it would be reasonable to say that the author as Theme is a normal but minor feature of the scientific article, but that the use of this type of Theme tends to wane towards the end of the twentieth century.

The other human feature is that of humans other than the author functioning as Theme. This occurs in four out of five articles in both the physical and biological sectors, in both the eighteenth and nineteenth centuries; and in the twentieth century it appears in all the articles. This feature occurs at about the same rate as the author type, a range (discounting those that have none) of 2 per cent to 20 per cent in the eighteenth century physical articles, and 4 per cent to 10 per cent in the corresponding biological articles. They occur rather less frequently in the nineteenth century, with a range of 1 per cent to 8 per cent in the physical sector, and a trace (less than 0.5 per cent) to 4 per cent in the biological sector. The corresponding rates for the twentieth century are 1 per cent to 5 per cent in the physical articles, and 1 per cent to 17 per cent in the biological articles. Hence, this type of Theme is normal, but in fairly restricted proportions, though individual authors occasionally use rather more. This is the case of Povey (1700), and Mummery (1920). Povey (1700) is a short early article, and two of the four human Themes refer to workers:

> **They** cast off not above twice in twenty four hours, (Povey, 1700)

Mummery gives a review of previous research in which he describes what others have done:

> **He** showed that MALASSEZ's epithelial rests in the peridontal membrane are part of the this sheath, (Mummery, 1920)

It is of interest to contrast the Themes dealing with the experimental group (Obj + Exp + Equip + Obs) with the Themes dealing with humans (Auth + Oth). This is done in Table 9.3.

It is noticeable that nowhere are the human Themes used to anything like the same extent as the experimental Themes. In over half of the cases the experimental Themes are used three to five times more frequently than the human Themes. Even in those twentieth century physical articles where there is a reduction in the rate of experimental Themes, there is also a reduction in the rate of human Themes. Hence I would hypothesize that the alleged impersonality of scientific writing is not a desire to avoid mentioning human agents, as is so often suggested. We see here that scientific writers

Table 9.3. Percentages of Themes in the experimental and human groups.

	Physical		*Biological*	
	Experimental	*Human*	*Experimental*	*Human*
1700	70	25	50	13
1720	90	10	71	17
1740	63	11	56	13
1760	74	16	73	10
1780	79	7	61	17
1800	71	14	94	2
1820	81	21	63	19
1840	62	18	57	13
1860	70	17	88	4
1880	35	13	74	8
1900	50	7	66	16
1920	68	9	64	20
1940	25	5	67	3
1960	32	6	65	7
1980	57	5	81	8

have no compunction about thematising themselves or other humans where it is appropriate to the needs of the discourse they are constructing. On the other hand, it is evident that there is a definite wish to thematise their study, in terms of the object of study and the process of experimentation or observation. This is the scientist's most frequent clausal starting point. It is evident that thematising elements of what I have called the experimental group will lead to an increase in the use of passive voice, since this is one of the formal resources which can place those items which are acted on, or which are under study, in thematic position. But, note, it is that way round. It is not the case that a choice of passive voice leads to the placing of experimental items in theme position, but that the thematisation of experimental items leads to increased use of the passive voice. It will be noted that thematisation of experimental items is, in general, much higher than the 30 per cent or so which is usually given as the proportion of passive clauses in this type of discourse. Thus, thematisation of these features does not necessarily lead to passive voice. Use of Relational process verbs, particularly the copula, is another choice which will frequently result from the thematisation of experimental items (Banks, 1987, 1994a), as is the use of these items as Subject with an active Material process predicator (Master,

1991). Thus the driving force behind the construction of the discourse, from this point of view, is the choices being made in thematic structure.

Textual reference

There might be some interference between references to other humans and references to other texts, particularly since texts are frequently referred to by naming their authors. References to other texts, despite the fact that this has become of crucial importance in the contemporary article, notably in the creation of a research space (Swales, 1990, 2004), do not rank high in terms of thematisation. They appear as Themes in only one of the eighteenth-century physical articles and in four of the biological articles from that century. In the nineteenth century, they appear in four of the physical articles but only two of the biological articles. And in the twentieth century, they appear in four of the physical articles and all five of the biological articles. Hence they seem to have become a virtually permanent feature in the physical article since the beginning of the nineteenth century, and since the beginning of the twentieth in the case of the biological articles. However, they never account for more than a very small proportion of the Themes. The highest rate in the corpus is 8 per cent for Barry (1840); and in the twentieth century the rate is never more than 1 per cent in the physical sector, and never more than 3 per cent in the biological sector. So, despite the sociological importance of this aspect of the text, it is not a matter for thematisation, at least not to any great extent.

The other textual feature that occurs as Theme is metalinguistic references or references to other parts of the same text. These occur in two of the eighteenth-century physical articles and four of the corresponding biological articles. In the nineteenth century, they occur in four of the physical articles and two of the biological. They occur in all of the twentieth century articles, so appear to have become a standard feature. However, like the intertextual references, they never account for a high proportion of the Themes; the highest rate is 9 per cent in Barry (1840), the same article that had the highest rate of intertextual Themes, and in Glazebrook (1880). In the twentieth century however, they appear a little more frequently than intertextual Themes, ranging from 1 per cent to 7 per cent in both the physical and biological sectors. In case it be thought that these should be included with the human element, but this is surely pushing the human element to the limit, the relevant figures are given in Table 9.4, where human + text is Auth + Oth + Meta +Inter.

Table 9.4. Percentages of Themes in the experimental and human/text groups.

	Physical		*Biological*	
	Experimental	*Human + Text*	*Experimental*	*Human + Text*
1700	70	25	50	13
1720	90	10	71	25
1740	63	19	56	23
1760	74	18	73	22
1780	79	12	61	24
1800	71	14	94	2
1820	81	21	63	19
1840	62	28	57	30
1860	70	23	88	4
1880	35	24	74	14
1900	50	5	66	20
1920	68	16	64	27
1940	25	12	67	13
1960	32	10	65	11
1980	57	9	81	11

Even here the rates for this extended human category are still far lower than those of the experimental category, inevitably, some will say, since this category already accounts in most cases for well over 50 per cent. Nevertheless, it can be noted that even this extended human category accounts for more than 25 per cent in only three cases.

In the mental category are elements relating to Mental processes and factors relating to the structure of the argumentation. If this relates to one of the other categories, that would be the metalinguistic category. This type of Theme appears in most of the articles in the sample. Only the first two physical articles in the eighteenth century and one biological article in the nineteenth have none. Otherwise the percentages vary fairly widely, 7 per cent to 11 per cent for the seventeenth-century physical articles that have some, and 1 per cent to 16 per cent for the biological articles; 3 per cent to 10 per cent for the physical and 4 per cent to 11 per cent for the biological articles of the nineteenth century; and 5 per cent to 12 per cent for the physical and 3 per cent to 15 per cent for the biological articles of the twentieth century. Thus the percentage is most frequently round about 6 per cent, fractionally more in the twentieth century. This indicates that this type of Theme has been a constant, if minor feature of the scientific journal article, and has, if anything, been reinforced in the twentieth century, where it never accounts for less than 3 per cent, and in three cases is over 10 per cent, with a maximum of 15 per cent in Lawrence 1940. Themes of this type most commonly function as Subject or Adjunct:

> **On the above hypothesis** this indicates that the synthesis of delphinidin requires at least one more stage than that of cyanidin. (Lawrence, 1940)

However, a significant number, eight out of 27 in the case of Lawrence (1940), have the form of an extraposition matrix:

> **It should be emphasized** that the hypothesis will be valid even if the end products are not directly synthesized from simple carbohydrates. (Lawrence, 1940)

Mathematics

Finally, we come to what is perhaps the most striking finding of this study of Themes in the *Philosophical Transactions* corpus, that is, the sudden explosion of mathematical Themes in the physical sector from the late nineteenth century on. The only early occurrence is Smith (1740), whose 2 per cent is a single rather complex example:

> **Then putting n, the Sine of Incidence = 100; m, the Sign of Refraction of the least frangible Rays, out of Glass into Air, = 154; and μ, the Sine of Refraction of the most refrangible Rays, = 156; as Sir *Isaac Newton* found them by Experiments**; we shall have,
>
> *PB*, the Focal Length of the Speculum with regard to the most refrangible Rays = 18.2926=, which will be somewhat increased by the Thickness of the Glass, when that is considerable. (Smith, 1740)

Otherwise, there are no examples before De la Rue (1860), where there are 2 per cent. In Glazebrook (1880), there is a sudden rise to 34 per cent, and with the exception of Duffield (1920), where the proportion is again 2 per cent, the percentage never drops below 27 per cent (which is the figure for Horai, 1980) in the physical sector. However, it will be noted that this phenomenon is virtually restricted to the physical sector, for there is only one single biological article in the whole of the corpus, which has any examples at all: that is the case of Joysey (1960), which has 9 per cent. It is evident that this is a major development in scientific writing. The importance acquired over a short period from the late nineteenth century on by the mathematical modelling of physical problems is reflected in the use of mathematical items as thematic choices:

> Hence $v = 72°44'39''$ [From Section III. (9).] (Glazebrook, 1880)

... **the minus sign** is of no significance, ... (Hartree, 1940)

Since $z < 1$ for all D-types, equation (2.11) shows that $v_1 < c_1 < a_1$ so that all D-type ionization fronts move subsonically relative to the fluid ahead. (Axford, 1960)

This factor, at least up to 1980, had not affected the biological sector. Joysey (1960) alone of the biological articles has examples of this type of Theme:

In the present equation, $y = a + bx$, it might appear at first sight that a represents the initial size difference between the variates, (Joysey, 1960)

Just as the biological sciences became experimental at a later date than the physical sciences, but have always continued to produce observational articles at the same time, it would be reasonable to hypothesise that the biological sector will follow the physical sector in becoming mathematical, but perhaps not to the same extent.

It was noted above that the percentage of Themes in the experimental group dropped in the physical sector in the twentieth century, in fact from 1880 onwards. It can now be seen that this fall coincides with the sudden influx of mathematical Themes. Thus the drop in Themes in the experimental group is compensated by the appearance of the mathematical group. In the physical sector the experimental group plus the mathematical group account together for about three-quarters of the Themes, whereas the proportion of Themes accounted for by the experimental group alone in the biological sector is slightly less (69 per cent on average). Moreover in the physical sector this group (experimental + mathematical) has slightly less variation than the experimental group of the biological sector; 70 per cent to 84 per cent for the physical sector, 64 to 81 per cent for the biological sector. To some extent the mathematical Themes dovetail with the object of study and the experiment. This is due to the fact that in some cases it is no longer clear, or perhaps no longer relevant, whether what is being dealt with is the mathematical model, or the physical phenomena which the model represents. From this point of view the fact that mathematical Themes have taken over part of the function of experimental Themes is not surprising.

Thus, while it is true that these scientific authors use a wide range of Theme types, it becomes increasingly evident that over time everything that concerns the object of study and the experiments or observations relating to it increasingly form the centre of his thematic interest. This is the starting point of the author's clausal construction; it is thus a major feature of this genre and the driving force in the construction of this type of discourse.

In choosing their clausal starting points, scientists naturally take them from the ongoing activity which they are dealing with in their articles. They take them from the situation, and more particularly from field, and just as in the cases of passives, personal pronouns, and nominalisation, the choice of Themes and the way they are used is derived from the situation, and is inseparable from it. Thus the language and the situation are in a mutually causal relationship: the situation has a causal role in creating the language which in turn has a role in remodelling the situation.

An Interpersonal coda

Ancients and Moderns

What has gone before gas been mainly concerned with two of the three types of meaning, first, ideational meaning, particularly relating to transitivity in the types of processes involved and the participants which occur with them, and, second, Textual meaning, involving thematic structure as a means of organizing the message. It would now seem appropriate to look at something of a more Interpersonal nature, in the form of the ways in which scientists refer to each other in their articles.

When we look back at historical changes, the vantage point our later position in time gives us can often telescope the events which actually took place. Thus, when new ideas replace old ones, particularly when those new ideas are ones which are now firmly established, the impression is usually one of rapid, even sudden, change, so that the new seems to oust the old because the new is just so obvious. This impression is obviously false, and new ideas take time to establish themselves, so that at times of change there may be a fairly lengthy period when old and new jostle for position in an uneasy relationship. So, when the new ideas of empirical science, espoused by the then Moderns began to take over from the old forms of thinking based on reference to the thinkers of antiquity, the Ancients, the tussle continued for quite some time. Even in the confines of the Royal Society, the fact that they were specifically set up to promote empirical science did not mean that the Ancients suddenly disappeared in the twinkling of a Newtonian prism. Thus in our corpus, we find Blair (1720) referring to the Ancients as a repository of knowledge:

> I cannot enough admire the Judiciousness and Sagacity of the Ancients, who, without any of those means made use of by the Moderns, have handed down to us such an account of the Virtues of those Plants, which by the unanimous Consent of all Physicians and Pharmacians, are more particularly dedicated for use in Physick, that all the laborious endeavours

of their inquisitive Successors, have never been able to outdo them. It must have been a long Tract of Experience, which enabled *Dioscorides* and *Theophrastus* to collect and receive from their wise Ancestors, such a lasting Catalogue of the Virtues of plants, as scarce any thing has been added to even to this day. The Royal Academy at *Paris*, has been at great pains to find out the Virtues of Plants by the Chymical Analysis, and several other Experiments, of which we have the Abstracts in *Tournefort's Histoire des Plantes aux environs de Paris*, and *Tauvry* his *Traité des Medicaments:* But these laborious Endeavours only serve to confirm what the Ancients advanced, without any new Discovery. (Blair, 1720)

Not only does he refer to the Ancients in praiseworthy terms, but, bizarrely from our perspective, he seems to be propounding precisely that philosophy which the Royal Society was set up to combat. This can be taken as a reflection of the fact that, on the ground, things are never as clear cut as they seem in retrospect. The last trace of this in the corpus seems to be in Smith (1740), who refers to the Moderns, but not to the Ancients. However, since the Moderns are the counterblast to the Ancients, one might think of the Ancients being implicitly present. The fact that they are not specifically mentioned then becomes significant in this context:

The Telescope is deservedly reckoned one of the most excellent of all the Inventions of the Moderns; (Smith, 1740)

So it would seem that the influence of the Ancients could still be felt well into the eighteenth century, more than a century after Bacon's death.

Epistolary framing

It was seen earlier that the *Philosophical Transactions* developed from the correspondence received by Oldenburg. The letter form naturally continued to play a large part in the contributions to the journal for quite some time. Indeed, Valle (1999) claims that examples continue to appear well into the nineteenth century. Since explicit letters were excluded from this corpus, it is perhaps not surprising that evidence of the letter form is rare here. However, one item, whose title does not explicitly betray it as a letter, does have some of the features of the letter format. This is the case of Wilson (1760), who begins with a standard letter opening:

To the Right Honorable the Earl of Macclesfield, President of the Royal Society.

My Lord,

In my letter upon the *Tourmalin,* which I had the honour of communicating to the Royal Society in December last, there are some experiments to shew, that glass is permeable by electricity. (Wilson, 1760)

And the piece ends with a standard valediction.

I am, my Lord,
    Your Lordship's
        most obliged
            and obedient servant,
                Benj. Wilson.   (Wilson, 1760)

So even though most of what appears between these two is cast as an experimental report, it does have this epistolary frame, and he slips back into this mode at appropriate points:

I shall now proceed to acquaint your Lordship with some other circumstances of as nice a nature, where the slightest, and almost imperceptible differences in the position, or in the force of the friction, of two bodies, produce in either of them, the plus electricity at one time, and the minus at another. (Wilson, 1760)

I might add other quotations of the same kind, but, as it would take up too much of your Lordship's time, I shall beg leave to refer to the letter itself. (Wilson, 1760)

Praise

In the early articles, notably in the eighteenth century, references to others are frequently expressed in highly laudatory terms. Thus Blair (1720) refers to a Dr Herman as 'that expert Botanist, and diligent Enquirer … the celebrated …', and to James Petiver as 'the late ingenious and accurate Natural Historian':

This induc'd that expert Botanist, and diligent Enquirer into the Knowledge of the *Materia Medica*, the Celebrated Dr. *Herman,* to lay down these general Maxims, *Quæcunque flore & semine conveniunt easdem possident virtutes:* And *Omnia semina striata sunt carminativa.* The late ingenious and accurate Natural Historian, sometime a noted Member of this Society, Mr. *James Petiver,* a few Years ago obliged us with a Discourse upon this Subject, printed in the Philosophical Transactions, in which he observes, that the *Plantæ Umbelliferæ, Galeatæ, Verticillatæ, Siliquosæ* and *Siliculosæ,* for the generality, have a tendency to the same Virtue and Use. (Blair, 1720)

Later in the same century, 'ingenious' is again the word which Cavallo (1780) uses to describe Professor Lichtenberg:

> The explanation of the ingenious Professor LICHTENBERG'S experiment now became very easy and natural; for the powder of rosin, being actually electrified negatively, could not be attracted, except by those parts of the electrophorus, which are in a contrary state, that is, electrified positively. (Cavallo, 1780)

And writers of this period were not beyond praising themselves, or at least their work, as Wilson (1760) does in describing experiments which he has carried out with Dr Hoadly as 'remarkable':

> And this confirms the reasoning upon the remarkable experiments related in the treatise published by Dr. Hoadly and myself. (Wilson, 1760)

This feature of praise seems to die out fairly early on. There are no examples in the corpus after the end of the eighteenth century. The only example which might be assimilated to them occurs in the late twentieth century in Miller (1980). Here the praise is to a certain extent indirect, since what is praised is not the scientist himself, that is, Campbell, but one of his photographs:

> Campbell's most striking photograph shows a specimen of *Phaciphacops birdsongensis* (Delo) (Campbell, 1975, pl. 5, fig. 3), having silicified laminae through which the top of the central core projected. (Miller, 1980)

Criticism

In the earlier articles, criticism is frequently accompanied by an attempt to find a reason, or even an excuse, for the supposed error. In the case of Wilson (1760) this is based on the conjecture that different types of wax may have been used. The fact that this is pure conjecture is interesting since it underlines the attempt to excuse other scientists. Perhaps one can see this as an early form of hedging:

> Now we find that the Dutch wax is softer than the English, and the Irish harder: and it is not improbable that the French wax, which I suppose the *Abbé Nollet* used, may likewise be different. (Wilson, 1760)

It will be noted that there are in fact two conjectures in this extract: first, that French wax does not have the same consistency as English wax, and secondly that the Abbé Nollet did indeed use this French wax. Home (1800) also wishes to excuse Professor Blumenbach. This is based on the quality of the zoological specimens which were available. It can be supposed that this was not an infrequent problem in those pre-refrigeration days!

> It was natural, under these circumstances, to reserve any observations which had been made upon this newly discovered quadruped, till the entire animal should be brought home preserved in spirit, and enable us to examine the structure of its different organs; but, finding that Professor BLUMENBACH has been led to believe that it was an animal without teeth, an opinion which must have arisen from the imperfect state of the specimen he examined, it appeared highly proper to do away the mistake, and lay before this learned Society, such observations respecting the head of this extraordinary animal, as I have been enabled to make. (Home, 1800)

Davy (1820) is similar to Wilson (1760), in that it is the precise chemical used which he supposes may have led to what he considers to be erroneous results:

> Mr. COOPER states the black oxide of platinum to consist of 100 platinum, with only 4.317 of oxygen;* but he has, I think, considerably under-rated the oxygen in it. ... [8 lines] ... Mr. COOPER, I presume, used a nitrate of mercury to decompose the muriate of platinum, but he seems to have overlooked the nitrous acid in stating his results. (Davy, 1820)

This feature of looking for excuses for others' errors seems to die out in the early nineteenth century and is replaced by muted criticism. Gassiot (1840) hedges his criticism of Professor Daniell with praise of the equipment he has developed:

> Although I must consider that Professor DANIELL laboured under some error when he describes the discharge passing in the form of a spark (8.) when the cells were approximated, yet I cannot but feel that it will be with the aid, and through the principles of this philosopher's scientific apparatus, which he has so appropriately denominated the constant battery, that the true principles of voltaic action will be correctly ascertained. (Gassiot, 1840)

The criticism of Taylor to be found in Axford (1960) might be thought of as being a more recent example of this phenomenon:

> Taylor (1950) has given some solutions for the external flow in waves having spherical symmetry,† but this work is not as complete as Goldsworthy's for ionization fronts, and no adequate diagrams are available showing all possible flow pattern solutions, such as figure 1. (Axford, 1960)

Disagreement can sometimes be expressed in much stronger terms. This occurs for example in the nineteenth century article, Barry (1840), where he discounts totally the opinion of Hunter:

> Should these facts be thought to confirm the opinion of HUNTER, that the Blood 'has life within itself,' or 'acquires it in the act of forming organic bodies,' because its corpuscles in certain altered states exhibit 'vital action,' still his assertion that 'the red globules' are the least important part of the blood, will appear to have no just foundation. (Barry, 1840)

The latest example of strong disagreement in the corpus occurs in Dawson (1900). At several points in her article she takes Frank to task in no uncertain terms:

> It is very difficult to understand how such results have led FRANK to this opinion, for they appear clearly to point to the conclusion that the Bacteroids *are* themselves the germs, whatever their contents may be. In this connection, too, FRANK reports the occurrence of Bacteroids in the parenchymatous tissues of aërial organs of lupine, pea, and bean, and in the cotyledons of the bean. I may at once state that, in accordance with SCHNEIDER and others, I have utterly failed to confirm these observations. In no case were Bacteroids visible in the cells of any other organs than the tubercles themselves. In addition, although I have made repeated attempts, using the methods which FRANK suggests, to determine the nature of the contents of the Bacteroids, I have been quite unable, even with high power objectives, to detect any structure which could justify the conclusion which he has drawn, viz., that they contain minute cocci, the true germs. (Dawson, 1900)

'very difficult to understand … utterly failed … in no case … repeated attempts … quite unable': it is difficult to imagine a more severe put-down in a scientific context; however, in fairness, it should be pointed out that elsewhere in her article Dawson quotes Frank with approval, so apparently he wasn't always wrong! This sort of strong disagreement is not overt in articles later than 1900. There is also, particularly in the nineteenth century, evidence of disagreement occurring in the context of an ongoing controversy. In the case of Barry, he names those with whom he agrees in the text, but those with whom he disagrees are relegated to a footnote:

> It may here be stated that my observations corroborate those of previous observers, that the blood-corpuscles in the Mammalia are biconcave; yet with HODGKIN and LISTER†, I find them in Man to be rounded at the edges‡, and not cut off abruptly as they have been described§. (Barry, 1840)

Similarly, in Matthiessen (1860), those with whom the author agrees are named, while those with whom he disagrees remain nameless:

> Several experimenters state, that when copper is heated in ammonia, the gas is decomposed and nitride of copper formed, a fact which SCHRÖTTER* disputes, and has been proved totally incorrect by DICK. We repeated the experiment by heating a copper wire, whose conducting power had been previously determined, for a quarter of an hour in a current of dry ammonia; when cold the conducting power was found the same, and the wire was as ductile as before. In all probability the reason why in the experiments of previous observers the copper became brittle, was (as already suggested by DICK) that they used copper containing suboxide. (Matthiessen, 1860)

It will be noted that the feature of finding possible reasons for previous error is again in evidence. This is the latest example of this in the corpus.

Community

Evidence of a close-knit community is in evidence in the eighteenth and nineteenth centuries. Wilson 1760 describes another scientist whom he refers to as 'my friend':

> I shall conclude with an experiment made by my friend *Mr. Hamilton,* professor of philosophy in the university of Dublin, as it seems to illustrate the doctrine of *resistances,* at least, so far as respects the air. (Wilson, 1760)

Davy (1820) refers to his now rather better-known cousin Humphry Davy:

> In my communication to Sir H. DAVY, Bart, 'On a new fulminating platinum,' which has been honoured with a place in the Transactions of the Royal Society,* I stated, that I had obtained some other new compounds of this metal: these have since occupied no inconsiderable portion of my leisure hours, and I now beg leave to lay the results of my inquiry before the Royal Society. (Davy, 1820)

It is interesting to note here that Davy refers to these activities as occupying his 'leisure hours'. This seems to indicate that the notion of science as a leisure activity, and hence the spirit of the *virtuosi,* was still alive in the early nineteenth century. It also seems to have been common practice for scientists of the nineteenth century to attend each other's experiments. Thus Gassiot attends the experiments of Daniell, and his own subsequent experiments are attended by Faraday:

> Having been, by the invitation of Professor DANIELL, witness on the 16th of February 1839 of the powerful effects obtained by a series of seventy of the large constant battery, I was induced to prepare 100 of precisely the same dimensions. On the first day, I excited that battery (14th of July), and when I was favoured with the company of Dr. FARADAY, I also excited 100 of the smaller cells already described (10.); but neither with these two powerful batteries combined, or separate, could any appearance of a spark be observed until contact was made and the circuit completed. (Gassiot, 1840)

These scientists would also lend each other substances, equipment, and specimens. Later in the same article, Gassiot, referring again to Daniell's experiments, uses titanium given to him by Faraday:

> Those who had the pleasure of witnessing the experiments of Professor DANIELL, at King's College, when a series of only seventy pairs of his constant battery was used, will no doubt recollect the brilliant effects produced with this powerful apparatus, and may form some idea of those obtained by using nearly one third increase of power. Titanium, which had been previously given to me by Dr. FARADAY,, volatized; and the flame from charcoal as well as from metallic electrodes was so intense as to render it indispensable that the eyes of those present should be protected by thick screens of black crape. (Gassiot, 1840)

An example of the lending of equipment occurs in Glazebrook (1880):

> The spectrometer was the same as that used in the experiments with aragonite, and was kindly lent me by Professor STOKES. (Glazebrook, 1880)

This type of close relationship seems to be dying out by the beginning of the twentieth century, but one example does occur in Mummery (1920):

> I was fortunate enough to obtain an excellent specimen of a lower molar tooth within the follicle, given to me by my friend Mr. DOLAMORE. (Mummery, 1920)

Although there is evidence of this close-knit community in the eighteenth and nineteenth centuries, it is unusual for technicians to be acknowledged, despite the fact that they obviously formed an important element of the scientific community. This however does occur once in the corpus, in the late eighteenth century:

> This instrument, the first hint of which I received from my ingenious friend THOMAS RONAYNE, Esq. after various trials, I brought to the present state of perfection as long ago as the year 1777; and immediately after several of them were made after my pattern by Mr. ADAMS, philosophical instrument maker in Fleet-street. (Cavallo, 1780)

Here, not only does Cavallo acknowledge the loan of a piece of equipment from his friend Thomas Ronayne, described as 'ingenious', the same word he used to describe Professor Lichtenberg, as was seen above, but he also acknowledges the instrument maker who produced his own improved model.

Provenance

There is one feature which seems to be common to the whole of the period under study, and that is the necessity to give the provenance of specimens. This fairly naturally applies more to the biological domain, particularly when specimens of animals and plants were being brought from newly discovered and exotic parts of the globe. But it is not restricted to that historical period, nor to the biological field. In the late eighteenth century we find Edwards (1760) giving the origins of a curious animal which is the subject of his article:

> It was brought from Surinam in South America, by the way of Barbadoes, to John Fothergill, MD of London, and is the animal, which Merian and Seba describe as changing from a frog into a fish. (Edwards, 1760)

Hunter (1780) refers to two specimens, one of which is still to be found in a private museum, and the second of which he examined:

> Some years ago one of these was sent to Dr. HUNTER, who gave me leave to examine it. I found, upon examination, that it had all the parts of the female peculiar to that bird. This specimen is still preserved in Dr. HUNTER'S Museum.
>
> Dr. PITCAIRN, having lately received a pheasant of this kind from Sir THOMAS HARRIS, exhibited it as a curiosity to Mr. BANKS and Dr. SOLANDER. I happened to be then present, and was desired to examine the bird. The following is the result of my examination. (Hunter, 1780)

It will be noted that, here, there is not just evidence of the provenance of the specimen, but also of the community; the specimen was given by Harris to Pitcairn, and shown to Banks and Solander; and moreover it was shown 'as a curiosity', showing the *virtuosi* spirit of the (gentle)men involved. The Banks referred to here is, of course, the same Joseph Banks discussed earlier. De la Rue (1860), almost a century later provides the same sort of information about his biological specimen:

> It had been contributed by Dr. STEPHENSON, of Manning River, N.S.W., who had obtained it from a species of *Ficus*, known as *F. rubiginosa*. The zealous Commissioner for New South Wales, Mr. (now Sir William)

MᶜARTHUR, brought this gum under our notice with the view of obtaining some information respecting its chemical properties. (De la Rue, 1860)

Also towards the end of the nineteenth century, Owen (1880) goes to even greater lengths to give the details of the origins of his zoological specimen:

> The female *Echidna* and her young, the subjects of the paper of 1865, were taken in Lolac Forest, Victoria, Australia, on the 12th August, 1864. Guided thereby, I noted, in correspondence with friends in localities frequented by the Echidnæ, the period when females in the impregnated state might be obtained, with instructions as to the parts to be preserved and transmitted, in alcohol, for examination; noting, also, the chief facts which remained to be determined§ in reference to the subject of the present communication. Among such friendly correspondents I have the good fortune to include GEORGE FREDERIC BENNETT, Esq., Corresponding Member of the Zoological Society of London, resident at a locality, Toowoomba, in Queensland, where individuals of the *Echidna Hysterix* were to be had. In a letter of September 23rd, 1878, Mr BENNETT writes:–
> 'You will have received, ere this reaches you, specimens of probably impregnated Echidna got on various dates – July 18th, 27th and August 9th.'
> The correspondent's father, my friend Dr. BENNETT, F.L.S., being in London when these specimens had arrived, I dissected them in his presence, but found not any ovum in either uterus. (Owen, 1880)

This question of provenance seems still to be in evidence in Miller (1980), who also is at pains to give a detailed history of his palaeontological specimens:

> The specimens of *Phacops rana milleri* are all from the Middle Devonian Silica Shale and were collected from the north quarry of the Medusa Portland Cement Company, Silica, Ohio. They include a uniquely informative slab collected by Mr Mullard Widener of Tulsa, Oklahoma, and registered AMNH 29282 (American Museum of Natural History). Other material was donated by Dr N. Eldredge and Dr R. Levi-Setti, and is deposited in the Royal Scottish Museum (R.S.M.). Cuticle and eye fragments of *P. rana africanus* Burton & Eldredge 1974 from the Eifelian of the Spanish Sahara, together with those from *P. rana crassituberculata* and *P. rana rana* from the Silica Shale, were also examined for comparative purposes, Professor A.D. Wright, Queen's University of Belfast (Q.U.B.), provided an early post-ecdysial specimen of *Cheirurus* sp. from the Silurian Wenlock Limestone of Dudley, England. (Miller, 1980)

Hence the question of traceability of specimens is an old one, and there is evidence of it throughout the period covered by the corpus.

Referencing

Providing references has become a major, and obligatory, feature of the contemporary scientific research article. The form of such references is now highly codified, down to the last comma, and each journal will have detailed instructions in its style-sheet of its own particular requirements in this area. This is a situation which has grown up over a long period of time, and consideration of the examples of referencing in the corpus gives some evidence of this, despite the fact that it necessarily can only give a very incomplete picture of all the ins and outs of this particular story.

In discussing reference to the Ancients, above, the article by Blair (1720) was referred to. Not only does Blair refer to two of the ancients by name, but he then goes on to two (for him) contemporary works, both in French. For each of these we have the name of the author and the title of the book. The relevant part of the quote is repeated here for convenience:

> It must have been a long Tract of Experience, which enabled *Dioscorides* and *Theophrastus* to collect and receive from their wise Ancestors, such a lasting Catalogue of the Virtues of plants, as scarce any thing has been added to even to this day. The Royal Academy at *Paris*, has been at great pains to find out the Virtues of Plants by the Chymical Analysis, and several other Experiments, of which we have the Abstracts in *Tournefort's Histoire des Plantes aux environs de Paris*, and *Tauvry* his *Traité des Medicaments*: But these laborious Endeavours only serve to confirm what the Ancients advanced, without any new Discovery. (Blair, 1720)

It may also have been noted that in the quote from later in this same article used to illustrate praise of others, Blair refers to an article by James Petiver. We are told that this appeared in an earlier issue of the *Philosophical Transactions*, but we are not given a precise reference. Again the relevant part of the quote is repeated here for convenience:

> The late ingenious and accurate Natural Historian, sometime a noted Member of this Society, Mr. *James Petiver*, a few Years ago obliged us with a Discourse upon this Subject, printed in the Philosophical Transactions, in which he observes, that the *Plantæ Umbelliferæ, Galeatæ, Verticillatæ, Siliquosæ* and *Siliculosæ*, for the generality, have a tendency to the same Virtue and Use. (Blair, 1720)

Presumably, Blair considered that his readers were sufficiently familiar with the contents of previous issues not to require precise reference details.

Only 20 years later, we do find Smith (1740) giving more detail in his references, even though these are to the work of Newton, who had, of course been President of the Royal Society, 1703–1727, and whose work was presumably well-known:

> The first of these Defects only, was known to the Writers of Dioptrics, before Sir *Isaac Newton*; for which Reason (as he informs us himself, *Opt. Lect.* 1, 2.) they 'imagined ...' (Smith, 1740)

> ... but rather discouraged any such Attempts, by declaring, 'that on this Account he laid aside his Glass-works', (*Phil. Trans.* No. 80.) 'and looked upon the Improvement of Telescopes, of given Lengths, by Refraction, as desperate' (*Optics*, 2d Edit. *p.* 91.). (Smith, 1740)

Here we have three fairly precise references, the third of which even gives the page number.

Another 20 years on, Wilson (1760) refers to a treatise written in Latin, giving its date but not the title:

> But I beg leave, first, to take notice, that our electrical apparatus is much improved, by the discovery of Father *Windelinus Ammersin*, of *Switzerland*, who, in a Latin treatise published in 1754, has shewn us, that wood, properly dried, till it becomes very brown, is a non-conductor of electricity. (Wilson, 1760)

He later refers to the work of Abbée Nollet, referring to the work simply as the 'thirteenth letter':

> The Abbé, in particular, who has taken remarkable pains to find out from whence this uncertainty arises, acquaints us, in the *thirteenth letter*, with his difficulties, and how much it perplexed him. (Wilson, 1760)

However, a few lines later he gives a quote from this document. The quote is about six lines long, in the original French and without any translation. So Wilson seems to expect his readers, not only to be familiar with the literature on this subject, but also to be sufficiently competent in French not to require a translation of six lines of text. When he refers to a work of which he is a co-author, he is rather more explicit, for although he does not give the title, he does give page references:

> And this confirms the reasoning upon the remarkable experiments related in the treatise published by Dr. Hoadly and myself. See p.27 to 34, and 46, 47. (Wilson, 1760)

So readers were apparently supposed to recognise which book was being referred to, and Wilson then directs them to precise passages.

Footnotes were already being used, and these could contain references. By the early nineteenth century, a reference could constitute the sole content of a footnote. For instance, in the following example, Davy gives a volume reference in a footnote:

> In my communication to Sir H. Davy, Bart, 'On a new fulminating platinum,' which has been honoured with a place in the Transactions of the Royal Society,* I stated, that I had obtained some other new compounds of this metal: these have since occupied no inconsiderable portion of my leisure hours, and I now beg leave to lay the results of my inquiry before the Royal Society.

> * Phil. Trans. 1817.   (Davy, 1820)

This is not the only example of this in Davy's article. The practice seems to have spread rapidly, and printers showed some ingenuity in finding distinguishing symbols when numbers of reference footnotes appeared on the same page. There are five such at the bottom of a single page of Gassiot (1840):

> *Philosophical Magazine, December, 1838, p. 401. † Philosophical Transactions, 1834, § 957
> ‡ Page 152   § Philosophical Transactions, 1809 || Page 153
>   (Gassiot 1840)

It will be noted that these references are fairly precise, with title, date and page number, where these were not already available in the text. This convention was still in use at the turn of the century, as this example from Townsend (1900) shows:

> It has been shown by Perrin* that the ionization produced by Röntgen rays in a gas in contact with a metal is considerably increased by allowing the rays to fall normally on the metal surface.

> *'Comptes Rendus,' vol. 124, p. 455.   (Townsend 1900)

It will also be noted that this reference is to a French publication, showing that scientists at this period were still expected to be competent in the major foreign languages.

At the same date, Dawson (1900) was using a new method of referencing:

> These observations were, in the main, confirmed by Prazmowski (7) in 1888, and again by Marshal Ward (6) in 1889. (Dawson, 1900)

The numbers in brackets refer to numbered entries in the bibliography at the end of her article. This is the earliest example in the corpus of this method of referencing, which is still in use. However, this must have taken some time to become conventional, since Duffield (1920), 20 years later, is still using the footnote method:

> In 1882 DEWAR† measured the hydrostatic pressure within the arc by using hollow carbons connected to delicate water manometers and found that 'during the maintenance of the steady arc the manometer connected with the positive pole exhibited a fixed increase of pressure corresponding to 1 to 2 mm. of vertical water pressure in different experiments and under varied conditions. The manometer connected with the negative pole shows no increase of pressure, but rather, on the average, a diminution.'
>
> † DEWAR, 'Roy. Soc. Proc.', xxxiii, 262, 1882.   (Duffield, 1920)

Hartree (1940) has the other method of referencing still in common use today, that is, that of giving name and date in brackets in the text, with full bibliographical details in a bibliography at the end of the article:

> The calculation pf approximate wave functions for the normal configurations of the ions O^{+++}, O^{++}, O^+, and neutral O, and the calculation of energy values from the wave functions, was carried out some years ago by Hartree and Black (1933).   (Hartree, 1940)

It will be noted that Hartree is himself one of the co-authors of the work referred to, so Hartree is referring to himself in the third person.

Changing patterns of referring

Thus we see that there are some types of reference which are short-lived in the corpus, and thus reflect a situation which persisted over a short period, while others are much longer-lived and cover much of the period of the corpus. References to the Ancients occur at the beginning of the period, but this dies out fairly quickly, and in Smith (1740) they are present only by implication.

Letters as such were excluded from this corpus; however, traces of an epistolary style remain in at least one mid-eighteenth-century article.

Mentioning others in laudatory terms is common in the earlier articles, but this too seems to wane fairly early on. There are no clear examples after the end of the eighteenth century.

Criticism might be thought of as an essential ingredient in scientific writing. This is true, but its expression has been couched in different terms over the centuries. In the early articles, criticism is frequently accompanied by an attempt to explain, or even excuse, the supposed error. This is particularly prevalent in the eighteenth century, but there are also some examples of it in the nineteenth century. As this practice dies out, criticism becomes more muted, but where there is serious disagreement this can be expressed in strong terms up to the end of the nineteenth century.

Evidence of a sense of community is present, particularly in the eighteenth and nineteenth centuries. Other scientists are frequently referred to as friends in the eighteenth century. Scientists attend each other's experiments, and they lend each other specimens and equipment. These practices continue into the early twentieth century.

A concern for the provenance of specimens, usually in the biological, but occasionally in the physical sector, can be felt throughout the period studied. The traceability of specimens seems to have been considered important from an early date, and to a certain extent, this continues to be the case.

Referencing other work has become an important and essential factor in contemporary scientific writing. In the corpus, from its beginnings as titles of appropriate works, to full detailed referencing, the development of reference systems can be seen, as well as the typographical techniques that have been used.

Thus the corpus illustrates a wide range of ways in which the relationships between scientific authors and other members of the scientific community are expressed.

By way of conclusion

The story so far

In the course of this book we have seen that the use of English to express scientific material begins with Chaucer's *Treatise on the Astrolabe*, which, although it is not research science, is of interest as the first technological text to have been written in English. More precisely, it is instructions for the use of the astrolabe, and is addressed to youngsters. When compared with a comparable present-day text, a teenager's 'how it works' book, we find that the rate of passives is roughly the same in both, but where in the modern text these are mainly of Material process, this is not the case in Chaucer's text. Chaucer uses a considerable number of personal pronouns, but these are rare in the modern text. Chaucer also uses a fair number of nominalised processes, but these too are rare in the present day text.

This then is the starting point, and Chaucer is a precursor is terms of the writing of scientific English. From here, we move to the seventeenth century, when, in the wake, and influence of Bacon, scientists started turning from Latin which until then had been the intellectual *lingua franca*, to English. In an extract from the writings of Boyle, it is found that where he uses nominalised processes, these tend to be mainly Material processes, as are the passives that he uses; when he uses first person pronoun subjects these tend to be with Verbal and Mental processes. In extracts from the work of Power and Hooke, it is seen that they use nominalisation to about the same extent, but much less frequently than Boyle, and neither of them uses passives to any great extent. Although Hooke uses more first person pronouns than Power, neither of them uses them as much as Boyle. The fact that Boyle is an experimental scientist, but the science of Power and Hooke (at least in these extracts) is observational seems to be significant in terms of the linguistic resources that they choose to use.

This leads up to the founding of the Royal Society in the early 1660s, and the publication of the first issue of the *Philosophical Transactions* in 1665. It was with these events that the use of English as a scientific medium really got under way. This was reinforced by the fact that the person of Newton dominates the science of the late seventeenth century. Although he was not a founding member, he had a significant influence on the Royal Society even before he became its President after the death of Hooke in the early years of the eighteenth century. While his dispute with Hooke led him to look for new ways of writing science, the possibility that he was influenced by the Latin, that he, like all scientists of the period used, cannot be excluded. It is notable that the nominalisations in the Latin of Newton's *Principia*, all remain nominalisations in Motte's (1729) English translation. When Newton's *Opticks* is compared with the French of Huygens' *Traité de la lumière*, a number of differences emerge. They obviously use passives to different extents because of general differences between the two languages, but, more interestingly, Newton's passives are more frequently Material than Huygens', whose passives contain a higher percentage of Verbal processes than Newton's. Newton uses rather more first person pronouns than Huygens, even taking into consideration the use of the French impersonal pronoun, *on*; but where Newton uses these fairly frequently with Material process, this is rare in Huygens, who has a higher percentage with Relational and Verbal process than Newton. They use nominalisation to a similar extent, but Newton uses more with Material processes than Huygens, who uses more with Mental processes than Newton. These differences can be traced to the fact that Newton is an empirical scientist, for whom experimentation is the starting point, whereas Huygens is working in the Cartesian tradition, where the theoretical hypothesis is paramount.

From this point on, the *Philosophical Transactions* provide us with a corpus of research articles covering the period 1700 to 1980. The corpus contains 30 articles selected at 20-year periods starting with 1700. Two articles represent each point in time, one of them from the physical sector, the other from the biological. Over time, there is a general tendency for the use of passives to increase, though the rate is usually rather less in the biological sector than the physical sector until the latter part of the twentieth century. The rate stabilises at about 30 per cent for the physical sector towards the turn of the twentieth century, and after 1920 in the biological sector. In the physical sector the use of passives occurs primarily with Material processes, and secondarily with Mental processes; there is a major change in the twentieth century with a rise in the rate of Mental process passives at the expense of Material process passives. In the biological sector Material process passives are the most common throughout the period, but less than in the physical sector in the eighteenth and nineteenth centuries, with Mental process passives being correspondingly more frequent.

The use of first person pronouns is limited throughout the period. Where they do occur, they tend to be with Material processes in the physical sector until the late nineteenth century, with increasing use with Mental processes from then on. In the biological sector, first person pronouns tend to occur with Mental processes until the mid-nineteenth century, with increasing use with Material processes from then on.

Nominalisation of processes has always been fairly frequent. In the physical sector this is of the order of one per 30 words from the mid-eighteenth century until 1920 when there is a sudden increase. In the biological sector the rate settles at about one per 30 words by the mid-nineteenth century. There is an increase in the twentieth century but not as marked as that in the physical sector. In general, the majority of nominalisations are of Material processes in both sectors, although the rate is rather higher in the physical than the biological sector, until the twentieth century. The use of nominalised processes as Modifiers is a twentieth-century phenomenon.

When thematic structure is considered, it is found that, as might be expected, the majority of topical Themes are unmarked, and hence conflate with the Subject, and the majority of marked Themes conflate with an Adjunct. Other types of topical theme occur only in small numbers, though extraposed matrices functioning as topical Theme constitute an interesting minor category. The use of textual themes has diminished over time from about 35 per cent of ranking clauses in the eighteenth century to a little over 20 per cent in the twentieth century. Interpersonal Themes are even less common than textual Themes, though they are a permanent, if marginal, feature from the mid-eighteenth century on. Extraposition matrices, and *let* as a mood marker are the commonest interpersonal Themes. The hypothesis that linear progression is more common than constant progression in this genre is confirmed; there are only six articles in the corpus where constant progression is more common than linear, and only one of these occurs later than 1840.

Consideration of a semantic categorisation of topical Themes reveals that those in the experimental and observational area, that is, object of study, experiment, equipment, and observation, account for about three-quarters of the topical Themes throughout the period in the biological sector, and in the eighteenth- and nineteenth centuries for the physical sector. This rate drops in the physical sector in the twentieth century, and is compensated for by the appearance and rapid increase of topical Themes of a mathematical nature. Topical Themes relating to humans (author and others) are not used to anything like the same extent, and these become even less frequent in the twentieth century for the physical sector, and from 1940 onwards for the biological sector than they had been previously. Even when the human

Themes are combined with textual Themes (metalinguistic and intertextual) this remains the case.

The way scientists refer to others in the early articles reveals traces of references to the Ancients, and of the epistolary form from which the scientific journal article developed. The first of these disappears rapidly. A feature which also seems to have died out early was the tendency to refer to others in highly laudatory terms. Rather longer lived was the strategy of accompanying criticism with an attempt to explain, and even excuse, the supposed error; this lasts until the mid-nineteenth century. There is also evidence of a close-knit scientific community, and examples of this type still occur in the early twentieth century. The traceability of specimens, particularly those of a biological, zoological or palaeontological nature, seems to be particularly important, and this appears to be constant throughout the period studied.

The general picture which emerges from this detailed study of linguistic features is one where the physical sciences are experimental from the late seventeenth century onwards, whereas the biological sciences were observational and remained so for a considerable time. It is only in the mid-nineteenth century that the biological sciences begin to adopt experimental procedures, and experiment and observation have cohabited in the biological sector since then. In the physical sciences, a major development occurs at the turn of the twentieth century, when the focus moves from the experiment as such to mathematical modelling. Thus, in the history of science over this period of three centuries, there are two major turning points, one in the mid-nineteenth century affecting the biological sciences, and a second at the beginning of the twentieth century concerning the physical sciences. It is study of the language used which here highlights these contextual features, but this means that the language itself is a reflection of the changing historical and scientific context within which it is produced. This underlines the social nature of language, and the way in which language and social situation are intimately intertwined. Thus the language is a reflection of the social situation of which it is a part.

Envoi

This book has to end, but the story it tells does not end. I am not so much concluding my subject, as abandoning it at this point, and floating it off to a reading public. But the story quite obviously goes on. It will continue to go on as long as science continues to be practised as a form of human endeavour, and the results of that practice are expressed in language. As long as that continues to happen, the social situation of science will continue to develop and change, and as long as it does so, the language produced within it will continue to change with it. I cannot predict what linguistic changes are going to occur as the scientific journal article continues to develop, but I know that whatever they are, they will provide a fascinating insight into the changing scientific world of which they are a part and a reflection.

Notes

1. Halliday (1988) is reprinted as Chapter 3 (pp. 54–68) of Halliday and Martin (1993), and as Chapter 5 (pp. 140–158) of Halliday 2004b.
2. Halliday (1987) is reprinted as Chapter 6 (pp. 106–123) of Halliday and Martin (1993).
3. Halliday (1994) also appears as Chapter 5 (pp. 86–105) of Halliday and Martin (1993).
4. Where appropriate, the relevant parts of examples have been highlighted in bold.
5. In all Tables, discrepancies in percentages are due to rounding.
6. Robertson's edition of *The Philosophical Works of Francis Bacon* uses the translations of Ellis and Spedding (1857).
7. The relevant extracts from Newton's *Principia*, in the original Latin and in Motte's (1729) English translation are available on the following website: http://www.maths.tcd.ie/pub/HistMath/People/Newton/
8. Translation of French examples is mine throughout, unless otherwise stated.
9. Scientific articles used only for analytical purposes, other than those in the *Philosophical Transactions Corpus*, are given in Appendix 1.

Appendix 1

Faraday, Michael (1838). 'Experimental researches in electricity – Thirteenth series', *Philosophical Transactions of the Royal Society*, 128: 125–168.

Krieger, Kenneth J. and M.F. Sigler (1996). 'Catchability coefficient for rockfish estimate from trawl and submersible surveys', *Fishery Bulletin*, 94: 282–288.

Lindsay, B.G., D.R. Sieglaff, D.A. Schafer, C.L. Hakes, K.A. Smith and R.F. Stebbings (1996). 'Charge transfer of 0.5-, 1.5-, and 5-keV protons with atomic oxygen: Absolute differential and integral cross sections', *Physical Review A*, 53(1): 212–218.

Millikan, R.A. (1910). 'A new modification of the cloud method of determining the elementary electrical charge and the most probable value of that charge', *The London, Edinburgh , and Dublin Philosophical Magazine and Journal of Science*, 6th series, 19(110): 209–228.

Sleigh, M.A., E.S. Edwards, A.W.G. John and P.H. Burkill (1996). 'Microzooplankton community structure in the north-eastern Atlantic: Trends with latitude, depth and date, between May and early August', *Journal of the Marine Biological Association of the United Kingdom*, 76: 287–296.

Thompson, James (1913). 'The chemical action of *Bacillus cloacæ* (Jordan) on citric acid and malic acids in the presence and absence of oxygen', *Proceedings of the Royal Society – Series B*, 86: 1–12.

Appendix 2

The *Philosophical Transactions* Corpus:

Axford, W.I. (1960). 'Ionization fronts in interstellar gas: the structure of ionization fronts', A, 253: 301–333.

Baker, Henry (1740). 'The Discovery of a perfect Plant *in Semine*', 457: 448–455.

Barry, Martin (1840). 'On the Corpuscles of the Blood', 595–614.

Blair, Patrick (1720). 'A Discourse concerning a Method of discovering the Virtues of Plants by their External Structure', 31:364: 30–38.

Cavallo, Tiberius (1780). 'An Account of some new Experiments in Electricity, with the Description and Use of two new Electrical Instruments', 70(1): 15–30.

Davy, Edmund (1820) 'On some combinations of Platinum', 108–125.

Dawson, Maria (1900). '"Nitragin" and the Nodules of Leguminous Plants', B, 192: 1–29.

De la Rue, Warren and Hugo Müller (1860). 'On the Resin of Ficus rubiginosa, and a new Homologue of Benzylic Alcohol', 150(1): 43–56.

Desaguliers, J.T. (1720). 'An account of an Experiment made on *Thursday* the last day of *June, 1720*. before the *R. Society*, to shew by a new proof, that Bodies of the same Bulk do not contain equal quantities of Matter, and therefore that there is an interspers'd Vacuum', 31(365): 81–82.

Duffield, W.G., Thos. H Burnham and A.H. Davis (1920). 'The Pressure upon the Poles of the Electric Arc', A, 220: 109–136.

Edwards, George (1760): 'An Account of the Frog-fish of *Surinam*', 51:2, 653–657.

Gassiot, John P. (1840). 'An account of Experiments made with the view of ascertaining the possibility of obtaining a Spark before the Circuit of the Voltaic Battery is completed', 183–192.

Glazebrook, R.T. (1880). 'Double Refraction and Dispersion in Iceland Spar: an Experimental Investigation with a comparison with HUYGEN'S Construction for the Extraordinary Wave', 2: 421–449.

Hartree, D.R., W. Hartree and B. Swirles (1940). 'Self-consistent field, including exchange and superposition of configurations with some results for oxygen', A, 238: 229–247.

Herschel, William (1800) 'Experiments on the Refrangibility of the invisible Rays of the Sun', 284–293.

Home, Everard (1800). 'Some Observations on the Head of the *Ornithorhynchus paradoxus*', 432–437.

Horai, K., J.L. Winkler Jr., S.J. Keihm, M.G. Langseth, J.A. Fountain and E.A. West (1980). 'Thermal conduction in a composite circular cylinder: a new technique for thermal conductivity measurements of lunar core samples', A, 293: 571–598.

Hunter, John (1780). 'Account of an extraordinary Pheasant', 70(2): 527–535.

Joysey, K.A. (1960). 'A study of variation and relative growth in the blastoid *Orbitremites*', B, 243: 99–125.

Knight, Thomas Andrew (1820). 'Upon different qualities of the alburnum of spring and winter-felled oak trees', 156–158.

Lafage, Mr. (1700). 'An Account of an Extraordinary Aneurisma of the Arteria Aorta near to the Basis of the Heart, with the symptoms thereof', 22(267): 666–668.

Lawrence, William John Cooper, James Robert Price, Gertrude Maud Robinson and Robert Robinson (1940). 'The distribution of anthocyanins in flowers, fruits and leaves', B, 230: 149–178.

Matthiessen, A. and M. Holzmann (1860). 'On the Effect of the presence of Metals and Metalloids upon the Electrical Conducting Power of Pure Copper', 150(1): 85–92.

Miller, J. and E.N.K. Clarkson (1980). The post-ecdysial development of the cuticle and the eye of the Devonian trilobite *Phacops rana milleri* Stewart 1927, B, 288: 461–480.

Mummery, J. Howard (1920). 'The Epithelial Sheath of Hertwig in the Teeth of Man, with Notes on the Follicle and Nasmuth's Membrane', B, 209: 305–320.

Owen, Prof. (1880). 'On the ova of the *Echnida Hystrix*', 3: 1051–1055.

Povey, Thomas (1700). 'The Method, Manner and Order of the Transmutation of Copper in Brass &c', 22(260): 474–475.

Smith, Caleb (1740). 'A new method of improving and perfecting *Catadoptrical Telescopes*, by forming the *Speculums* of *Glass instead of Metal*', 456: 326–340.

Townsend, John S. (1900). 'The Diffusion of Ions into Gases, A, 193: 129–158.

Wilson, Benjamin (1760). 'Farther Experiments in Electricity', 51(2): 896–906.

References

Atkinson, Dwight (1999). *Scientific Discourse in Sociohistorical Context: The Philosophical Transactions of the Royal Society of London, 1675–1975*. Mahwah, NJ: Lawrence Erlbaum Associates.

Auffray, Jean-Paul (2000). *Newton, ou le triomphe de l'alchimie*. Paris: Le Pommier.

Banks, David (1987). 'Copulation and the passive', in André Joly (ed.), *La Transitivité, domaine anglais* (Travaux CIEREC 52). Saint-Etienne: Publications de l'Université de Saint-Etienne, pp. 127–140.

Banks, David (1994a). *Writ in Water: Aspects of the Scientific Journal Article*. Brest: ERLA.

Banks David (1994b). 'Hedges and how to trim them', in M. Brekke, Ø. Andersen, T. Dahl and J. Myking (eds), *Applications and Implications of Current LSP Research*, Vol. 2. Bergen: Fagbokforlaget, pp. 587–592.

Banks, David (1994c). 'Clause organization in the scientific journal article', *Unesco ALSED-LSP Newsletter*, 17(2): 4–16.

Banks, David (1995). 'There is a cleft in your sentence: less common clause structures in scientific writing', *ASp, la Revue du GERAS*, 7/10: 3–11.

Banks, David (1996). 'Joseph Banks and the development of scientific writing', in Gerhard Budin (ed), *Multilingualism in Specialist Communication, Proceedings of the 10th European LSP symposium, Vienna 1995*, Vol. 2. Vienna: IITL/Infoterm, pp. 697–705.

Banks, David (1997a). 'Little Lewis and Chaucer's astrolabe: instructions for use in the fourteenth century', in David Banks and Alain Tsédri (eds), *Sons et sens: mélanges offerts à Jean François Raoult*. Brest: ERLA, pp. 56–72.

Banks, David (1997b). 'Your very first ESP text (wherein Chaucer explaineth the astrolabe)', *ASp, la Revue de GERAS*, 15/18: 451–460.

Banks, David (1998). 'Vague quantification in the scientific journal article', *ASp, la revue du GERAS*, 19/22: 17–27.

Banks, David (1999). 'Aspects of the development of grammatical metaphor in scientific writing', *Les Cahiers de l'APLIUT*, 19(1): 5–25.

Banks, David (2001a). 'The reification of scientific process: the development of grammatical metaphor in scientific discourse', in Felix Meyer (ed.), *Language for Special Purposes: Perspectives for a New Millenium*, Vol. 2. Tübingen: Gunter Narr, pp. 555–563.

Banks, David (2001b). 'Vers une taxonomie de la nominalisation en anglais scientifique', in David Banks (ed.), *Le Groupe nominal dans le texte spécialisé*. Paris: L'Harmattan, pp. 53–64.

Banks, David (2003a). 'A note on modality in French', *Word*, 54(3), 325–334.

Banks, David (2003b). 'The evolution of grammatical metaphor in scientific writing', in Anne-Marie Simon-Vandenburgen, Miriam Taverniers and Louise Ravelli (eds), *Grammatical Metaphor: Views from Systemic Functional Linguistics*. Amsterdam: John Benjamins, pp. 127–147.

Banks, David (2004a). 'Philosophy, science, ideology, and the establishment of science as a profession', *ASp, la revue du GERAS*, 43/44: 69–80.

Banks, David (2004b). 'Degrees of Newness', in David Banks (ed.), *Text and Texture, Systemic Functional Viewpoints on the Nature and Structure of Text*. Paris: L'Harmattan, pp. 109–124.

Banks, David (2004c). 'Anglophone systematists and French enonciativists: shall the twain never meet?', *Language Sciences*, 26(4), 392-410.

Banks, David (2005a). 'Emerging scientific discourse in the late seventeenth century: a comparison of Newton's *Opticks* and Huygens' *Traité de la lumière*', *Functions of Language*, 12(1), 65–86.

Banks, David (2005b). 'The historical origins of nominalized process in scientific text', *English for Specific Purposes*, 24(3), 247–257.

Banks, David (2005c). *Introduction à la linguistique systémique fonctionnelle de l'anglais*. Paris: L'Harmattan.

Banks, David (2007). 'L'évolution de la phrase en anglais scientifique', in David Banks (ed), *La Coordination et la subordination dans le texte de spécialité*. Paris: L'Harmattan, pp. 203–221.

Banks, David (forthcoming). 'The position of Ideology in an SFL Model', in Carys Jones and Eija Ventola (eds), *Exploring Meaning-making, Field and the Ideational Function*. London: Equinox.

Banks, Joseph (1768–71 [1962]) (ed J.C. Beaglehole). *The Endeavour Journal of Joseph Banks, 1768–1771*, 2 vols. Sydney: Angus and Robertson.

Barber, C.L. (1962). 'Some measureable characteristics of scientific prose', in F. Behre (ed.), *Contributions to English Syntax and Philology*. Stockholm: Almquist and Wiksell, pp. 21–43.

Baugh, Albert C. (1959). *A History of the English Language*, 2nd edn. London: Routledge and Kegan Paul.

Bazerman, Charles (1988). *Shaping Written Knowledge: The Genre and Activity of the Experimental Article in Science*. Madison: University of Wisconsin Press.

Berry, Margaret (1996). 'What is Theme? – An(other) Personal View', in Margaret Berry, Christopher Butler, Robin Fawcett and Guowen Huang (eds), *Meaning and Form: Systemic Functional Interpretations, Meaning and Choice in Language: Studies for Michael Halliday*. Norwood, NJ, Ablex, pp. 1–64.

Bloor, Thomas and Meriel Bloor (1995). *The Functional Analysis of English, A Hallidayan Approach*. London: Arnold.

Boyle, Robert (1661 [2003]). *The Sceptical Chymist*. Mineola, NY: Dover.

Brunot, F. and C. Bruneau (1969). *Précis de la grammaire historique de la langue Française*. Paris: Masson.

Burnie, David (1990). *Machines and How They Work*. London: Dorling Kindersley.

Butterfield, Herbert (1957). *The Origins of Modern Science*, 2nd. edn. London: G. Bell and Sons.

Cameron, Hector Charles (1952). *Sir Joseph Banks: The Autocrat of the Philosophers, 1744–1820*. London: Batchworh Press.

Carnet, Didier (1997). 'La détermination passive et quelques thématisations particulières en anglais médical', *ASp, la revue du GERAS*, 15/18, 505–524.

Carter-Thomas, Shirley (2000). *La cohérence textuelle: pour une nouvelle pédagogie de l'écrit*. Paris: L'Harmattan.

Chapman, Allan (2005). *England's Leonardo: Robert Hooke and the Seventeenth-century Scientific Revolution*. Bristol: Institute of Physics Publishing.

Chaucer, Geoffrey (1391 [1957]). 'A treatise on the astrolabe', in Geoffrey Chaucer (ed. F.N. Robinson), *The Complete Works of Geoffrey Chaucer*, 2nd edn. London: Oxford University Press, pp. 544–563.

Cooke, Ray (1993). 'Learning to publish in English: how can French researchers bridge the gap?', *ASp, la Revue du GERAS*, 1, 463–475.

Cooray, Mahinda (1967). 'The English Passive Voice', *English Language Teaching*, 21(3), pp. 203–210.

Crépin, André (1972). *Histoire de la langue anglaise*, 2e. éd. Paris: Presses Universitaires de France.

Crompton, Peter (2004). 'Theme in discourse: "Thematic progression" and "method of development" re-evaluated', *Functions of Language*, 11(2), pp. 213–249.

Curry, Walter Clyde (1960). *Chaucer and the Medieval Sciences*, 2nd edn. London: George Allen and Unwin.

Darwin, Charles (1839 [1989]) (ed and abr Janet Browne and Michael Neve). *Voyage of the Beagle*. Harmondsworth: Penguin.

Dalton, John (1827 [1965]). *New System of Chemical Philosophy*, London: Peter Owen.

Davies, Martin (1986). 'Literacy and Intonation', in Barbara Couture (ed), *Functional Approaches to Writing: Research Perspectives*. London: Pinter, pp. 199–220.

Dear, Peter (1985). '*Totius in verbum*, Rhetoric and Authority in the Early Royal Society', *Isis*, 76, pp. 145–161.

Eco, Umberto (1994)(trans Jean-Paul Manangaro). *La recherche de la langue parfaite*. Paris: Editions du Seuil.

Eggins, Suzanne (1994). *An Introduction to Systemic Functional Linguistics*. London: Pinter.

Fairclough, Norman (2003). *Analysing Discourse, Textual Analysis for Social Research*. London: Routledge.

Fara, Patricia (2002). *Newton: The Making of Genius*. London: Picador.

Fara, Patricia (2003). *Sex, Botany and Empire: The Story of Carl Linnaeus and Joseph Banks*. Cambridge: Icon Books.

Farrington, Benjamin (1949 [1951]). *Francis Bacon: Philosopher of Industrial Science*. London: Lawrence and Wishart.

Fawcett, Robin (2000). *A Theory of Syntax for Systemic Functional Linguistics*. Amsterdam: John Benjamins.

Fawcett, Robin and Guowen Huang (1995). 'A functional analysis of the enhanced theme construction in English', *Interface, Journal of Applied Linguistics*, 10(1), 113–144.

Fennell, Barbara A. (2001). *A History of English: A Sociolinguistic Approach*. Oxford: Blackwell.

Firbas, Jan (1992). *Functional Sentence Perspective in Written and Spoken Communication*. Cambridge: Cambridge University Press.

Gascoigne, John (1994). *Joseph Banks and the English Enlightenment: Useful Knowledge and Polite Culture*. Cambridge: Cambridge University Press.

Gleik, James (2003). *Isaac Newton*. London/ Fourth Estate.

Gosden, Hugh (1992). 'Discourse functions of marked theme in scientific research articles', *English for Specific Purposes*, 11(3), pp. 207–224.

Gotti, Maurizio (1996). *Robert Boyle and the Language of Science*. Milano: Guerini.

Gross, Alan G. (1996). *The Rhetoric of Science*, 2nd edn. Cambridge, MA: Harvard University Press.

Gross, Alan G., Joseph E. Harmon and Michael Reidy (2002). *Communicating Science: The Scientific Article from the 17th Century to the Present*. Oxford: Oxford University Press.

Hall, Marie Boas (1962 [1994]). *The Scientific Renaissance, 1450–1630*. New York: Dover.

Halliday, M.A.K. (1978). *Language as Social Semiotic: The Social Interpretation of Language and Meaning*. London: Arnold.

Halliday, M.A.K. (1987). 'Language and the order of nature', in Nigel Fabb, Derek Attridge, Alan Durant and Colin McCabe (eds), *The Linguistics of Writing: Arguments between Language and Literature*. Manchester: Manchester University Press, pp. 135–154.

Halliday, M.A.K. (1988). 'On the language of physical science', in Mohsen Ghadessy (ed.), *Registers of Written English: Situational Factors and Linguistic Features*. London, Pinter, pp. 162–178.

Halliday, M.A.K. (1994). 'The construction of knowledge and value in the grammar of scientific discourse, with reference to Charles Darwin's *The Origin of Species*', in Malcolm Coulthard (ed.), *Advances in Written Text Analysis*. London: Routledge, pp. 136–156.

Halliday, M.A.K. (1998). 'Things and relations. Regrammaticising experience as technical knowledge', in J.R. Martin & Robert Veel (eds), *Reading Science, Critical and functional perspectives on discourses of science*, London, Routledge, pp. 185–235.

Halliday, M.A.K. (rev. Christian M.I.M. Matthiessen) (2004a). *An Introduction to Functional Grammar*, 3rd. edn. London: Arnold.

Halliday, M.A.K. (ed. Jonathan Webster)(2004b). *The Language of Science, The Collected Works Vol. 5*, London, Continuum.

Halliday, M.A.K. and J.R. Martin (1993). *Writing Science: Literacy and Discursive Power.* London: The Falmer Press.

Halliday, M.A.K and Christian M.I.M. Matthiessen (1999). *Construing Experience through Meaning: A Language-based Approach to Cognition.* London: Cassell.

Henry, John (2002). *Knowledge is Power: Francis Bacon and the Method of Science.* Cambridge: Icon Books.

Huygens, Christiaan (1690 [1992]). *Traité de la lumière.*, Paris: Dunod.

Hyland, Ken, (1998). *Hedging in Scientific Research Articles.* Amsterdam: John Benjamins.

Jones, Richard Foster (1961 [1982]). *Ancients and Moderns: A Study of the Rise of the Scientific Movement in Seventeenth-century England.* New York: Dover.

Katzen, May F. (1980). 'The changing appearance of research journals in science and technology: an analysis and a case study', in A.J. Meadows (ed.). *Development in Science Publishing in Europe.* Amsterdam: Elsevier, pp. 177–214.

Kronick, David A. (1976). *A History of Scientific and Technical Periodicals: The Origins and Development of the Scientific and Technical Press, 1665–1790*, 2nd edn. Metuchen, NJ: Scarecrow Press.

Knowles, Gerry (1997). *A Cultural History of the English Language.* London: Arnold.

Le Ru, Véronique (2005). *Voltaire Newtonien: le combat d'un philosophe pour la science.* Paris: Vuibert/ADAPT.

Lock, Graham (1996). *Functional English Grammar: An Introduction for Second Language Teachers.* Cambridge: Cambridge University Press.

Master, P.(1991). 'Active verbs with inanimate subjects in scientific prose', *English for Specific Purposes*, 10(1) 15-33

Martin, J.R. (1992). *English Text: System and Structure.* Amsterdam: John Benjamins.

Martin, J.R., Christian M.I.M. Matthiessen and Clare Painter (1997). *Working with Functional Grammar.* London: Arnold.

Martin, J.R. and David Rose (2003). *Working with Discourse: Meaning Beyond the Clause.* London: Continuum.

Matthiessen, Christian (1995). *Lexicographical Cartography: English Systems.* Tokyo: International Language Sciences.

Maxwell, James Clerk (1881 [2005]). *An Elementary Treatise on Electricity.* New York: Dover Publications.

McCabe, Anne (2004). 'Thematic progression patterns and text types in history textbooks', in David Banks (ed.), *Text and Texture: Systemic Functional Viewpoints on the Nature and Structure of Text.* Paris: L'Harmattan, pp. 215–237.

McDonald, Philip B. (1929). *English and Science.* Kingsport, TN: D. Van Nostrand.

Mossé, Fernand (1959). *Manuel de l'anglais du moyen age: des origines au XIVe siècle*, Vol. 2, *Moyen-anglais.* Paris: Aubier.

Newton, Isaac (1730 [1979]). *Opticks*. New York: Dover.

O'Brian, Patrick (1988). *Joseph Banks: A Life*. London: Collins Harvill.

Ormrod, Janet (2001). 'Construction discursive de noms composé dans les textes scientifiques anglais', in David Banks (ed.), *Le groupe nominal dans le texte spécialisé*. Paris: L'Harmattan, pp. 9–23.

Ormrod, Janet (2004). 'Creation and subsequent usage of terms for discourse purposes in the scientific research article', in *Actes de GLAT-Barcelona 2004, La production des textes spécialisés: Structure et enseignement*. Brest: GLAT, pp. 51–60.

Oxford English Dictionary, 2004, CD-ROM version 3.1, London: Oxford University Press.

Panza, Marco (2003). *Newton*. Paris: Les Belles Lettres.

Perrot, Nolwenn (1998). 'The evolution of grammatical metaphor in the life sciences', unpublished Masters' dissertation, Université de Bretagne Occidentale, Brest.

Quirk, Randolph, Sydney Greenbaum, Geoffrey Leech and Jan Svartvik (1972). *A Grammar of Contemporary English*. Harlow: Longman.

Quirk, Randolph, Sydney Greenbaum, Geoffrey Leech and Jan Svartvik (1985). *A Comprehensive Grammar of English*. Harlow: Longman.

Quirk, Randolph and C.L. Wrenn (1955). *An Old English Grammar*. London: Methuen and Co.

Ravelli, L.J. (1988). 'Grammatical Metaphor: An initial analysis', in E.H. Steiner and R. Veltman (eds), *Pragmatics, Discourse and Text: Some Systemically-inspired Approaches*. London: Pinter.

Rissanen, M. (1999). 'Syntax', in R. Lass (ed.), *The Cambridge History of the English Language*, Vol 3 *1476–1776*. Cambridge: Cambridge University Press.

Robertson, John M. (ed)(1905). *The Philosophical Works of Francis Bacon*. London: George Routledge and Sons/New York, E.P. Dutton.

Salager-Meyer, Françoise (1994). 'Hedges and textual communicative function in medical English written discourse', *English for Specific Purposes*, 13(2), pp. 149–170.

Salager-Meyer, Françoise (1998). '"I think that perhaps you should": a study of hedges in scientific discourse' *The Journal of TESOL-France*, 2(2), pp. 127–144.

Salager-Meyer, Françoise and Gérard Defives (1998). 'From the gentleman's courtesy to the scientist's caution: a diachronic study of hedges in academic writing (1810–1995)', in Immaculada Fortanet, Santiago Posteguillo, Juan Carlos Palmer and Juan Francisco Coll (eds), *Genre Studies in English for Academic Purposes*. Castelló de la Plana: Publicacions de la Universitat Jaume 1, pp. 133–172.

Salager-Meyer, Françoise, Gérard Defives and Miguel Hamelynk (1996). 'A diachronic study of hedges in medical English written discourse', in Gerhard Budin (ed.), *Multilingualism in Specialist Communication, Proceedings of the 10th European LSP symposium, Vienna 1995*, Vol. 2, Vienna: IITL/Infoterm, pp. 267–286.

Savory, Theodore H.(1953). *The Language of Science: Its Growth, Character and Usage*. London: André Deutsch.

Skeat, Walter W. (1900). 'Introduction to a Treatise on the Astrolabe', in Geoffrey Chaucer (Walter W. Skeat (ed.)). *The Complete Works of Geoffrey Chaucer*, Vol. 3, London: Oxford University Press, pp. lvii–lxxx.

Sprat, Thomas (1667 [2003]). *The History of the Royal-Society of London, for the Improving of Natural Knowledge*. Whitefish, MT: Kessinger.

Strang, Barbara M.H. (1970). *A History of English*. London: Methuen and Co.

Swales, John M. (1990). *Genre Analysis: English in Academic and Research Settings*. Cambridge: Cambridge University Press.

Swales, John M. (2004). *Research Genres: Exploration and Applications*. Cambridge: Cambridge University Press.

Taverniers, Miriam (2003). 'Grammatical metaphor in SFL: a historiography of the introduction and initial study of the concept', in Anne-Marie Simon-Vandenbergen, Miriam Taverniers and Louise Ravelli (eds), *Grammatical Metaphor: Views from Systemic Functional Linguistics*. Amsterdam: John Benjamins, pp. 5–34.

Teilhard de Chardin, Pierre (1955). *Le phénomène humain*. Paris: Editions du Seuil.

Thompson, Geoff (2004). *Introducing Functional Grammar*, 2nd edn. London: Arnold.

Turner, G.W. (1972). 'The passive construction in English scientific writing', *Journal of the Australasian Universities Language and Literature Association (AUMLA)*, 18, pp. 181–197.

Valle, Ellen (1999). *A Collective Intelligence: The Life Sciences in the Royal Society as a Scientific Discourse Community, 1665–1995*. Turku: Angliana Turkuensia.

Ventola, Eija (1996). 'Packing and unpacking of information in academic texts', in Eija Ventola and Anna Mauranen (eds), *Academic Writing: Intercultural and Textual Issues*. Amsterdam: John Benjamins, pp. 153–194.

Vickers, Brian (ed)(1987). *English Science: Bacon to Newton*. Cambridge: Cambridge University Press.

White, Michael (1997). *Isaac Newton: The Last Sorcerer*. London: Fourth Estate.

Author Index

Subject Index